OCEAN LINERS

OCEAN LINERS

SPEED AND STYLE

EDITED BY

DANIEL FINAMORE AND GHISLAINE WOOD

V&A PUBLISHING IN ASSOCIATION WITH
THE PEABODY ESSEX MUSEUM,
SALEM, MASSACHUSETTS

The exhibition *Ocean Liners: Speed and Style* is co-organized by the Peabody Essex Museum, Salem, Massachusetts (on view 20 May – 9 October 2017) and the Victoria and Albert Museum, London (on view 3 February – 17 June 2018). At the Victoria and Albert Museum it is supported by Viking Cruises.

First published by V&A Publishing, 2017
Victoria and Albert Museum
South Kensington
London SW7 2RL
www.vandapublishing.com

This UK edition first published by V&A Publishing, 2018

Distributed in North America by Abrams, an imprint of ABRAMS

Exhibition edition (UK only) hardback
ISBN 978 1 85177 949 9

Exhibition edition (UK only) paperback
ISBN 978 1 85177 953 6

10 9 8 7 6 5 4 3 2 1
2021 2020 2019 2018

Designer: Peter Dawson, www.gradedesign.com
Origination: DL Imaging Ltd, London
Copy-editor: Jane Ace
Index: Hilary Bird

New photography by Richard Davis,
V&A Photographic Studio

Printed in China

A catalogue record for this book is available from the British Library.

MIX
Paper from responsible sources
FSC
www.fsc.org FSC® C008047

V&A Publishing
Supporting the world's leading museum of art and design, the Victoria and Albert Museum, London

FRONT COVER
Detail from '*Empress of Britain*', poster for Canadian Pacific Railways, designed by J.R. Tooby, printed by Sanders, Phillips & Co.
London, United Kingdom, c.1930–1
Colour lithograph
GIVEN BY THE CANADIAN PACIFIC RAILWAY CO.
V&A: E.2215–1931

BACK COVER
Bound for Hawaii, photograph by Edward Steichen for *Vogue*
1934
Gelatin silver print
CONDÉ NAST COLLECTION: CN00018611

CONTENTS

DIRECTORS' FOREWORD

IN JULY 1840, RMS *BRITANNIA* departed Liverpool for Boston on the voyage that would initiate transatlantic steamship service on a regular schedule. So began the transatlantic connection between Europe and North America that became the great age of ocean liner travel and that, after more than 175 years and thousands of ocean liner crossings, is celebrated in *Ocean Liners: Speed and Style*.

This groundbreaking exhibition, and its accompanying book, frame ocean liners in an international context. The project explores many fascinating aspects of ocean liners' design; from architecture, engineering and interiors, to the lifestyle on board and their cultural impact as archetypal symbols of the modern era. The exhibition is the result of a collective interdisciplinary investigation on the part of art, design and maritime historians. We would like to thank all the staff from both institutions involved in the organization of this exhibition, particularly the curatorial teams led by Daniel Finamore, The Russell W. Knight Curator of Maritime Art and Culture at the Peabody Essex Museum (PEM), and Ghislaine Wood, Fellow of the Research Department at the Victoria and Albert Museum and Deputy Director of the Sainsbury Centre, University of East Anglia. We would also like to thank V&A Museum of Design Dundee for providing invaluable curatorial support.

The collaboration between PEM, founded in 1799 and one of America's fastest growing art museums with a rich and diverse collection of global art and culture, and the V&A, the world's leading museum of art, design and performance, has capitalized on the strengths of both institutions. It has allowed access to richer collections, ideas and perspectives than each institution could have provided alone. In recognising this important partnership, we are grateful to Stephen Lash, Chairman Emeritus of Christie's Americas, and Martin Roth, former V&A Director. It was Stephen's passion for ocean liners and his unique perspective as a preeminent collector of liner material that brought PEM and the V&A together.

Cultural memory of the liner era is made manifest today in the collections of former travellers, maritime history devotees and aficionados of twentieth-century graphic and decorative arts. Though today these collections foster reflection upon the past, their significance lies not in nostalgia, but in documenting the experience of modern life.

PEM was actively collecting art and design related to ocean liners by at least 1870, building holdings of paintings, prints, posters and models that today number in the thousands. The majority of PEM's vast collection of ocean liner ephemera was bequeathed by Howard Galvin who worked in the Thomas Cook travel office in Boston from the 1930s to the 1970s.

At the V&A, the history of collecting ship-related material reaches back to the origin of the museum in the 1850s. Ship models and technology patents were collected by the South Kensington Museum (later renamed the Victoria and Albert Museum) with the purpose of improving Britain's commercial and manufacturing advantage. Many of these objects were acquired from the international expositions, including the Great Exhibition of 1851, and are now held by the Science Museum. In the twentieth century, the V&A acquired a range of ocean liner material, including posters and ephemera, ceramics, textiles, metalwork and furniture, with the aim of representing good design.

We are greatly indebted to the foresight of our predecessors, whose vision included ocean liner design in their collecting goals, and to the generous institutional and private lenders whose actions to preserve the rich design culture of the liner have made this book and exhibition possible. Finally, we would like to thank our sponsor, Viking Cruises, for their support.

DR TRISTRAM HUNT
DIRECTOR,
VICTORIA AND ALBERT MUSEUM, LONDON

DAN L. MONROE
THE ROSE-MARIE & EIJK VAN OTTERLOO EXECUTIVE DIRECTOR & CEO,
PEABODY ESSEX MUSEUM, SALEM, MASSACHUSETTS

SPONSOR'S FOREWORD

AT VIKING WE HAVE ALWAYS BELIEVED that cruising should connect you with your destination – not just take you to places on a map. For us, the perfect voyage immerses travellers in local cultures; the ideal journey nourishes and enriches – and even changes the way you see the world.

Our journey began on Russia's waterways over 20 years ago, when we founded Viking River Cruises in the spirit of discovery that inspired the Vikings. Today our modern Viking ships ply both rivers and oceans around the world, delivering experiences designed for the curious traveller.

The Viking vision on the oceans is to bring the destination back to cruising, with a range of exciting itineraries that span the globe, and a fleet of state-of-the-art, Scandinavian-inspired ships, designed to be both elegant and inviting.

It is with great pleasure that we are partnering with the V&A in this exhibition, and we invite you to join us as we celebrate the joy of ocean travel, past and present.

TORSTEIN HAGEN
CHAIRMAN, VIKING CRUISES

INTRODUCTION

DANIEL FINAMORE AND GHISLAINE WOOD

WRITING IN 1871, THE FRENCH AUTHOR Jules Verne vividly brought to life the experience of travelling to America on board Isambard Kingdom Brunel's epoch-defining ocean liner, *Great Eastern* (1859)[1] [1].

> This steam-ship is indeed a masterpiece of naval construction; more than a vessel it is a floating city, part of the country, detached from English soil, which after having crossed the sea, unites itself to the American Continent. ... the 'Great Eastern' is not merely a nautical engine, but rather a microcosm, and carries a small world with it, an observer will not be astonished to meet here ... all the instincts, follies and, passions of human nature.[2]

Verne's fascinating novel *Une Ville Flottante* (A Floating City, 1871) described a transatlantic voyage in great detail and was the eighth work in his 'Voyages Extraordinaires' series, which also included the more fantastic *Twenty Thousand Leagues Under the Sea* (1870) and *Around the World in Eighty Days* (1872). His voyage on the *Great Eastern* was no less full of wonder, however, and Verne was not alone in marking the significance of the ocean liner as a symbol of progress and as the most visceral experience of modernity. Eleven years earlier the English author William Makepeace Thackeray had also signalled the advent of a new era in his essay, 'De Juventute' (1860):

> We are of the age of steam. We have stepped out of the old world on to 'Brunel's' vast deck, and across the waters *ingens patet tellus*.[3] Towards what new continent are we wending? to what new laws, new manners, new politics, vast new expanses of liberties unknown as yet, or only surmised?[4]

Brunel's great ship bears humanity into a new era, where technological progress will transform law, politics and the very fabric of society. The ocean liner metaphorically conveys man into this brave new age while also being the embodiment of it – gigantic machines, whose complex systems and idealized societies provided models for new ways of living, while also shaping the cultural imagination. As microcosms of society, or as liminal spaces free from the conventions of terra firma, ocean liners inspired authors as diverse as Thackeray, Verne, F. Scott Fitzgerald and Stefan Zweig.

The great age of ocean travel has long since passed, but ocean liners remain one of the most powerful and admired symbols of twentieth-century modernity. No form of transport was as romantic, remarkable or contested, and ocean liner design became a matter of national prestige as well as an arena in which the larger dynamics of global competition played out. This book explores the design of liners – their architecture, engineering, interiors and lifestyle on board – within a broad cultural context and from a range of perspectives. Ocean liners are central to the narratives of modernity for they lie at the intersection of progressive design and populist notions of opulence. Liner design operated as a fantasy environment that fulfilled the desires and aspirations of millions, while responding to new markets and changes in the social, political and economic fabric.

The advent of steam power transformed many industries and none more so than transport. The nineteenth century saw the development of networks, both on land and at sea, which effectively connected the world in an unprecedented way. Before ocean-going steam vessels were the norm, sailing ships, or packets, plied the North Atlantic Ocean, advertising regular departure dates but with little assurance of a date of arrival. The ocean liner, a ship that carries passengers between ports according to a fixed schedule, transformed the transatlantic journey, reducing the crossing time and allowing for increasing numbers of travellers. In 1837, the Peninsular Steam Navigation Company (soon to become the Peninsular and Oriental Steam Navigation Company – P&O)

1 ABOVE

The Great Eastern *(Wheel and Chain Drum)*,
photograph by Robert Howlett
United Kingdom, 1857
Albumen print from collodion negative

V&A: PH.259–1979

INTRODUCTION

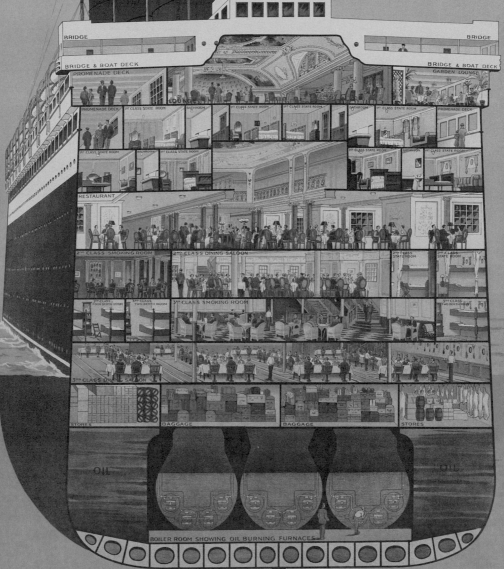

was awarded a contract by the Admiralty to deliver mail from Britain to the Iberian Peninsula and Gibraltar according to a fixed schedule. Three years later Samuel Cunard's new company ran its first mail steamer *Britannia* from Liverpool to Halifax and Boston.[5] Shipping companies in other countries were quick to follow suit and a number of national lines were established, including: the Hamburg-Amerikanische Packetfahrt Actien-Gesellschaft (known as Hamburg-American Line or HAPAG) in 1847, Norddeutscher Lloyd (North German Lloyd) in 1857, the Compagnie Générale Transatlantique (shortened to the CGT or French Line) in 1861, the International Navigation Company of Philadelphia (known as the Red Star Line) in 1871 and the Italian company Lloyd Sabaudo in 1906.

The distinctive character of travel on ocean steamships long predates the invention of the actual ocean liner. Passengers who stepped on board steam vessels of the early nineteenth century associated the experience with industrialization, but not always on pleasant terms. Ocean passages under sail were always fraught with hazards from rocks and weather, but steam engines introduced an entirely new element of potential disaster in the form of boiler explosions and fire. In June 1816, long before steamships had reached most waters of the world, an explosion from a faulty boiler valve on the Ohio River steamboat *Washington* (1816) brought the hazards of this newfangled technology to wide attention. That story was repeated many times over. In *Life on the Mississippi* (1883), Mark Twain wrote of his brother's painful death following a boiler explosion on *Pennsylvania* (1854), while 1,800 deaths following boiler explosions on *Sultana* (1863) in 1865 is still considered the worst maritime disaster in United States history.[6]

Even when accomplished in safety, steamship passages were often considered less comfortable than sailing vessels, with narrow hulls that rolled more and fewer masts and sails to act as stabilizers. Charles Dickens wrote about his 1842 passage on *Britannia*: 'what the agitation of a steam vessel is, on a bad winter's night in the wild Atlantic, it is impossible for the most vivid imagination to conceive.'[7] The dramatic evolution in scale, reliability, safety and comfort of ocean liners over the following century marks the liner as a symbol of the modern era. This project aims to map that evolution, marking the significance of the ocean liner over the course of the late nineteenth and twentieth centuries.

The historiography of ocean liners is a rich field but studies have tended to focus on the development of maritime technologies, the histories of shipbuilding, whether by nation or individual shipping company, or most commonly the design of individual ships. This book and the accompanying exhibition explore the design of liners by adopting a more integrative and holistic approach, employing an interdisciplinarity that is unique in the literature. It draws on the expertise of design, technology, fashion, maritime, architectural, art and cultural historians to provide a rich examination of the subject, outlining the design of liners in the broadest terms. The main developments in technology, interior design, publicity and the sociology of the design of ships, and the unique rituals and behaviours that evolved on board are all explored. This is one of a handful of volumes to embrace the material culture of liner design. A number of key works have provided the foundation for this study, including Louis-René Vian's *Arts Décoratifs à Bord des Paquebots Français, 1880–1960* (1992), the books of Philip Dawson, notably *The Liner: Retrospective and Renaissance* (2005), Anne Wealleans's *Designing Liners: A History of Interior Design Afloat* (2006), and the many books by Bruce Peter, markedly *Ship Style: Modernism and Modernity at Sea in the Twentieth Century* (2010) co-edited with Philip Dawson.

No prior exhibition projects have taken such an international perspective on the design and cultural impact of the ocean liner and, to date, no other ocean liner exhibition has travelled internationally. A watershed exhibition at the Cooper Hewitt Museum in New York City called *The Oceanliner: Speed, Style, Symbol* (1980) was the first to highlight the ocean liner as a

2 OPPOSITE

'Cunard Line – To all parts of the world', poster,
printed by Thos. Forman & Sons
Nottingham, United Kingdom, 1920s,
Chromolithograph
GIFT TO THE AMERICAN FRIENDS BY LESLIE,
JUDITH AND GABRI SCHREYER AND ALICE
SCHREYER BATKO
V&A: E.1829–2004

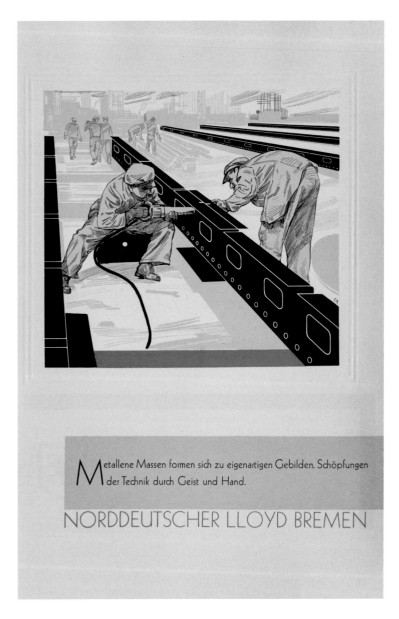

Metallene Massen formen sich zu eigenartigen Gebilden. Schöpfungen der Technik durch Geist und Hand.

NORDDEUTSCHER LLOYD BREMEN

consummately designed object involving the contributions of hundreds of designers, artists, skilled and semi-skilled craftsmen, but, unfortunately, only a slim booklet was produced to document the central concepts of that show. This project shares comparably ambitious goals. When the Cooper Hewitt exhibition was held, two ships – *Stefan Batory* (1968) and *Queen Elizabeth 2* (1969, also known as *QE2*) – were still carrying passengers across the Atlantic on a fixed schedule. A prominent review in *Art in America* magazine concluded that 'no exhibition could really do justice to the subject, for only a crossing on a great liner can really suffice'.[8] The author's perspective was one of unrepentant nostalgia for an era on the wane. Exhibitions in following years offered close examinations of individual ships, including *Fantastic Voyage* (1996) at the Suntory Museum of Art in Tokyo and *DecoDence* (2010) at the South Street Seaport Museum in New York City – both of which focused on

Normandie (1935) – and *Paquebot France* at the Musée national de la Marine in Paris (2011). A few exhibitions have explored the cultural impact of liners of a single nation, such as *Paquebots de Légende, Décors de Rêve* (1991–2) also held at the Musée national de la Marine in Paris and *Six Wonderful Days* (2002–3) at the Palazzo della Nuova Borsa, Museo dell'Accademia Ligustica di Belle Arti in Genoa. Nostalgia often motivated visitors to these exhibitions who, like the reviewer for *Art in America*, wished to remember their own experiences on board. Today, enough time has passed that only a small minority of museum visitors (and practically no one under the age of 30) has ever travelled on an ocean liner – the era of nostalgia has given way to one of history, and the academic study of ocean liners and their role in cultural history has taken on a new legitimacy.

While charting the trajectory of ocean travel, this book adopts a thematic approach. Uniquely, the significance of the ocean liner is mapped through the surviving material culture. Over 200 objects – from furniture and interior fittings removed from the ships themselves, to sculpture, design drawings, models, posters, paintings, books, photography and publicity ephemera – document the wider industry. The volume opens with a close examination of the extraordinary promotional material created to attract passengers. Described as one of the greatest public relations successes in the history of industry, transoceanic steamship travel was transformed in the public imagination from a dangerous, dirty and sickening experience into a highly desirable and glamorous leisure activity within only a few decades. By 1900, new ships, classes of service and improved amenities were advertised with high-quality and progressive graphics in unified design schemes that maximized the visual impact of their message. Advertising posters and brochures, ship models, and the architecture of shipping offices and port buildings are each discussed as separate modes in the strategy designed to convey a taste of the high style a passenger would experience on board. The arrangement of this chapter focuses attention on the interrelated methods and goals of those who designed the material culture of promotion.

Ocean liners were monumental feats of engineering that played a key role in the status of a nation. The large shipbuilding industries of Britain, Germany, France and Italy were vital to the national economies of those countries and shipping companies frequently benefited from state loans for the construction of fast liners [3]. As key military assets the technological progress of ships became not just a matter of prestige but a national imperative and helped to drive the industry forward. Within the liner trade, that narrative was consistently one of striking the optimal balance between the

5 ABOVE

Hales Blue Riband trophy, designed by Charles
Holliday, made by James Dixon & Sons
Sheffield, United Kingdom, 1935
Silver, gilding and green onyx
Neptune and Amphitrite flank Victory who supports
a globe topped by two Titans battling for a liner.
DANISH SHIPOWNERS' ASSOCIATION,
COPENHAGEN

sometimes conflicting interests and concerns of the traveller, but the passenger experience was always paramount in driving the developments that were to be adopted. Cunard's Chairman Sir Percy Bates (1879–1946) announced 'I deprecate any emphasis on speed' at the maiden voyage of *Queen Mary* in 1936, although the ship still went on to capture the Blue Riband, the fiercely-competed-for award rewarding the fastest transatlantic crossing [4 & 5]. The public of all shipbuilding nations clamoured for ever faster and larger ships, feeding national pride in the latest accomplishments, while each liner disaster – whether through collision, warfare or fire – inspired inventions and design developments to make subsequent ships safer.[9] Passenger comfort remained at the core of design decisions, and, while speed was often seen as the enemy of safety, it was also frequently sacrificed for increased luxury. No matter what luxuries were available to distract passengers from the realities of rocking on the sea, however, they generally found a faster passage appealing and looked forward to stepping ashore at their destination. On the maiden voyage of Hamburg-American's *Imperator* in 1913, the lavish ornamentation was found to make the ship so top-heavy that the first-class marble bathrooms had to be stripped back and other heavy furniture replaced with lighter wicker. International competition and divergent visions of modernity also led to distinctive refinements in the design of hulls, funnels, propellers and engines, reaching a pinnacle with the ultra-streamlined form of SS *United States* (1952).

Until the First World War, the design of ocean liners was predominantly geared towards the need to service the empires of various European nations and the large-scale emigration to America. Over 11 million people emigrated from Europe to the United States between 1900 and 1914, often in very poor conditions, while colonies around the world required regular and scheduled services. Achieving the right balance between the different classes of accommodation determined profitability and shipping companies were quick to make changes if profits were down. The introduction of new immigration regulations in the United States after the First World War shifted the economic factors driving the industry and the focus moved from the accommodation of emigrants to the need to appeal to wealthy passengers. A key strategy for attracting them was through the interior design of ships.

Although P&O ships incorporated elaborate decorations early on – *Hindostan* (1842), for example, boasted painted papier-mâché panels and finely carved woodwork in the passenger spaces – the first ship interiors designed by architects appeared in the late nineteenth century [6].[10] The elaborate historicist designs evoked

6 ABOVE

Arcade enclosing Mosque and Minarets,
tile panels, probably trial pieces or duplicates for
a P&O passenger ship, by William De Morgan
United Kingdom, *c.*1888–97
Polychrome tile

SOUTHWARK HERITAGE SERVICE, SOUTHWARK
COUNCIL, LONDON: CE008, CE009, CE010

LE GRAND SALON

Décorations murales de Jean Dupas (peintures sur glace ; voir plus loin le détail d'un panneau). Colonnes et grande porte entre le salon et le fumoir en laque d'or par Jean Dunand.
Au centre, piste de danse. Grands appareils lumineux en verre de Labouret.
Aquarelle de J. SIMONT.

Bouwens de Boijen et Expert, architectes.

the opulent palaces and castles of Europe and fostered an aura of luxury and comfort that denied the reality of the surroundings on the sea, with its attendant vulnerabilities and potential for discomfort and danger. The major shipping lines modelled their first-class interiors on grand hotels to create the most luxurious experience, and, like hotels, historicism characterized ship design throughout the Victorian and Edwardian eras.

Writing in 1928 the British designer Charles A. Richter (1876–1945) declared his independence from the historical styles that were being questioned in the face of post-First World War Modernism.

When we start designing our ship we are full of reminiscences, and that is why traditional forms linger long after the purposes they once expressed have passed away ... Reminiscences of bygone forms, once the outcome of structure and purpose, combined with an insatiable love of representation, leads us into many absurd extravagances ... If on the other hand we frankly and cheerfully accept the new materials and methods of construction for what they are, not seeking to disguise them, the new style is within our reach, nay, must inevitably result, for the aesthetic sense freed from all pretence, will evolve from these elements new melodies of line, new harmonies of proportion and arrangements of masses which will remain for all time the truest and most fitting expressions of our era.[11]

Richter marked the pivotal moment when ship designers and industry management confronted the traditional tenets of their profession and looked to the future of oceanic travel. Three chapters that follow trace the highly mediated and often contentious process through which shipping lines of different nations embraced stylistic changes, from the Arts and Crafts and Beaux-Arts palaces designed

7 OPPOSITE

The first-class grand salon on *Normandie*,
illustration by J. Simont, from *L'Illustration*,
special issue on *Normandie* (June 1935)

8 ABOVE

Panel from *The Rape of Europa* for the first-class
grand salon on *Normandie*, by Jean Dupas,
made by Jacques-Charles Champigneulle
France, 1934
Verre églomisé (glass, paint, gold, silver
and palladium leaf)
MIOTTEL MUSEUM, BERKELEY, CA

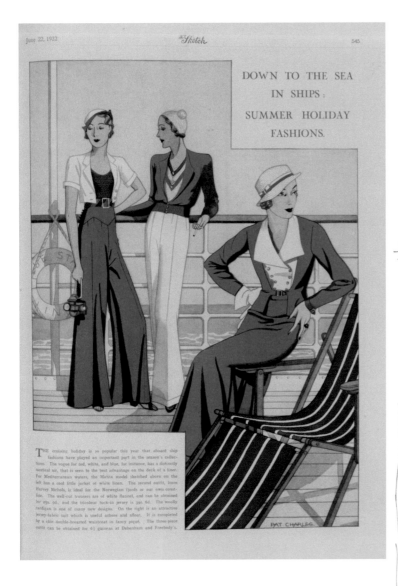

One critic in 1932 noted that:

> from the interior decorative point of view, it is observable that the Italians still feel in their bones the classic tradition. The Germans are modifying a little their extreme ideas of ugly Cubist forms. The French are uncompromisingly *Moderne* with a Teutonic flair. The Swedes and Danes, of all the nations adopting the *Moderne* look, have produced the most beautiful rendering infused with classic grace. The British have refused to be stampeded by a fashion, and have produced many ships of traditional comfort, and only in a few instances have indulged in a half-hearted way the *Moderne* treatment.[12]

Increasingly, designers faced the challenge of evoking a nation's values while also reflecting the greater internationalism that characterized contemporary experience as ocean liners became both an agent and mirror of a globalizing world.

To travel on a twentieth-century ocean liner was to enter a realm of transformative glamour and escapist fantasy. 'Spectacle' was a key idea, and for many travellers the highlight of each day at sea was the theatrical *grande descente* into the dining salon, where passengers could see and be seen by one another. Fashion was central to the experience, with the poolside, deck, smoking lounge, bar, gymnasium, ladies' salon and winter garden all requiring specific attire and codes of behaviour [7 & 9]. Passengers caught sight of, and even had opportunities to speak with, celebrities who were also travelling abroad. The use of space on board shifted as the requirements of new markets changed attitudes, leading to an increase in specialized activity areas. Strict class distinctions were eroded and new spaces were created, developing a greater flow in the plan of ships. Two chapters explore life on board and the etiquette that developed, from children's spaces and deck activities to dining and eveningwear.

The advent of cruising and the increased demand for leisure activities also affected the design of the liners. Cunard's primary

largely for British and German lines, through the sleek French and British Art Deco interiors of the interwar period, to the American streamlined industrial Modernism and festive high style of the Italian ships that followed the Second World War. This section of the book draws upon new research and previously unpublished works that reveal the increasing competition between lines and countries and the resulting impact on design, as the great ships came to represent both a nation's aspirations and political ideology.

---

9 ABOVE
'Down to the Sea in Ships: Summer Holiday Fashions', illustration by Pat Charles, from *The Sketch* (22 June 1932)

10 OPPOSITE
Cities: Moving New York, 1964, by Ron Herron 1964
Photography, ink drawing and pencil on board
RON HERRON ARCHIVE

EACH WALKING UNIT HOUSES NOT ONLY A KEY
ELEMENT OF THE CAPITAL , BUT ALSO A LARGE
POPULATION OF WORLD TRAVELLER-WORKERS.

A WALKING CITY

post-war advertising declared that 'Getting there is half the fun!'. The ship one chose was no longer 'just a method of transportation but a way of life. She's a floating resort, a great hotel, a gay night club, a rendezvous for lovers of good food, a chic shopping centre, a sports pavilion, a quiet club … she is anything you want her to be!'.

As the largest moving objects ever built, ocean liners became a symbol of technological progress and provided a model for new ways of living, capturing the imagination of artists, engineers and architects. The final three chapters highlight some of the ways in which ocean liners inspired key developments in Modernism, from the intense new iconography of the American Cubist Realist painters to Norman Bel Geddes's fantastical proposal for a futuristic liner. Le Corbusier's liner-inspired housing and the proposal for *Walking City* (1964) by Archigram's Ron Herron epitomize how liners helped shape approaches to architecture, art and design throughout the twentieth century [10]. The ocean liner provided a model for such seminal ideas as high-density living and the 'serviced' megastructure, helping to shape both social and technological visions of the future. Liners also provided a fantasy space for Hollywood, and innumerable films were set onboard – or sets built to emulate them. It is perhaps through the dystopian visions of liners, explored in such movies as Ronald Neame's *The Poseidon Adventure* (1972) and James Cameron's *Titanic* (1997),

that the popular imagination has been most thoroughly captured. *Titanic* remains one of the most successful films ever made and ironically proved a huge impetus to the cruise line industry.

Technological developments during the Second World War meant that air travel had become much faster, safer and commercially viable by the late 1950s.[13] However, liners encapsulated the social, political and economic dynamics of their age. Moreover, they have continued to haunt the cultural imagination, dramatically influencing the built environment and becoming a literary and visual leitmotif. From Jules Verne to the more recent science fiction of Iain M. Banks and his 'Culture' series or Alessandro Baricco's *Novecento* (1998), which follows the life of a pianist who from birth to death never leaves the ship, their hermetic cultures have proved rich terrain. For F. Scott Fitzgerald they encapsulated the human experience:

On the long-roofed steamship piers one is in a country that is no longer here and not yet there … the future is the glowing mouth in the side of the ship … Up the gangplank and the vision of the world adjusts itself, narrows. One is a citizen of a commonwealth smaller than Andorra, no longer sure of anything… Next the loud mournful whistles, the portentous vibration and the boat, the human idea—is in motion.[14]

CHAPTER 1
PROMOTING LINERS

ADVERTISING THE OCEAN LINER

CATHERINE FLOOD

IN THE 1860S AND '70S the steamship held a powerful fascination for a public enthralled by technological achievement. As an object it embodied the thrilling progress of modern technology. As a mode of transport, however, it represented danger, discomfort and disease. While new steamships were celebrated in the pages of the illustrated press with detailed reports on their engineering innovations, the same publications were quick to sensationalize steamship disasters or to detail the poor conditions endured by passengers at sea. To build the now-popular image of the ocean liner as the epitome of luxury involved tremendous vision on the part of the shipping lines and required a huge shift in public perception. Over the following decades a flood of printed advertising materials and extensive public-relations budgets were employed to revolutionize the image of steamship travel and establish the unique profile of the ocean liner in visual culture. Both the expansion of commercial advertising in the latter years of the nineteenth century and the emergence of Modernism were to play important roles in this achievement.

STEERAGE AND SALOON

In the 1860s the shipping lines promoted themselves simply by announcing their services through press advertisements and posters embellished with basic reassurances of safety, speed and moderate comfort. Speed was a promise of getting an uncomfortable journey over with as quickly as possible, but was also a statement of technological prowess. The Blue Riband, an unofficial accolade awarded for the fastest crossing of the Atlantic Ocean, kept the public keenly engaged with the engineering race between the shipping lines to build ever-faster ships.

When the British shipping company White Star Line entered the transatlantic passenger trade in 1870 with the launch of *Oceanic* it needed a fresh marketing strategy to stand a chance against its more established competitors. The company approached this challenge by building a reputation – supported by extensive advertising – for providing better on-board facilities than its rivals for both steerage and saloon (first-class) passengers. For the former, this meant promises of daylight and innovations such as separate sleeping quarters for single men and single women. For the latter, it meant the introduction of a wholly new concept of luxurious accommodation that gained momentum as successive liners offered a constantly escalating range of comforts and impressive interiors. The dual character of the ocean liner was thus established: within a single, albeit carefully segregated, structure, it embodied the economic upheavals of emigration on the one hand and an exaggerated display of wealth on the other.

Social distinctions were clearly reflected in the hierarchy of White Star's advertising materials. In the late 1870s the company published promotional literature lavishly illustrated with colour lithographs of first-class interiors being enjoyed by fashionable passengers. In cheaper, mass-printed advertising, however, the options for illustrating the ocean liner were limited. Around 1874, White Star printed a simple leaflet advertising its steerage services that featured a black and white wood engraving of one of its liners on the cover [12].

COLOUR POSTERS

A dramatic shift in the image of the liner occurred in the last quarter of the nineteenth century when advances in printing by colour lithography made it viable to print large-scale pictorial posters in full colour. Earlier posters for the shipping lines were printed in black and white by letterpress. Any pictorial content was generally restricted to a broadside-view, wood engraving of the ship (of the kind used in the White Star leaflet), usually sandwiched between rigid blocks of text. Colour lithography, however, could deliver a painterly portrait of an ocean liner built up from multiple over-printings in different colours with text integrated into the image. The form of the ship expanded to occupy most of the sheet and, since the majority of posters continued to favour a portrait format, the ocean liner was manoeuvred into a new and more

11 PREVIOUS

'*Rex* and *Conte di Savoia*', poster for Italia Flotte
Riunite, designed by Giovanni Patrone, printed
by Barabino & Graeve
Italy, 1932
Colour lithograph
COLLECTION OF MARIO J. PULICE

12 ABOVE

'White Star Line: Liverpool to New York every
Thursday', leaflet, published by Ismay, Imrie & Co.
Liverpool and London, United Kingdom, *c.*1874
Wood engraving and letterpress
PHILLIPS LIBRARY,
PEABODY ESSEX MUSEUM: MH O.211

13 ABOVE

'Allan Lines Royal Mail Steamships', poster, printed
by Donaldson Brothers
New York, United States, 1893
Colour lithograph
ELWIN M. ELDREDGE COLLECTION
MARINERS' MUSEUM AND PARK,
NEWPORT NEWS, VA: LP3254

dramatic perspective. The horizontal profile gave way to an angled view, with the sharp vertical line of the ship's hull cutting through the water towards the viewer.

Indeed, the consistency with which the image of the ship dominated the advertising posters of the shipping lines is remarkable – no other genre of contemporary travel poster honed in on the means of transport to the same extent. The promotion of the ocean liner had to span a vast social range and, while leaflets and brochures could target a particular class of passenger, the poster as a public medium was potentially visible to everyone. The shipping lines needed posters that would appeal to emigrants, upon whom their profits depended, without jeopardizing the increasingly glamorous image of first-class ocean travel. In this context the exterior of the ship was a common denominator, a wonder of the modern age that could be enthusiastically celebrated as a universal symbol of technical achievement.

The act of emigration itself represented a more precarious underside of modernity and was largely avoided by poster designers. In the mid-nineteenth century the departing emigrant had been repeatedly fetishized in paintings as a sentimental figure associated with poverty, despair, regret, nostalgia and loss.[1] With this iconographical heritage it is perhaps unsurprising that the person of the emigrant rarely makes an appearance in ocean liner posters. One exception is a poster for the Scottish Allan Line from around 1900 featuring the head and shoulders of an attractive young woman framed inside a ship's wheel. It is an emotionally contained image. The figure is suspended in time and space, neither departing nor arriving, wearing a slight but calmly confident smile [13].

The 1890s witnessed a burst of excitement about the artistic possibilities of the poster when a number of avant-garde, Paris-based artists, led by the example of Henri de Toulouse-Lautrec (1864–1901), began experimenting with its design, drawn to it as a medium that felt intrinsically modern. Contemporary critics hailed the poster as a new art form with the potential to transcend a purely commercial purpose. Among the shipping lines, the Red Star Line and the American Line stand out for posters commissioned from the Belgian Art Nouveau artist Henri Cassiers (1858–1944) that applied a consciously artistic approach to the task of promoting the liner. In Cassiers's posters a cast of different characters (a fashionable mother and daughter, male workers, a line of peasant women) is depicted turned away from the viewer, transfixed by the sight of an ocean liner [14]. Whether the viewer is meant to identify with these figures as potential passengers or whether they simply represent casual observers is ambiguous. As a compositional device

American Line

New York
Southampton

they frame the ocean liner as an object of fascination while allowing
for more artistic interest than a straightforward image of the
ship. The Red Star Line promoted these posters as decorative
and collectable items in their own right. In 1907 they were
reproduced on its menu cards with a notice informing passengers
that the posters themselves could be ordered from the printers
– a nod to a brief but avid craze for poster collecting in the early
twentieth century.

In the 1900s, Germany was widely acknowledged to be
producing the most aesthetically progressive poster art. Designers
such as Lucian Bernhard (1883–1972), Julius Klinger (1876–1942)
and Ludwig Hohlwein (1874–1949) developed a bold approach
based on minimal text and the simplification of images. Following
the Deutscher Werkbund's (the German Association of Craftsmen)
philosophy that form should be determined by function, their
designs favoured clear communication over the decorative clutter
that characterized most commercial art of the day. The German

14 ABOVE

'American Line: New York, Southampton', poster,
designed by Henri Cassiers
New York, United States, c.1900
Colour lithograph
GIFT OF FRANCIS B.C. BRADLEE, 1928
PEABODY ESSEX MUSEUM: M6959

R. M. S. Aquitania (Cunard Line).
Length 902 ft. Breadth 97 ft.
Depth 92 ft. 6 inches.
Tonnage 47,000. Speed 23 knots.

shipping line Norddeutscher Lloyd made a number of forays into modern design, including commissioning a poster by Hohlwein for its Mediterranean route in 1913 [16].

In general, however, posters by the likes of Cassiers and Hohlwein remained the exception rather than the rule among the shipping lines. Looking at the vast majority of ocean liner posters from the period before the First World War, it is clear that the safest commercial choice was considered to be a painterly picture of the ship procured from one of the commercial marine artists who were based around the ports and shipyards.

POSTCARDS

Another new format in which the image of the ocean liner flourished at the turn of the twentieth century was the picture postcard. From the 1890s to the outbreak of the First World War, the postcard enjoyed enormous popularity as an attractive and inexpensive form of communication that was intimately bound up with the new international geographies of immigration. Among the many topical subjects depicted on postcards, the ocean liner was a particularly fitting theme since it represented a vital link in the transnational mail service, upon which the postcard phenomenon relied.

The shipping companies were quick to capitalize on the potential of the ocean liner postcard and began issuing their own, which were sold on the dockside and on board. Buying and sending farewell postcards to friends and families left behind became part of the ritual of departure. For the shipping companies, these postcards were a lucrative line in merchandise and a clever means of dispatching their advertising messages directly into the hands of more potential passengers. For emigrants, they tapped into the anxieties of parting and offered reassurance – the liner depicted on the postcard not only carried you away from loved ones, but it was also the means by which you could stay connected.

On some postcards this message was emphasized by a popular motif known as 'Hands Across the Sea', in which a male and a female hand are shown clasped in the sky above the ubiquitous image of the liner [15]. The ships themselves realized the visual connection by transporting the card from one hand to another. The success of these postcards in combining their promotional purpose with such intimate moments rendered these relatively humble objects a triumph of advertising strategy.

NATIONAL RIVALRY

While ocean liner postcards tapped into personal feelings, the shipping lines were also able to exploit political themes for emotional impact, particularly during the years of heightened nationalism in Europe preceding the outbreak of the First World War. Hohlwein's poster for Norddeutscher Lloyd's Mediterranean cruises in 1913 played on racial stereotypes that appealed to Germany's identity as a relatively new colonial power [16]. The poster depicts an ocean liner steaming along the horizon as a black boy riding a donkey turns to look back at the ship in amazement, and possibly fear. The white viewer is flattered by contrast through his or her assumed familiarity with the liner as a sharply modern and civilized mode of transport. The location of the scene is left vague – indicated only by a line of camels on the shoreline. Printed two years after the Agadir crisis (when Germany had sent the gunboat *Panther* to the port in reaction to the deployment of French troops in Morocco) it may have both evoked an exotic destination and reminded contemporary viewers of Germany's ambitions on the world stage.

Indeed the ocean liner was itself becoming an issue of national rivalry – particularly between Britain and Germany. As such, advertising materials began actively to encourage the public to embrace new ocean liners as national monuments, aligning corporate priorities with patriotic fervour. Around 1907 promotional booklets published by Cunard pictured the *Mauretania* and *Lusitania* alongside iconic British landmarks such as the Houses of Parliament, St Paul's Cathedral and a number of famous town halls. A Hamburg-American Line brochure for *Imperator* in 1913 described the launch of the liner as 'an event of national significance' for Germany and reproduced a photograph of Kaiser Wilhelm II (1859–1941) christening the ship.

15 OPPOSITE

Aquitania postcard with 'Hands Across the Sea'
motif, published by Cunard, 1913

16 ABOVE

'Mittelmeer-Fahrten' (Mediterranean cruises),
poster for Norddeutscher Lloyd, designed by
Ludwig Hohlwein, printed by Vereinigte Druckereien
und Kunstanstalten
Munich, Germany, 1913
Colour lithograph
MÜNCHNER STADTMUSEUM: B 17/152

PUBLIC RELATIONS

The success of a new liner was determined not only in the shipyards, but also in the marketing departments of the shipping lines that invested time and energy into making their ships into media stars. As an article in *The Times* reported on the maiden voyage of *Imperator* in 1913: 'much depends on the public reception of the ship; for there is all the difference in the world between a vessel that becomes a popular favourite with the Transatlantic public and one that for some reason or other, does not "catch on".'[2] By this time the launch and the maiden voyage of a new liner were carefully staged media events attended by tens of thousands of people, and for which the press were carefully courted and primed. On the maiden voyage of *Imperator* a group of international journalists and writers travelled as VIP guests in order to report on the experience. Through the pages of the press, a broad section of the public was able to consume descriptions of ocean liners and to participate in the social fantasies they conjured.

As well as working to secure press coverage, the shipping lines published a great array of their own printed literature all designed to keep the ocean liner in the public eye. This ranged from celebratory company histories to booklets issued in conjunction with significant events such as coronations and world fairs, to deck plans and logbooks intended for passengers to use on board and then keep as souvenirs. In the late nineteenth century, several shipping companies produced weighty guidebooks that combined information about their ships and services with world maps, star charts and essays on topical themes such as navigation and nature at sea. In the early twentieth century however, the brochure emerged as the set piece in promoting the liner, typically issued for the maiden voyage of a new ship or after any major refit. Brochures allowed people to see inside the liner, to explore the complexities of its structure in detailed sectional plans and to browse its lavish interiors through photographs and illustrations. Dominated by images, these brochures encouraged the idea that the ocean liner was a site for visual pleasure.

OCEAN LINERS AND SKYSCRAPERS

As we have seen, the speed of an ocean liner had always been an important factor in capturing the public's imagination – a record-breaking crossing of the Atlantic grabbed headlines and increased passenger numbers. Size and comfort, however, were becoming

17 OPPOSITE

'Surpassing the Greatest Buildings and Memorials
on Earth', White Star Line promotional image
for *Titanic*, 1912

18 ABOVE

'The Big 3 to France and England',
Cunard tourist office sign depicting *Berengaria*,
Aquitania and *Mauretania*, designed and
executed by Kay of Austria
c.1925
Painted wood

COLLECTION OF STEPHEN S. LASH

THE DINING SALOON

FLOTTE RIVNITE ✕ COSVLICH ✕ LLOYD SABAVDO ✕ NAVIGAZIONE GENERALE

19 ABOVE
'The Dining Saloon', from a first-class brochure for
Rex, designed by Vittorio Accornero de Testa and
Edina Altara, printed by Richter & C., published by
Ufficio pubblicità Italia
Naples, Italy, 1932
HOWARD GALVIN STEAMSHIP EPHEMERA
COLLECTION
PHILLIPS LIBRARY, PEABODY ESSEX MUSEUM

20 OPPOSITE
'Cunard Line: Europe-America', poster, designed
by Kenneth Shoesmith, printed by Thos. Forman
& Sons
Nottingham, United Kingdom, 1925
Colour lithograph
GIFT OF FRANCIS B.C. BRADLEE, 1928
PEABODY ESSEX MUSEUM: M11215

increasingly important competitive factors and the Hamburg-
American Line decided around 1910 to make these its priorities
by commissioning a new generation of giant liners. As ocean
liners grew to proportions that challenged traditional modes of
representation, the shipping lines needed new visual strategies
to convey the superlatives of size. As the brochure for *Imperator*
exclaimed, in trying to describe the ship 'all comparisons of size
fail'. One popular solution was to measure the liners against the
world's tallest buildings. In 1899 a drawing depicted *Kaiser Wilhelm
der Grosse* (1897) upended alongside a number of tall buildings –
including the newly completed St Paul Building in New York (1898)
– all of which the ship outstrips. This comparison between an
upended liner and the latest New York skyscraper became a much-
repeated trope in the postcards and brochures of shipping lines.
In around 1908, *Lusitania* was depicted topping the Singer Building
and in 1913 *Imperator* was demonstrated to be 'taller' than the new
Woolworth Building. And the comparison worked both ways.
When Alfred Stieglitz (1864–1946) photographed the Flatiron
Building in New York in 1902–3, he did so from an ocean-liner
perspective, so that the triangular corner of the building towered
above the viewer like the prow of a great ship.

Ocean liners and skyscrapers were two almost overwhelming
monuments of modernity, and as such they could inspire a mix
of exhilaration, dislocation and anxiety about change. One visitor
to New York commented in 1913: 'The huge ocean liners and the
gigantic skyscrapers seem to stimulate growth reciprocally. Amazed
one asks where and when the final limit will be reached.'[3] One
image produced by the White Star Line to promote *Titanic* (1912)
in brochures and on postcards provided a variation on the familiar
ocean liner/skyscraper theme that addressed this question [17].
The ship is placed vertically in the middle of the picture between a
succession of four New York skyscrapers on the left and a group of
celebrated historical monuments on the right. The liner, therefore,
represents, not a break with the past, but a connection between the
old world and the new. Its extraordinary size is presented as part
of an ongoing tradition of technical innovation stretching back to
ancient Egypt.[4]

TOURISM, LUXURY AND CONSUMPTION

In 1921, the United States tightened controls on immigration,
resulting in a dramatic shift in the demographic of transatlantic
travel. From now on the shipping companies' appeals to emigrants
were specifically targeted. In the 1920s, for example, the White Star
Line issued a series of posters in line with a scheme sanctioned by
the Canadian government for the admission and assisted passage

21 ABOVE

'*Empress of Britain*', poster for Canadian Pacific
Railways, designed by J.R. Tooby, printed by Sanders,
Phillips & Co.

London, United Kingdom, *c.*1930–1

Colour lithograph

GIVEN BY THE CANADIAN PACIFIC RAILWAY CO.

V&A: E.2215–1931

22 OPPOSITE

'*Normandie*: Le Havre–Southampton–New York',
poster for the Compagnie Générale Transatlantique,
designed by A.M. Cassandre

Paris, France, 1935

Colour lithograph

V&A: E648–2017

of farm labourers and domestic workers. Displayed at agricultural fairs in England, the posters were an active call to emigrate, featuring rosy scenes of men and women enjoying a full and productive rural life in a new country. In general, however, the transatlantic shipping lines adjusted their business model to focus on the luxury tourist market. Steerage was replaced with more first- and second-class cabins and a 'tourist third cabin' was introduced to cater for the newly prosperous section of American society who could now contemplate travelling to Europe on holiday.

The creation of tourist class necessitated marketing campaigns to present the new service as both affordable and aspirational. As the trade magazine *The Ocean Ferry* commented in reference to a series of White Star press advertisements in 1926, 'the idea of seeing Europe inexpensively is put forth but there is no suggestion that tourist third cabin is "cheap" excepting from the monetary standpoint'. Such adverts took pains to define the social profile of the new tourist. The confined space of the ocean liner had always provoked anxieties about social mixing and advertising copy reassured potential tourists that 'in tourist third cabin you will enjoy the companionship of cultured men and women from college and professional circles'.[5]

As ocean travel became more firmly linked with tourism, the marketing of the liner became entwined with an associated culture of commodities. One of the main display sites for shipping line posters had always been in the windows of company offices and travel agencies, which were also sometimes embellished by elaborate desk signs and purpose-designed fittings bearing the name of the line [18]. In the 1920s, however, department stores and retailers began to take posters from the shipping lines to integrate into travel-themed displays of apparel, books and luggage. The shipping companies gained free advertising space for their posters, while the image of the liner conferred added glamour on the retailers' wares. In turn, shipping line brochures cultivated the idea of the liner as a feminized milieu of luxury consumption. A 1931 brochure for the Italian liner *Rex*, for example, could be mistaken for a series of fashion plates from an upmarket ladies' magazine [19]. The illustrations for the brochure were commissioned from Vittorio Accornero de Testa (1896–1982) and his wife Edina Altara (1898–1983), who was both an illustrator of fashion magazines and a fashion designer. Accornero drew the lavish interiors that served as stage settings for Altara's detailed depictions of modish clothing.

NORMANDIE

Cⁱᵉ Gᵉ TRANSATLANTIQUE
French Line

LE HAVRE — SOUTHAMPTON — NEW-YORK
SERVICE RÉGULIER
PAR PAQUEBOTS DE LUXE
ET A CLASSE UNIQUE

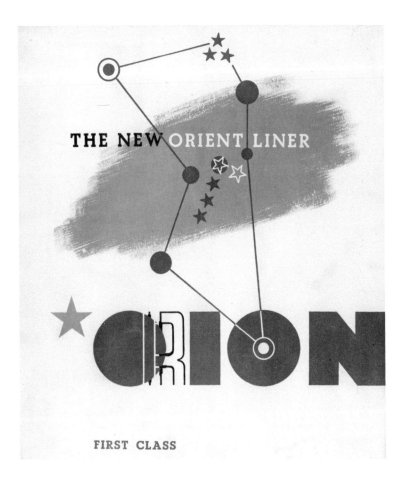

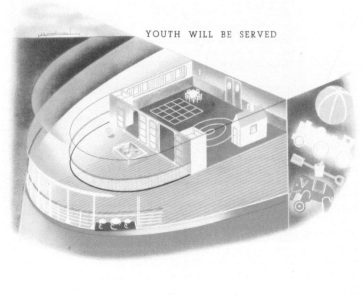

MODERN DESIGN

Until the 1920s the aesthetic style in which the ocean liner was both
decorated and depicted had lagged behind its meaning as a symbol
of modernity. In the pages of ocean liner brochures before the First
World War photographs of gleaming turbines and engine rooms sat
next to illustrations of lavish interiors decorated in the grand style
of *belle-époque* hotels. There was a clear disjunction between the
sense of modernity inspired by the form and technology of the
ocean liner and the design of first-class accommodation that
disguised the characteristic lines of the ship and drew its affluent
ambience from the decorative styles of the past. In a similar
fashion, the image of the ocean liner had been rendered on posters,
brochures and postcards in a style that looked to a conservative
tradition of marine painting.

The Paris Exhibition of 1925, however, marked a turning point
for European design in which the work of artists and designers,
energized by the technologies and artefacts of modern life, gained
new currency as an expression of style and luxury. In the late 1920s
and early '30s, the ocean liner was embraced both as a source of
inspiration by painters, designers and architects and as a site for
Modernist design commissions. This included a bolder, modern
approach to the design of posters and graphics [20 & 21].

For the French painter and commercial artist A.M. Cassandre (1901–68), advertising represented a more authentic response to modern life than easel painting. 'Advertising', he wrote, 'can no more be summed up in a snap judgement than it can be viewed in Museums and Collections. It is like Love. One does not JUDGE it one EXPERIENCES it ... it is one of the finest expressions of contemporary life'.[6] Inspired by architecture and the experiments of avant-garde art, Cassandre developed a poster style based on clean lines, geometric shapes and pared-down colour schemes. It was an approach that worked with the logic of printing technology rather than obscuring the means of production by striving to simulate a painterly effect. According to his son and biographer, Cassandre was inspired in the late 1920s and early '30s by 'all that was new, daring and awe-inspiring in the contemporary scene ... all that seemed to extend the boundaries of man's world'.[7] The ocean liner delighted him as a subject that gave the perfect scope for exploring a machine aesthetic through poster design.

Cassandre treated the unique forms of the ocean liner from a number of angles, playing with perspective and scale. In a poster advertising the new Dutch liner *Statendam* in 1928 he focused in on an abstracted detail of smokestacks and ventilators that almost seem to suck the viewer into the poster (a composition that was almost certainly inspired by *Boatdeck*, a painting by the American artist Gerald Murphy (1888–1964), exhibited at the Salon des Indépendants in Paris in 1924) [215]. In 1935, Cassandre gave the Compagnie Générale Transatlantique ship *Normandie* a towering frontal view that emphasized the symmetrical geometry of the ship's lines [22]. A sense of the colossal scale is created by the way the prow soars into the top of the sheet and by a tiny flock of gulls passing across the mass of the hull.

Normandie was a tour de force of Art Deco style that showcased the best contemporary work of French architects, decorators, artists and craftsmen. A poster by Cassandre, the most celebrated poster artist of the day, was a natural choice to promote the ship. Ocean liners now functioned as ambassadors of a nation's design achievements and the publicity materials that introduced them needed to match the message.

In Britain, *Orion* (1935), completed in the same year as *Normandie*, was also an exercise in modern design, but in a very different vein. More understated in style than the French ship, the revolutionary thing about the design of *Orion* was its totally co-ordinated approach. Under the guidance of the young Colin Skelton Anderson (1904–80) of the Orient Line, who went on to become an important figure in the post-war art world, every fitment 'down to the publicity materials, menus, ship's information and the stewards

buttons' was designed from scratch to contribute to an integrated whole.[8] Edward McKnight Kauffer (1890–1954) – one of the most influential graphic designers of the inter-war period who had translated the challenging visual languages of Cubism, Futurism and Surrealism into successful commercial art – produced the ship's graphics (including posters, brochures and luggage labels), which guided passengers into a seamless experience of modern design before they even stepped aboard [23]. The *Orion*'s brochure was illustrated by Ceri Richards (1903–71), a British Surrealist artist who also worked in advertising. His stylish airbrushed images perfectly captured the linear economy of *Orion*'s interiors [24].

In Italy, Art Deco style developed under the influence of Futurism and Fascism. While Futurism celebrated industrial society and expressed a particular affinity with advertising, most commercial advertisers rejected the anarchic aesthetics of the

movement in its pure form. Certain dynamic aspects of Futurism, however, did find their way into mainstream graphics. In Giovanni Patrone's (1904–63) poster for the inaugural voyages of the liners *Rex* and *Conte di Savoia* in 1932, the hulls of the two great Italian vessels appear almost to leap out of the poster frame, while the angled alignment of the text gives the composition additional energy [11]. Patrone established a strong reputation for ocean liner publicity, and worked for the Italian Line for the next two decades. A poster by Gino Boccasile (1901–52) for the Cosulich Line in the mid-1930s represented a more figurative tendency in Italian graphic design. Boccasile is known for both pin-up style illustrations of glamorous women on magazine covers such as *Le Grandi Firme* and for the propaganda posters he produced for Mussolini's regime. His poster for the shipping line has political echoes in its portrayal of the Fascist ideal of the healthy, sporting female form and in the rousing optimism of the composition [25].

END OF AN ERA

After the Second World War the building of new ocean liners and refitting of existing ones played a role in the reconstructing of national identities, but the relevance of the ocean liner as a mode

of transport soon dwindled in the face of commercial air travel. The dynamics of commercial art were also changing as design groups and advertising agencies better suited to the corporate structures of the second half of the twentieth century began to replace the individual graphic artists and designers who had put their personal stamps on the image of the ocean liner. For the *QE2* (1969), an integrated system of graphics and signage to guide passengers through the maze of the ship's corridors was devised by graphic designers Alan Fletcher and Colin Forbes who were part of Crosby/Fletcher/Forbes, a new kind of multidisciplinary design group including architect Theo Crosby [26].[9] In around 1968, John Bainbridge (1919–78) produced a striking poster for *France* (1962) [27]. Like Cassandre's poster for *Statendam* 40 years earlier, it focused on an architectural detail of the ship (in this case a distinctive winged funnel), but did so in a style that evoked the contemporary aesthetics of Op art and pop culture. And yet the poster was something of an anachronism – *France* was among the last great, purpose-built ocean liners while Bainbridge belonged to a fading generation of designers for whom the poster was a defining part of their output. The zeitgeist of graphic art now lay with the energy of the counterculture rather than the exhilaration of the machine age.

26 ABOVE
QE2, brochure with branding possibly by Crosby/
Fletcher/Forbes, designed by Mando Arts Ltd,
published by Transart Ltd
London, United Kingdom, 1969
Paper, board and plastic
P&O HERITAGE COLLECTION, LONDON:
CH/01989/00

27 OPPOSITE
'SS *France*-Le Havre-New York', poster for the
Compagnie Générale Transatlantique, designed by
John Bainbridge
United Kingdom, c.1968
Colour offset lithograph
V&A: E.250–1981

BAINBRIDGE
SS FRANCE
LE HAVRE
NEW YORK
FRENCH LINE
COMPAGNIE GENERALE
TRANSATLANTIQUE
CROISIERES

A CLOSE-UP PICTURE OF A MIGHTY PROJECT: PROMOTIONAL EXHIBITION MODELS

GEORGE SCHWARTZ

[I]n the distant past, even as now ... models were ever fascinating to the beholder.

Easy, then, it is to understand why our great Masters of the Marine in the present day employ models to attract, one might say compel, the attention of [a] travelling public more critical and better provided for than ever in history.[1]

FROM THE MID-NINETEENTH CENTURY, many shipyards began to establish divisions exclusively devoted to constructing a new type of promotional model. Known as 'builders' models', these works presented vessels as pristine objects with glossy finishes and were intended for display in the shipyard's offices or boardrooms.[2] Modelling workshops also created many builders' models made specifically for exhibition at the great industrial expositions of the later nineteenth century. These fairs permeated popular culture, presenting emerging artistic talents and national cultural achievements to the world. Steamship companies displayed models alongside recreated interior spaces and visual art to promote innovations in design and technology. A model of Isambard Kingdom Brunel's (1806–59) *Great Britain* (1845) – 'made of tin, neatly executed and painted' – was exhibited in the north-western gallery of the 'Crystal Palace' during London's Great Exhibition in 1851.[3]

Models were popular attractions at these fairs, and steamship lines exploited them as a new tool to advertise their companies. In the Machinery Hall at the 1876 *Centennial International Exhibition* in Philadelphia, a model of the Inman Line's *City of Berlin* (1875) was displayed in the British section of the building and admired for its 'remarkably fine and exquisitely finished' workmanship.[4] Of all the exhibits mentioned in a *Harper's Weekly* column dedicated to the fair, this object was deemed worthy of illustration; a testament to the popularity of ship models [28]. Perhaps in anticipation of a future voyage, a mother and her two children carefully examine the intricate details of the vessel. By the end of the century, Cunard,

White Star, Norddeutscher Lloyd and other international lines occupied specially designed wings, or, in some cases, their own separate buildings at these fairs. In each display, their current and past ships were presented as models.

By 1900, the appeal of models on public display had led to their appearance in booking offices to offer customers a taste of the ships on which they might book passage. Willy Stöwer (1864–1931), a German marine artist and illustrator who created works used in Norddeutscher Lloyd and Hamburg-American promotional materials, accurately captures this experience in a scene showing Norddeutscher Lloyd's office in Berlin [29]. A large model of *Kaiser Wilhelm II* (1889) fills the street-front window of the booking office, while a family peers through the glass to study a world map showing the company's route network. On these lines are miniature models of the Norddeutscher Lloyd fleet, which were moved every morning to denote their current position on the seas, allowing the public to follow the daily movements of the fleet and perhaps follow friends and family on their travels.[5]

The steamship lines' desire for sleek and finely rendered models of varying scales gave rise to professional modelling companies that focused solely on creating promotional ship models while established model makers also began incorporating them into their portfolios. A select few emerged as the premier manufacturers of exhibition-quality models, and liner companies invested heavily in having their ships portrayed in intricate detail for public consumption. Christopher de Groot, New England representative of Norddeutscher Lloyd in the 1920s and '30s, noted:

the price ranges from around $5,000 to well above $25,000, depending both upon the size and the type of the model executed. Of course it is possible to produce a cheaper model, but this is seldom done. Practically all steamship companies prefer to have their ships shown in fitting style.[6]

28 ABOVE

'The Centennial-Model of the Steam-Ship *City of Berlin* in Machinery Hall' at the *Centennial International Exhibition*, Philadelphia, 1876, from *Harper's Weekly* (8 July 1876)

29 TOP
Wood engraving of a dispay window
at the Norddeutscher Lloyd Office, Berlin,
by Willy Stöwer, 1893

30 ABOVE
'Craftsmen at Art Model Studios in Mount Vernon,
New York, at work on a model of *Leonardo da Vinci*.
In the foreground are models in for repair, from left:
SS *United States*, *Cristoforo Colombo*, *Queen Mary*
and *Independence*', published in *The New York Times*
(3 April 1960)

Similarly, Associated Press writer Devon Francis reported in 1935: 'Modest fortunes are being sunk again in steamship models' that 'go the rounds of the steamship agencies of the principal cities to help up passenger business'.[7]

In 1907, Cunard commissioned Robert Smith and his associates in Newcastle upon Tyne to make two models for their London office: one of *Mauretania* (1907), recently built at the Swan Hunter & Wigham Richardson shipyard near their workshops, and another of her sister ship *Lusitania* (1907).[8] Around the same time, Gebrüder Fleischmann of Nuremberg, founded in 1887 and still renowned today, began to produce scale models of ocean liners. In 1906, they received a commission from Norddeutscher Lloyd for at least six models of its liner *Kronprinzessin Cecilie* (1907) for display in American booking offices.[9] A 1908 Fleischmann catalogue declares that these models were built to such a degree of accuracy that they could be used for educational purposes at a university.[10] The model that decorated the Norddeutscher Lloyd office in Philadelphia has a hull cast in three pieces of pewter that were soldered together, tin decks, and was internally illuminated, allowing viewers to catch a rare glimpse of the ship as it would appear at night [32].[11]

In the inter-war period, other model companies arose devoted primarily to making models for smaller regional offices and travel agents. Like ocean travel, creating these models was an international affair and makers often crafted works for shipping lines of other nations. In Italy, Ditta Giacomo Patrone of Genoa, founded in the late nineteenth century by Giacomo and Erasmo Patrone, made models for Italian, American and other international shipping companies from the 1920s to the mid-1960s.[12] In the United States, Arthur G. Henning's Art Model Studio of Mount Vernon, NY, produced around 200 models a year, many of which were displayed in the offices of United States Lines, Cunard, the Italian Line and others [30].[13] Its portfolio included full and half hull models, ranging from twelve inches to twelve feet in length.

The finest model-making company during the golden age of ocean-liner travel was Bassett-Lowke Ltd of Northampton, Great Britain (operating from 1898 to 1965). Founded by Wenman J. Bassett-Lowke (1877–1953) as a business devoted to model railway engines and parts, the firm added a ship-modelling division before the First World War. In the inter-war period they gained international recognition for their high-quality models and were contracted by Cunard, White Star, the Compagnie Générale Transatlantique (CGT) and others to create models for booking offices in the United Kingdom, France and the United States. They also made models of interior spaces on board liners and other novel creations for display in regional fairs and international exhibitions.

For the British Pavilion at the 1937 *Exposition Internationale des Arts et Techniques dans la Vie Moderne* in Paris, Bassett-Lowke presented Britain's commercial and naval fleet in miniature. The models moved across a painted backdrop and were viewed through 'two life-size port-holes ... so realistically portrayed that as the onlooker gazes, he finds it hard indeed to realise that he is not inside a big ocean-going liner watching through his port-hole the ships at sea'.[14]

Bassett-Lowke clearly understood the importance of high-calibre models in liner promotion. In an advertisement entitled 'Ideal Publicity for Ships: Illuminated Scale Models', the company proclaims, 'MODELS are wonderful publicity agents – real INVESTMENTS – as many shipping companies have proved'.[15] Specifically, Bassett-Lowke calls attention to a 10-ft illuminated model of *Normandie* (1935) created for the windows of the CGT offices on Cockspur Street, London, 'which day and night draws crowds of interested spectators ... showing all her wonderful amenities in a comprehensive form'. To further their international marketing, Bassett-Lowke found representatives on the continent to carry their products, such as E.P. Malaret & Co., who owned a toyshop on the Rue de Rivoli in Paris called 'Au Paradis des Enfants'.[16]

Bassett-Lowke's model of *Queen Elizabeth* (1940) represents the apex of ocean-liner exhibition models [31]. Billed as the largest model ever made, and based upon the biggest liner of the time, it was created for Cunard's palatial offices at 25 Broadway in New York. Every piece of the 1:48 scale (1/4 in. to 1 ft) model was handcrafted over the course of a year. The hull was carved from a large log of West African obeche specially obtained for the project, and the final assembly took a five-man team 12 weeks to complete.[17]

Attesting to the popular allure of ship models and the complexity of this monumental project, Britain's Pathé News filmed the completion of this 'schoolboy's dream come true'.[18] The narrator mentions the model's 900 handcrafted fittings, all made 'to the minutest detail', and the 20 coats of paint required to create this 22-ft 'baby sister to a queen of the seas'. The film not only celebrates the new model, but also promotes model making in general as 'an old and proud craft'. To complete the promotional tableau, Bassett-Lowke produced an illustrated brochure, declaring that the purpose of the model was to 'provide a close-up view of a mighty project'.[19]

The model was inspected and approved by a Cunard naval architect before it was accepted and sent to New York on its liner *Parthia* (1948) to grace the company's office. After walking through the door, prospective voyagers would be greeted by the 'lions' of the Cunard Line with *Queen Elizabeth* on the right and a sister model of *Queen Mary* (1936), constructed by Bassett-Lowke almost 15 years

31 ABOVE

Queen Elizabeth, 1:48 promotional model,
made for Cunard by Bassett-Lowke Ltd
Northampton, United Kingdom, 1949
West African obeche, gunmetal and brass
GIFT OF CUNARD LINE LTD, 1970
PEABODY ESSEX MUSEUM: M14220

32 LEFT

Kronprinzessin Cecilie, 1:96 illuminated model, made
for Norddeutscher Lloyd by Gebrüder Fleischmann
Nuremberg, Germany, *c.*1906
Pewter, metal, wire, plastic, thread and paint
GIFT OF EDWARD W. ROSENBAUM
MARINERS' MUSEUM AND PARK,
NEWPORT NEWS, VA: MD73

before, on the left. After marvelling at these creations, customers would proceed to the office's Great Hall, which stretched 'the entire width of a block, with booking counters on each side, the whole closely resembling the nave of a massive cathedral' [33].[20] More models of various Cunard liners past and present filled the hall: a historical snapshot of the company and a three-dimensional affirmation of its brand.

In addition to the standard full-hull treatment, ship models were made in a variety of forms. A model of the Cunard liner *Berengaria* (previously *Imperator* (1913) built for the Hamburg-American Line) attributed to Bassett-Lowke, with a port-side longitudinal section cutaway, was exhibited in Cunard's Atlanta office in April 1939 [151]. This unusual display technique allowed would-be patrons to examine the internal arrangement of the vessel as painted by Montague Birrell Black (1884–1964). Black was a British painter, illustrator and poster artist who created works for White Star, the CGT and United States Lines, in addition to other British rail- and travel-related advertising art. This style of model was usually displayed in a mirror-backed case so that exterior features such as portholes and ventilators could be viewed at the same time as interior cabin arrangements.

Waterline models, which give the appearance of a ship at sea, were another popular form used for promotion. These types of models were displayed in smaller offices as their hulls were often hollow and they were lighter and easier to move. When Norddeutscher Lloyd opened their new Boston office on 252 Boylston Street in 1931, they incorporated 'the general motif of the ultra-modern steamship *Bremen*' (1929) into the office design.[21] In the street-facing window, a large model of *Bremen* speeding through an artificial sea epitomized this industrial modern aesthetic and extended these progressive ideas to the front office [34].

It was noted as attracting 'interested spectators continuously' and, with illumination spilling from cut-through portholes and windows, it gave an impression of the liner 'cruising along after dark'.[22]

Models were not only displayed in booking offices, but also in public spaces such as department stores and banks. In 1936, Cunard loaned a 6-ft illuminated model of *Queen Mary* to the Boggs & Buhl department store in Pittsburgh, Pennsylvania, for a display on its fashion floor advertising 'clothes for travel, including the new "Cunard Red"'.[23] Sometimes models were used to promote new vessels in advance of their maiden voyage. A 19½-ft model of *Titanic* (1912) built by eight employees of the Harland & Wolff shipyard in Belfast, for example, was sent to the United States in 1911 and exhibited in a few cities across the country.[24] On other occasions, liner companies actually encouraged the public to make models as a means of promoting recent launches. In 1936, the CGT created a worldwide contest to construct a model of *Normandie*. Of the 2,000 models submitted, the top 100 were exhibited in the Rockefeller Center in New York City and judged by a committee headed by the French Consul General. The top three entrants were announced on board *Normandie* when the liner arrived in New York on 21 April 1936.[25]

With the end of the ocean-liner era, the world-class models that were the face of many shipping lines were jettisoned from closing offices or scrapped. A few fortunate examples found homes in museum collections, but the majority were lost or have fallen into disrepair, only noticed by a discerning eye that can see beyond weathered hulls and broken decks. Some surviving examples are now on contemporary cruise ships, displayed in areas devoted to nostalgic reminiscences of the golden age of ocean liners. And within these spaces the models serve to 'arouse the wanderlust' in ocean travellers once again.[26]

---

33 OPPOSITE
The Great Hall of the Cunard Building (1921),
25 Broadway, New York, designed by Benjamin
Wistar Morris, from the *Description of the Great Hall*
booklet

34 OVERLEAF
Bremen, 1:144 illuminated waterline model,
possibly the one displayed in the Norddeutscher
Lloyd Boston office
c.1931–3
Wood and metal
GIFT OF LEON LAWRENCE SIDELL, 1969
PEABODY ESSEX MUSEUM: M13662

CUNARD BUILDING
25 BROADWAY · NEW YORK CITY

THE ARCHITECTURE OF PROMOTION

BRUCE PETER

THE GROWTH OF LINER SHIPPING – the operation of scheduled overseas transport services – required an extensive shore-based infrastructure to feed cargoes and passengers, filling vessels to capacity. Thus, networks of cargo agencies, freight forwarders and travel agents spread out from the ports. Often, the design of liner companies' ticketing bureaus sought to give potential passengers an appealing foretaste of the kinds of atmosphere and service that they would experience onboard ship, if only they could be persuaded to purchase travel. As such, architecture played a key role in shipping lines' marketing strategies.

For much of its long history, sea travel had an image problem; the oceans were stormy and potentially dangerous, so, for a majority of travellers, a liner voyage was something to be done only out of necessity. Just as the railways sought to reinvent themselves in the public's imagination as 'safe' and 'respectable' through the targeted deployment of grand architecture for stations, so too did the liner companies. Subsequently, however, it was found that they could also generate welcome secondary revenue streams through property development.

Britain's Peninsular & Oriental Steam Navigation Company (P&O) – which pioneered liner services by steamship from London to Mediterranean ports, and subsequently east of Suez to India – was an early patron of grand architecture. The London-based architect Thomas Edward Collcutt (1840–1924) designed part of P&O's offices in Leadenhall Street (1893) and went on to produce public rooms for over a dozen of the company's liners, including *Himalaya* and *Australia* (both 1892) [36]. His designs for first-class music rooms, dining areas and lounges were richly decorated with oak or mahogany and complemented by stained glass, fine plasterwork and murals. This opulent approach to decoration was also employed in other important shipping buildings of the period, including Lloyd's Register (1901) on Fenchurch Street, on which many leading Arts and Crafts designers and sculptors worked.

While P&O was established in the City, other liner companies developed offices on Cockspur Street, between Trafalgar Square and Pall Mall in Westminster. This short thoroughfare was well located to attract potential passengers of all classes, as well as being conveniently near to London's most exclusive gentlemen's clubs, where shipping directors hobnobbed with financiers and politicians.

Sir Henry Tanner (1849–1935), whose London-based firm had produced numerous imposing post offices for the government's Office of Works, designed White Star Line's Oceanic House (1906) [35]. With ticketing on the ground floor and administration above, this was not dissimilar to the post offices in terms of spatial and structural characteristics. The façade of Oceanic House, however, was grandly ornate, mixing Greek and Baroque motifs, the top three storeys being particularly boldly modelled. The interior was by Waring & Gillow, a prominent decorator and furnishing company that subsequently designed spaces on board *Lusitania* (1907), *Queen Mary* (1936) and *Queen Elizabeth* (1940) among others.

Between 1906 and 1908, the Hamburg-American Line employed Arthur T. Bolton (1864–1945) to remodel an existing building at 14–16 Cockspur Street. It was another Baroque affair, adorned with splendid, nautically inspired architectural sculpture by William Bateman Fagan (1860–1948) [37]. Upon the outbreak of the First World War, however, the government requisitioned the building and Hamburg-American's employees were sent home as enemy aliens. Retained as a war reparation, the building was acquired by P&O, which modified the iconography of its exterior to reflect the change of use from a transatlantic liner company to one serving the British Empire. P&O added sculptures by Ernest Gillick (1874–1951) depicting 'Britain' and 'The Orient' above the main entrance to the ticket office [38]. By the 1920s, with numerous other shipping companies in residence, Cockspur Street had become to liner travel what Harley Street was to medicine and Savile Row was to tailoring.

Before the First World War, Hamburg-American was an exceptionally powerful company and its Director General, Albert

OFFICES·FOR·THE·P·&·O·STEAM·NAVIGATION·COMPANY·LTD
LEADENHALL·STREET·E.C.

T.E·COLLCUTT·F·R·I·B·A·ARCHt

36 LEFT
Engraving of the P&O offices (1893), 128 Leadenhall
Street, London, designed by Thomas Edward
Collcutt, from *The Building News* (June 1894)

37 OPPOSITE LEFT
*View of the P&O Office and Booking Hall
at 14–16 Cockspur Street*, artist unknown
United Kingdom, *c*.1920
Watercolour on paper
P&O HERITAGE COLLECTION, LONDON:
AC/04453/00

38 OPPOSITE RIGHT
Main entrance to the P&O office and booking hall,
14–16 Cockspur Street, London, with sculptures
by Ernest Gillick, photograph by J.W.C. for Bedford
Lemere & Co., 1921

Ballin (1857–1918), was a member of Kaiser Wilhelm II's inner circle. In Hamburg, Ballin helped to finance the construction of the Hotel Atlantic, a Neoclassical building located next to the Alstersee, in which first-class transatlantic passengers were accommodated in appropriately grand surroundings. The hotel was designed by the Bremen architects Friedrich Wellermann (1865–1951) and Paul Fröhlich (1874–1946), and completed in 1909. For third-class migrants, Hamburg-American also developed barracks-type accommodation in single-storey timber buildings with romantic Tyrolean roof details. Located near the port, they provided shelter for those leaving Europe to begin new lives in the United States.

While Hamburg-American's closest rival, Cunard, stopped short of investing in a hotel in Liverpool, it did purchase terraced housing in the city in which migrants were quartered prior to embarking on board its liners. As with Hamburg-American's migrant accommodation, Cunard's housing was necessary for logistical reasons, but was nonetheless promoted to third-class passengers as an added benefit available for their comfort and peace of mind at little extra cost.

Revenue from liner operation fluctuated with the wider economy, and liners themselves were expensive, long-term investments, so an attractive alternative revenue stream for the shipping companies

was in property onshore. In Liverpool, Cunard took the opportunity in 1913 to purchase a very prominent site at Liverpool Pier Head between the recently constructed Dock Offices (also known as the Port of Liverpool Building, 1907) and the Royal Liver Building (1911). Cunard's intention was to develop a grand corporate headquarters and passenger terminal to process their customers embarking from the nearby landing stage. In addition, there would be a significant amount of space available for lease to other businesses from which Cunard could earn rent.

At that time, Cunard was anticipating the delivery of a new flagship liner, *Aquitania* (1914), the interiors of which were being designed by Arthur Joseph Davis (1878–1951) of the Anglo-French architectural partnership of Mewès and Davis. They were best known for having designed the Ritz Hotel in London's Piccadilly and hotel-like liner interiors for Cunard's major rival, Hamburg-American. So impressed were Cunard's directorate by these projects that Davis was invited to design the Liverpool headquarters, working in collaboration with local architects, Willink and Thicknesse (who had previously designed interiors for Cunard's *Franconia* and *Laconia*, 1911 and 1912). Whereas the Ritz hotels were in the French manner, for the Cunard Building Davis produced an American-inflected, Italian Renaissance-style 'palazzo', constructed of concrete and faced with

dressed Portland stone [39]. Subsequently, Willink and Thicknesse became involved in the project to carry out the detailed design.[1] The Cunard Building was completed in 1917, with the clear intention that would-be passengers could be reassured by the obvious heft and bold modelling of its stonework and should associate these characteristics with the seaworthiness of the company's liners:

> the walls are battered, thus giving a striking appearance of massive strength and solidity, suggestive of the receding face of a fortress. The masonry below the wave course is heavily rusticated each piece being distinguished by a broad surrounding channel, while the chiselling of the protuberant stone faces is rough, thus increasing the impression of rugged strength and forcefulness ...[2]

On the ground floor, tall axial corridors linked to a double-height central hall with fluted Doric columns and a leaded-glass roof. Passenger facilities were split into the same three classes as found on board. First class occupied marble-lined spaces at ground level, while the second and third classes were confined to the basement, where baggage was also gathered for loading. Of the three large edifices at the Pier Head, the Cunard Building won most praise from within the architectural profession for its monumentality and poise, the neighbouring Dock Offices and Royal Liver Building being considered over-ornamented and a little vulgar by comparison.[3]

Gratified by the success of their Liverpool headquarters, Cunard next sought to build an even larger and grander 22-storey office block on Broadway in New York, for which it employed the architect Benjamin Wistar Morris (1870–1944) [40]. Originally from Oregon, Morris had studied in Paris at the École des Beaux-Arts, and went on to join the New York firm of Carrère and Hastings just before the turn of the century. Although he had set up his own practice in 1900, Morris continued to collaborate with them on large projects, including the Cunard Building, for which plans were completed in 1919 with inauguration two years later. As in Liverpool, the Italian Renaissance style was selected with an axial internal plan, but, this

being New York, the building's scale was considerably bigger. Of the many imposing internal spaces, the ticket office [33] and its ante-rooms were the most spectacular, as *Architecture and Building* records:

> The Great Hall is entered ... through a monumental opening at its eastern end; and the eye and mind are at once impressed with a sense of space and dignity unusual in a room designed for the transaction of business. ... The floor, walls and counters are simply done in Travertine [and feature] Barry Faulkner's [1881–1966] maps on the walls of the four niches. These are ... masterpieces of mural decoration ... Surmounting the Travertine walls is a cornice thirty-five feet from the floor and above it soar the intersecting curves and surfaces of the ceiling, a stupendous orchestration of colour, line and harmony by Ezra Winter [1886–1949].[4]

Come the Great Depression that followed the 1929 Wall Street Crash, Cunard would have been glad for the rentable floor space in its Liverpool and New York headquarters, since the property market recovered faster than the shipping business. When, in the mid-1930s, Cunard finally was able to complete its new flagship liner, *Queen Mary*, it retained Morris to advise on an interior design that would appeal to the American market.

While Morris successfully made the transition from Renaissance styles to Art Deco in the early 1930s, elsewhere in the architecture and design worlds more fundamental shifts in approach were under way as Modernism emerged to challenge the old order. Arguably the first British liner to attempt a Modernist-inspired interior design was Orient Line's *Orion* (1935), the architect of which, Brian O'Rorke (1901–74), was subsequently retained to design the interiors of the company's office building in Sydney within a shell by local architects Fowell & Mansfield [41]. Reflecting on the circumstances of O'Rorke's commissions from the vantage point of the 1960s, Orient Line's Chairman, Sir Colin Skelton Anderson (1904–80), recalled:

> I was still young enough to be critical of the Established Order (I was in my late-twenties) and, because ours was a family business, was able to make my remarks in circles more authoritative than are usually available to young reformers … I felt I needed someone with whom I could identify myself and … the choice fell on a young New Zealander working in England, Brian O'Rorke, who had almost as clean a sheet of achievements to his name as I had.[5]

Orient Line's Sydney offices were completed in 1938 and, as with *Orion*, they were warmly received by the design press for their clean lines, light colours and crisp detailing – indeed the journal *Art in Australia* went as far as to state that the building was 'the most valuable contribution to the architecture of Sydney yet seen'.[6] The booking hall's smooth expanses of polished wood veneer were complemented with modern, etched-glass panels by the London-based illustrator Lynton Lamb (1907–77), who had previously designed menu covers and other graphic work for *Orion*.

LINER TERMINALS

From the late 1920s onward, the advent of a new generation of much larger transatlantic liners, aimed primarily at the business and tourist markets rather than the migrant trades, brought a need for commensurately bigger and better-designed, shore-based facilities. Hitherto, liner terminals were often little more than cargo warehouses with waiting rooms inserted. Edwardian-era railway companies operating packet steamers between Channel ports, however, had set the precedent for smooth train-to-ship interchanges. At Dover, Folkestone, Calais and Boulogne, passengers arriving by train experienced grand edifices, faced in dressed stone, through which they were efficiently processed via emigration and directly to a waiting steamer. The fact that the entire infrastructure belonged to a single company was advantageous in achieving a high level of integration. For the liner trades, however, ships, ports and railways more typically belonged to entirely separate organizations.

It was in France and in Italy – where the state and regional authorities either owned or strongly influenced all three components – that there was the best possibility of providing an almost seamless travel experience. At Cherbourg, a new *gare maritime* was inaugurated in 1933. This replaced an existing timber-framed structure dating from 1912, which was built to serve the

largest Compagnie Générale Transatlantique (CGT), Cunard and White Star liners of the Edwardian era. Plans were prepared in 1924 by the local architect René Levavasseur (1881–1962), who was a graduate of the École des Beaux-Arts in Paris. For the Gare Maritime de Cherbourg, Levavasseur's atelier worked in partnership with the well-known road and bridge engineer Marcel Chalos (1895–1992), but their initial design was judged too costly on account of its decorative enrichments and a second version of greatly simplified design was produced. This maintained the original's spacious dimensions and facilities – comprising a train shed, a customs hall capable of processing up to 1,000 passengers per hour, passenger circulation and waiting rooms. These included a 'grand salon' in the Art Deco style for first-class travellers with interior decoration by Marc Simon, who had also made liner interiors.[7] Additionally, a baggage hall and warehousing were located beneath the customs hall. As eventually completed in 1933, the 280-m-long complex possessed an austere, cathedral-like splendour.[8] In terms of size, it was France's second-largest building; only the Château de Versailles was bigger. The station's largely unadorned reinforced concrete construction emphasized the interplay of light and shade while a slender campanile, 70-m-tall, underlined its civic importance.

In Le Havre – France's other main Atlantic liner port – an even more impressive *gare maritime* was under construction; this project was in anticipation of the completion in 1935 of the CGT's flagship liner *Normandie* (1935) [43]. The building's architect, Urbain Cassan (1890–1979), had studied at the École des Beaux-Arts and at the École Polytechnique, thereafter being employed in-house by the Compagnie des chemins de fer du Nord (the French Northern Railway Company) for whom he mainly designed station buildings. Though conceptually and structurally similar to the Cherbourg complex, the Gare Maritime du Havre was streamlined in style. Indeed, it effectively complemented *Normandie*'s clean-lined external design. Dramatic horizontals and verticals, comprising columns, balconies and lift towers, characterized the lofty spaces within.[9] The CGT, like many companies, went on to build tourist and booking offices in many countries that adopted streamlined architectural styling in an echo of their liners. These buildings manifested the glamour and style that was to be experienced onboard.

In Italy, meanwhile, equally impressive *stazioni marittima* terminal facilities were developed in Genoa and Naples for the Italian Line's transatlantic vessels. The Genoa complex had late-nineteenth century origins, but was greatly extended from 1914 onward mainly to accommodate large numbers of migrants bound for the USA; this structure was decorated in the Baroque manner, reflecting the

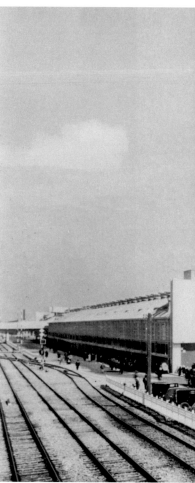

first class shipboard style of the era's Italian liners. Between 1931 and 1933, a further extension was built to a design by the architect Luigi Vietti (1903–98). This new annexe was, by contrast, of rather futuristic appearance, being entirely of reinforced concrete with streamlined details.

In 1936, the Naples terminal was completed to a design by Cesare Bazzani (1873–1939) in the so-called 'littorian' manner – stripped-back Neoclassicism with *moderne* detailing – a design approach commonly used for public buildings during the later years of Fascist rule and, of course, also applied to the interiors of recent Italian liners, most notably *Conte di Savoia* (1932) [42].

Whereas the French terminals provided rail-to-sea interchanges with train sheds on one side and ships' berths on the other, the Italian *termini* were built on piers protruding into the harbour basins and were accessible from the front, primarily by road vehicles or on foot. Liners were therefore able to berth on both sides, the planning being consequently symmetrical with passengers passing through an axial sequence of ticketing, baggage and customs spaces before being directed to the appropriate class of waiting room on one side or the other. As elsewhere, cargo was handled at ground/pier level with passengers above. The Genoa building was accessed from the city via bridges spanning railway

---

42 ABOVE
Stazione Marittima, Naples (1936), designed by
Cesare Bazzani

43 OPPOSITE
Gare Maritime du Havre for the Compagnie
Générale Transatlantique (1935), designed by
Urbain Cassan. *Normandie* is in dock behind the
Gare Maritime.

tracks, while in Naples passengers entered by a vast staircase with marble treads, giving intimidatingly monumental first and last impressions of the Fascist state.

The coming of *Normandie* and *Queen Mary* also required significant infrastructural investment in New York, where the Hudson River was lined on both sides by liner piers. On the midtown Manhattan shore, a series of new piers was commissioned in the mid-1930s, all measuring 335 m in length (a little longer than the new French and British superliners). The size and Art Deco end façades were the only distinguishing characteristics of these piers, however, as otherwise they were fairly standard 'double deck' structures, just like most of the others in the ports of New York and New Jersey.

Since the mid-1930s and the advent of *Queen Mary*, England's Southern Railway had wished to construct a liner terminal in Southampton similar to those at Cherbourg and Le Havre, but economic and political uncertainty in the lead up to the Second World War had delayed its plans. It was not until the late 1940s that the project went ahead, albeit in a context of post-war austerity and materials rationing. In the circumstances, the Ocean Terminal's

completion in 1950 was a considerable achievement. The design was by the Docks Engineer J.H. Jellett, assisted by the Docks Architect C.B. Dromgoole, and it followed the established approach to liner terminal planning in having cargo and luggage handling at ground level with passenger check-in and waiting areas above.

At its landward end, the Ocean Terminal's otherwise plain exterior was enlivened with a semicircular 'streamline moderne' tower feature, the design of which was reminiscent of late-1930s British and American commercial architecture [44]. *The Architects' Journal* was scathing:

> From now on the [new Ocean Terminal] will be the first view a large number of visitors – especially American visitors – get of contemporary English architecture. Being a building of considerable public importance ... its undistinguished character, inside and out, is disappointing.[10]

The terminal's designers understandably were most upset by the negative tone of the review and each wrote a lengthy and pained letter to justify their approach. The terminal certainly

complemented the style of the remaining 1930s liners that would use it most regularly, particularly *Queen Mary* and *Queen Elizabeth*. Indeed, the interiors of the passenger circulation spaces – with their polished woodwork and concealed lighting – were arguably a perfect prelude to embarkation on either vessel [45].

In New York, the Marine and Aviation Department completed a very innovative pier in 1962 for the Holland-America Line's freight and passenger liners, which had hitherto berthed in Hoboken, New Jersey, on the Hudson River's opposite side [46]. The new Pier 40 was a reinforced concrete structure, which was square in plan and consequently allowed berths on three sides. Within, there were ramps enabling vehicles to reach all three levels and its central area had ample parking space for trucks, the idea being to speed

up cargo-handling operations. State of the art though it was when first completed, subsequent profound changes in liner shipping methods meant that the pier operated for only 20 years.

The period from the late 1950s until the mid-1970s was a torrid time for British liner companies, who needed to adjust to the effects of the Suez Crisis, the loss of empire and the so-called 'shipping revolution' through which general cargo liners were superseded by specialized container and roll-on, roll-off vessels. The advent of the jet age, meanwhile, quickly destroyed the companies' traditional passenger operations. By the 1960s, P&O had become a sprawling conglomerate with substantial interests in nearly all aspects of merchant shipping. At the end of the decade, it became clear to the directorate that property was a more lucrative investment area.[11]

44 OPPOSITE
Ocean Terminal, Southampton (1950), designed by
J.H. Jellett and C.B. Dromgoole

45 ABOVE
Interior of Ocean Terminal, Southampton (1950),
designed by J.H. Jellett and C.B. Dromgoole

In 1962, P&O opened a new Sydney office tower, designed by Fowell, Mansfield & Maclurcan. It had 20 storeys, the majority for lease to other businesses. Next, P&O demolished its London headquarters in Leadenhall Street in 1964, replacing it with a 15-storey office block in the 'International Style' by the Gollins Melvin Ward Partnership, London-based architects specializing in offices and other commercial developments, which was completed in 1969. The six uppermost floors were occupied by P&O and its subsidiaries, the remainder being leased to banks and insurance companies. A company brochure produced for its inauguration warned office workers of the dangers of clutter to the building's clean-lined aesthetic:

> To create a uniform appearance, the offices ... have been designed by the same firm of architects who designed the building ... Much thought has been given with regard to design and colour in the provision of such items as clocks, calendars, ashtrays, writing pads, pen and clip trays, in and out trays, pictures etc., and such individual items as bric-a-brac should not be imported ...[12]

Soon, however, what remained of P&O's traditional passenger liner operations were closed down and, by the mid-1970s, the company's activities consisted of container shipping, ferries, cruise ships, bulk shipping – and property development. The design of P&O's new offices – which externally were undistinguishable from those of conglomerates operating in sectors other than shipping – reflected this new reality.

46 RIGHT

Pier 40, New York (1962), designed by the New York
City Department of Marine and Aviation, c.1965

COMPAGNIE GÉNÉRALE TRANSATLANTIQUE: IDENTITY THROUGH TIME

DORIAN DALLONGEVILLE

In French minds the legendary Compagnie Générale Transatlantique (CGT, or popularly shortened to 'Transat' and known in English as the 'French Line') is still strongly associated with the idea of large luxury liners sailing to New York. This affiliation is no accident, of course, since the Transat ships, evocative of a particular art of luxurious living, were key to building the company's identity over many decades.

In 1855, as capitalism boomed under France's Second Empire, brothers Émile (1800–75) and Isaac Pereire (1806–80) founded the Compagnie Générale Maritime, which became the Compagnie Générale Transatlantique in 1861. Faced with stiff European competition, the company used every means of promotional communication at its disposal, from posters, leaflets and brochures, to issuing cross-section views and portraits of its flagship liners. The best poster designers and official painters of the French navy were brought in to create advertisements combining images of power, elegance, modernity, exoticism and adventure.

Particular attention was paid to the company monogram, the distinctive sign with which each piece of gold, silver, glass or porcelain on board was marked. The care taken over the elegant monogram design and ensuing updates contributed to the prestige of the company and all its liners. The initials 'CGT' first appeared in the final decades of the nineteenth century, gracing a wide variety of items, including the crew's uniforms and the iconic red livery of the bellboys.

A discreet presence on the lapel of a maître d'hôtel, at the top of a poster or on the corner of an ashtray, the company's signature evolved with the changing fashions. The monograms of the late nineteenth and early twentieth centuries with their *rinceaux*, ribbons and ropes gave way to more contemporary designs when the liners *France* (1912) and *Paris* (1921) came into service [48]. An enamelled stoneware planter by Émile Muller & Cie, from the grand-luxe apartment on board *France*, is a perfect example of the monogram's Art Nouveau incarnation [47]. Art Nouveau, however, was rarely a major element of Transat decor and was soon replaced

French Line

by Art Deco, the style that had triumphed at the Paris Exhibition of 1925. The monogram evolved in line with the trend and when *Île-de-France* came into service in 1927, the Transat initials were elegantly intertwined on a stylized anchor designed by Luc Lanel (1893–1965).

In addition to Lanel, Artistic Director at Christofle, Transat hired renowned French decorative artists to design its dinner services, such as ceramicist Jean Luce (1895 –1964), silversmith Jean Puiforcat (1897–1945), and master glass designer René Lalique (1860–1945) and his daughter Suzanne Lalique-Haviland (1892–1989). Transat would order separate dinner services for use in different classes on the same liner, the most extreme example being for *Normandie* (1935), which not only carried one for each of its three classes, but also a complete service specially designed for the four grand-luxe apartments. The company monogram appeared on every piece.

The fashion of the mid-1930s was for pure lines and simple forms and the monograms designed for *Normandie*'s different classes reflect this bold aesthetic. The extraordinary second-class monogram, square or rectangular according to the type of piece it marks, is in itself undoubtedly a small masterpiece of Art Deco design. First class featured the so-called 'circular' monogram, another icon of Art Deco style, in which the letters CGT appear one inside the other. This simple but clever design was to prove a lasting success, adapting and changing colour according to the different objects and documents it marked. It survived for several decades and continued to signify the prestige of the Transat line until *France* (1962) was decommissioned in 1974 [49].

---

49 ABOVE
Detail of French Line letterhead paper showing the
circular CGT monogram, printed by the Imprimerie
Transatlantique, 1925–50

50 RIGHT
Fashion shoot for Maison Rodier on *France*, 1962

CHAPTER 2

SHIPBUILDING: SPEED, SAFETY AND COMFORT

SHIPBUILDING: SPEED, SAFETY AND COMFORT

JOHN R. HUME

THE GREAT LINERS OF THE nineteenth and twentieth centuries were exceptional objects of engineering and naval architecture at the cutting edge of the era's capabilities. Underlying the experience of travel on board was the vast endeavour of shipbuilding and design, which utilized a tremendous range of knowledge and skills to ensure a fast, safe and comfortable voyage. From design, through construction, to the operation of these liners, huge workforces were required as well as major investments from companies and governments, which in turn affected the national economies of shipbuilding nations [52]. The development and operation of the 'first-class' liner was therefore a complex phenomenon, inextricably linked with the ambitions of entrepreneurs, designers, companies and countries, and vulnerable to shifts in the structure of world power and colonialization.

MATERIALS: FROM WOOD TO ALUMINIUM

Innovations in construction materials starting in the mid-nineteenth century were instrumental to the building of liners in the next century. Vessels made between the mid-1850s and the early 1880s moved away from hulls constructed entirely from wood to incorporate wrought iron, also called malleable iron. Iron ships, such as Cunard's first transatlantic liner *Persia* (1855), were made on the same principle as wooden ships, with keel, ribs, deck beams, and bow and stern frames defining the form of the hull [53]. Iron plates were used to form the exterior shell and, since iron was much stronger than wood, the hulls could be made stiffer. The process of making wrought iron was extremely labour intensive, however, requiring lumps of iron weighing about 60 kg to be rolled out and welded together by dedicated, skilled teams to make pieces large enough to form plates, sections and machinery parts. Iron plates allowed longer vessels to be constructed, which led to the development of a new form of propulsion – the screw propeller. In addition, as engines became more powerful, the strength of engine beds and of supports for the propeller shafts became a major consideration.

Isambard Kingdom Brunel (1806–59) designed *Great Eastern* (1859) for the Australian trade [54]. His vision was for a vessel large enough to carry fuel for the entire journey from the United Kingdom round the Cape of Good Hope to Ceylon (Sri Lanka), since intermediate coaling stations had not yet been established. Single sets of engines large enough to propel a vessel of 14,000 gross tons could not be constructed at that time, so the ship carried three different forms of propulsion: sails, paddle and screw propeller. There were two sets of engines, one driving the paddle-wheels and the other driving the screw propeller. When it became apparent that the vessel would not be a commercial success as a passenger liner – apart from anything else she rolled badly in rough weather [55] – she was adapted to lay underwater telegraph cables, including the first successful one across the Atlantic. It would not be until the end of the nineteenth century that ships the size of *Great Eastern* were built again.

The increased demand for transatlantic passages by the late 1800s, however, meant that such large vessels could now be profitable, and the achievement of ever-faster crossings became both a major commercial endeavour and a matter of national prestige. Beginning with the Cunard liner *Servia* (1881), hulls started to be made of steel and powered by high-pressure steam engines.[1] The introduction of steel had an enormous impact on shipbuilding: substituting steel for iron reduced a vessel's weight by 20 per cent, permitting the construction of faster and more economical ships.[2] Steel plates and rolled sections used in forming frames and beams could be larger and thicker, and reduced the number of rivets needed to fasten them. Steel was also employed in boiler making, for large components of marine engines and for propeller shafts. In particular, the use of steel in boilers allowed much higher pressures to be developed and saved on fuel consumption.

New construction materials necessitated the introduction of specialist machines for cutting and forming plates and sections, as well as techniques for forming ribs and 'joggling' them to the shape

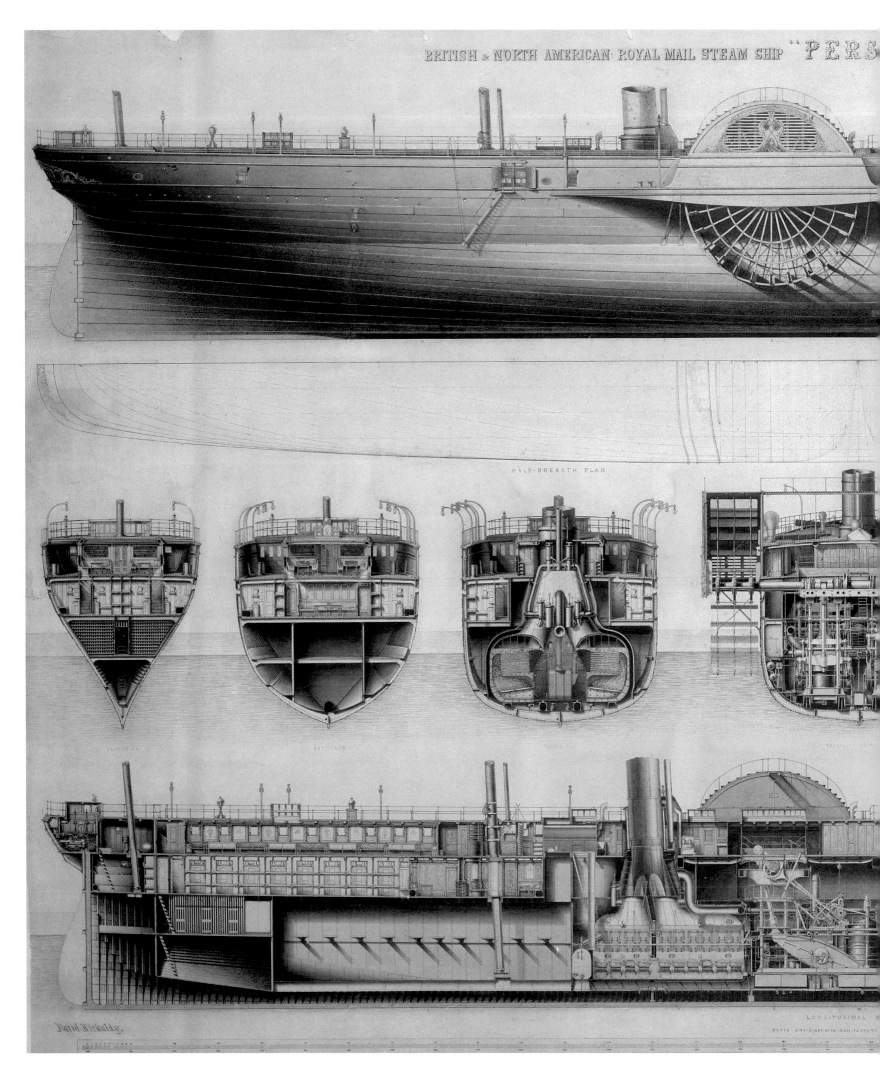

HALF-BREADTH PLAN

SECTION N°A   SECTION N°B   SECTION N°C   TRANSVE

David Kirkaldy.

LONGITUDINAL

SCALE ONE-EIGHT OF AN INCH TO THE

CONSTRUCTED BY MESSRS R. NAPIER & SONS, GLASGOW.

HALF-BREADTH PLAN

Glasgow 4 July 1860.

of the hull [57]. Riveting was the method employed to fasten the components of hulls together and was utilized from the beginning of iron shipbuilding until after the Second World War. Stanley Spencer's (1891–1959) *Riveters* (1941, from his series of war-artist commissions documenting shipbuilding on the Clyde) depicts a riveter at work in the confined space of a mast tube [56]. Riveting was a labour intensive job in the shipyards, and only replaced by welding in the last days of liner construction. Four million rivets alone were required for the building of *Queen Mary* (1936), attesting to the monumental task of creating a liner.

Welded steel would be replaced after the Second World War with aluminium in the construction of some liners, including SS *United States* (1952) and *Canberra* (1961), to reduce the weight of their superstructures. This lighter material, utilized in the interior and exterior of SS *United States*, combined with her advanced hull design and powerful engines, made her the fastest liner ever constructed. In 1952, she crossed the Atlantic in just three days and 10 hours.

HULL DESIGN

Alongside the structural strength of a liner's hull, stability was also a serious concern. The British naval architect William Froude (1810–79) had shown that stability could be tested by using models in long tanks of water, also employed to calculate the hull resistance of a full-sized vessel. This aid to hull design was first applied to warships, but in 1879 a test tank was built in Dumbarton, Scotland, for use in designing merchant vessels [58]. Cutting machines were utilized to transfer the drawn lines of the design to a wax model and, from this point forward, tank testing became an essential feature in the design of hulls and propellers for speed and seaworthiness. The study of the efficiency of hull forms led to the realization that the longer the vessel, the greater the economical speed, which became a very powerful factor in designing ever-larger and faster liners.

Increasingly streamlined and hydrodynamic hulls were essential in the international race across the Atlantic. Further efficiency studies led to the development of the bulbous bow (a rounded protrusion at the front of the hull hidden below the waterline) [51]. By altering the flow of water around the hull of a ship and reducing resistance, it increased speed. First used in warships at the end of the nineteenth century, it was applied to *Bremen* (1929) and *Europa* (1930), which both broke speed records with their Atlantic crossing times. Together with its famous streamlined hull, *Normandie* (1935) also featured a bulbous bow designed by Russian émigré engineer Vladimir Yourkevitch (1885–1964). Later liners, such as

51 PREVIOUS P.71
Canberra's bulbous bow photographed in Southampton's King George V dock, photograph by Stewart Bale, May 1961

52 PREVIOUS P.73
La Costruzione Navale di Sestri Ponente (Shipbuilding at Sestri Ponente), by Giuseppe Mazzei
*c.*1926
Pastel on paper
WOLFSONIANA, PALAZZO DUCALE FONDAZIONE PER LA CULTURA, GENOA: GX1993.466

53 PREVIOUS PP.74–5
Presentation drawing of *Persia*, showing outboard and inboard longitudinal profiles and sections with inboard detail, by David Kirkaldy
United Kingdom, 1860
Ink and wash on paper
NATIONAL MARITIME MUSEUM, ROYAL MUSEUMS GREENWICH: DKY0001

54 OPPOSITE ABOVE
Great Eastern, fully rigged 1:44 model with working internal steam engine
*c.*1858
Brass, copper, cotton, paint, tin, varnish and wood
NATIONAL MARITIME MUSEUM, ROYAL MUSEUMS GREENWICH: SLR0901

55 OPPOSITE BELOW
'The Disaster to the Great Eastern: State of the Grand Saloon during the Gale'
London, United Kingdom, *c.*1860
Colour lithograph
GIFT OF FRANCIS LEE HIGGINSON, 1992
PEABODY ESSEX MUSEUM: M25925

SHIPBUILDING: SPEED, SAFETY AND COMFORT

77

56 ABOVE

Shipbuilding on the Clyde: Riveters (detail),

by Stanley Spencer

United Kingdom, 1941

Oil on canvas

Canberra and *Queen Mary 2* (2004), were conceived with even more pronounced bulbous bows.

ENGINES

As the length of vessels increased so did the power needed to propel them. The harnessing of steam power was a crucial advance that enabled the establishment of lines offering regular and reliable crossings. Before the development of mechanical propulsion when ships were reliant on wind power, a crossing from Liverpool to New York could take more than three weeks. The length of the journey dwindled to a few days with the introduction and development of steam power.

A significant incentive to develop faster vessels was the Blue Riband. This measure of supremacy in speed rewarded the vessel that achieved the fastest east-to-west crossing of the Atlantic. The accolade was unofficial until 1934 when Harold K. Hales (1868–1942), a British politician and owner of the Hales Brothers shipping company, established a trophy that was awarded to the titleholder. Therefore, larger and more powerful marine engines were developed that could propel these great vessels.

The Clyde firm of J. & G. Thomson had created the first vertical layout for steam screw engines in the 1850s, which went on to become the industry standard. The earliest engines of this type were 'simple' – that is to say, the cylinders employed steam at boiler pressure. Soon, though, compound marine engines were developed. These used steam in two or more successive cylinders and were more efficient, wasting less steam power. Further developments of this principle were the triple- and quadruple-expansion engine, the adoption of which was made possible by the introduction of mild steel in boiler construction [59]. By the end of the nineteenth century, however, the potential of the reciprocating steam engine to deliver ever-higher speeds had effectively been exhausted.

To satisfy the demand for faster travel, the steam turbine, which directly produced rotary power, was adopted. Steam turbines had already been used on a small scale on board ships for generating electricity for lighting. Larger turbines had also been developed for generating electricity on land and it was from these that the engineer Charles Parsons (1854–1931) developed the marine steam turbine. In 1894, Parsons designed *Turbinia*, a 30-m-long experimental ship intended to demonstrate the use of steam turbines. During a test in 1897, she achieved over 32 knots (37 mph) and became the fastest ship in the world. Both the British navy and commercial shipping companies were quick to see the benefits. The first transatlantic liners with turbine propulsion were Cunard's *Lusitania* and *Mauretania* of 1907.

57 TOP
Shipyard workers using a joggling press to form the plates so that they fit the frames, Greenock and Grangemouth Dockyard Company, *c.*1900

58 ABOVE
Employees preparing to test a model in the Test Tank at William Denny & Bros, Dumbarton, Scotland, 1935

59 ABOVE

Model of quadruple expansion tandem engine,
designed by Walter Brock, made by David Carlaw
for William Denny Brothers, Dumbarton, Scotland
United Kingdom, 1887
Wood, metal and brass
GLASGOW MUSEUMS: T.1962.10

SHIPBUILDING: SPEED, SAFETY AND COMFORT

Until the end of fast liner services in the 1960s, steam turbines continued to be used in all the largest vessels. The first turbines drove the ships' propellers directly, and so the turbine rotors had to be large in diameter. In the White Star liners *Olympic* (1911), *Titanic* (1912) and *Britannic* (1915), the exhaust steam from their reciprocating engines was used in enormous steam turbines. After the First World War, however, gearing allowed the size of turbines to be reduced, and this arrangement was thereafter used in most large liners. Between the wars, an alternative to the geared turbine was turbo-electric propulsion. Here turbines drove the electric generators powering the propellers' electric motors. The largest vessel employing this method was the French liner *Normandie*. Although steam power was dominant for most larger ships, the diesel engine had a role in smaller liners, and Harland and Wolff built two such motor vessels, the *Britannic* (1930) and the *Georgic* (1932). When in the late 1920s the White Star Line contemplated building a new liner, Harland and Wolff produced a design with a number of medium-sized diesel engines driving generators to supply current to motors driving the four propellers. Similar systems are still used in the largest cruise liners since they enable speed to be varied precisely, optimizing fuel economy.

PROPULSION

In the earliest transatlantic liners, paddlewheels with fixed blades were used for propulsion. Paddlewheels, however, were susceptible to storm damage, especially in North-Atlantic winters. The screw propeller was not subject to this disadvantage, required less space and was more efficient, but it took some time to develop engines that could drive them. Once the principle of screw propulsion, introduced in Brunel's *Great Britain* (1843), had been established much effort was devoted to designing efficient propellers for greater power. This became critical in the early twentieth century, when the largest liners tended to suffer from vibrations caused by the propellers' inability to handle the power developed by their engines. Propellers became an important area of research with different designs delivering variable results. For instance, when a submerged

object damaged a propeller on the *Mauretania* on 2 May 1908, Cunard seized the opportunity to replace those on both inner shafts with four-bladed propellers. *Mauretania* left Liverpool on 23 January 1909 and by April of that year she had captured both the eastbound and westbound records and continued to hold the Blue Riband until July 1929.[3] The conception and construction of new propellers was therefore often a closely guarded secret, as was the case with the four- and five-bladed designs by the engineer Elaine Kaplan for SS *United States*.

63 OPPOSITE

'The Largest Steamers in the World', poster for
Olympic and *Titanic*, White Star Line

1911

Colour lithograph

GIFT OF CUNARD STEAMSHIP CO. LTD,

BOSTON OFFICE, 1955

PEABODY ESSEX MUSEUM: M8708

THE LARGEST STEAMERS IN THE WORLD
WHITE STAR LINE

"OLYMPIC"
(IN SERVICE JUNE, 1911)

882½ FEET LONG

92½ FEET BROAD

45,000 TONS REGISTER

66,000 TONS DISPLACEMENT

HEIGHT FROM KEEL
TO TOP OF FUNNELS
175 FEET

"TITANIC"
(BUILDING AT BELFAST)

882½ FEET LONG

92½ FEET BROAD

45,000 TONS REGISTER

66,000 TONS DISPLACEMENT

HEIGHT FROM KEEL
TO TOP OF FUNNELS
175 FEET

FOUR ELECTRIC ELEVATORS
THREE IN FIRST CLASS
ONE IN SECOND CLASS

SUN DECK
FIRST AND SECOND CLASS PROMENADE
DECK GAMES
GYMNASIUM
OFFICERS' QUARTERS

UPPER PROMENADE DECK "A"
FIRST AND SECOND CLASS PROMENADE
VERANDAH CAFE AND PALM COURT
PHOTOGRAPHIC DARK ROOM
FIRST CLASS LOUNGE
FIRST CLASS READING AND WRITING ROOM
FIRST CLASS SMOKE ROOM
FIRST CLASS STATEROOMS

PROMENADE DECK "B"
(GLASS ENCLOSED)
FIRST AND SECOND CLASS PROMENADE
FIRST CLASS A LA CARTE RESTAURANT
FIRST CLASS SUITES AND CABINS WITH BATH
FIRST CLASS STATEROOMS
SECOND CLASS SMOKE ROOM

UPPER DECK "C"
FIRST CLASS APARTMENTS AND CABINS DE LUXE
ENQUIRY OFFICE
SECOND CLASS LIBRARY
SECOND CLASS PROMENADE
THIRD CLASS SOCIAL ROOM
THIRD CLASS SMOKE ROOM
MAIDS' AND VALETS' SALOON

SALOON DECK "D"
FIRST CLASS DINING SALOON
FIRST CLASS RECEPTION ROOM
FIRST CLASS STATEROOMS
SECOND CLASS DINING SALOON
SECOND CLASS STATEROOMS
THIRD CLASS ROOMS

MAIN DECK "E"
FIRST CLASS STATEROOMS
SECOND CLASS STATEROOMS
THIRD CLASS ROOMS

MIDDLE DECK "F"
TURKISH AND ELECTRIC BATH ESTABLISHMENT
SALT WATER SWIMMING POOL
TENNIS AND HANDBALL COURT
SECOND CLASS STATEROOMS
THIRD CLASS DINING SALOON
THIRD CLASS ROOMS

LOWER DECK "G"
SEA POST OFFICE
THIRD CLASS ROOMS

TWO LOWER DECKS
CARGO - COAL BUNKERS
BOILERS - ENGINES

DOUBLE BOTTOM

FOUR ELECTRIC ELEVATORS
THREE IN FIRST CLASS
ONE IN SECOND CLASS

SUN DECK
FIRST AND SECOND CLASS PROMENADE
DECK GAMES
GYMNASIUM
OFFICERS' QUARTERS

UPPER PROMENADE DECK "A"
FIRST AND SECOND CLASS PROMENADE
VERANDAH CAFE AND PALM COURT
PHOTOGRAPHIC DARK ROOM
FIRST CLASS LOUNGE
FIRST CLASS READING AND WRITING ROOM
FIRST CLASS SMOKE ROOM
FIRST CLASS STATEROOMS

PROMENADE DECK "B"
(GLASS ENCLOSED)
FIRST AND SECOND CLASS PROMENADE
FIRST CLASS A LA CARTE RESTAURANT
FIRST CLASS SUITES AND CABINS WITH BATH
FIRST CLASS STATEROOMS
SECOND CLASS SMOKE ROOM

UPPER DECK "C"
FIRST CLASS APARTMENTS AND CABINS DE LUXE
ENQUIRY OFFICE
SECOND CLASS LIBRARY
SECOND CLASS PROMENADE
THIRD CLASS SOCIAL HALL
THIRD CLASS SMOKE ROOM
MAIDS' AND VALETS' SALOON

SALOON DECK "D"
FIRST CLASS DINING SALOON
FIRST CLASS RECEPTION ROOM
FIRST CLASS STATEROOMS
SECOND CLASS STATEROOMS

MAIN DECK "E"
FIRST CLASS STATEROOMS
SECOND CLASS STATEROOMS
THIRD CLASS ROOMS

MIDDLE DECK "F"
TURKISH AND ELECTRIC BATH ESTABLISHMENT
SALT WATER SWIMMING POOL
TENNIS AND HANDBALL COURT
SECOND CLASS STATEROOMS
THIRD CLASS DINING SALOON
THIRD CLASS ROOMS

LOWER DECK "G"
SEA POST OFFICE
THIRD CLASS ROOMS

TWO LOWER DECKS
CARGO - COAL BUNKERS
BOILERS - ENGINES

DOUBLE BOTTOM

Sectional View
(AMIDSHIP)

THE TRIPLE SCREW SEA GIANTS
"OLYMPIC"   "TITANIC"
IN SERVICE JUNE, 1911   BUILDING AT BELFAST

STABILIZERS

An uncomfortable feature of ships of the early twentieth century was a tendency to roll from side to side in rough seas. It was a key ambition of ship designers to counteract this in order to attract customers seeking more comfortable crossings. One approach employed a gyroscope – a device that used a flywheel to reduce the ship's plane of rotation. First adopted on the Italian liner *Conte di Savoia* in 1932 the gyroscopes were located in the lower part of the hull [64]. The ship was extensively marketed on the smooth passage generated by the gyroscope, and a brochure published by the Italian Line's New York publicity department in 1933 announced: 'the first liner with a gyroscopic stabilizing unit ... silent, little giants, deep in the ship, that hold the fleet liner steady and on an even keel in any weather. In this respect the Italian Line has again brought out an innovation which establishes a new era in ocean travel'.[4]

In 1903, William Denny & Bros at Dumbarton and Sir William Wallace (1881–1963) of Brown Brothers in Edinburgh developed another stabilization device, the fin stabilizers. The 'Denny-Brown' stabilizer utilized underwater fins that could be extended from the side of the ship to counteract roll. It was soon adopted for liners of the largest class including Cunard's *Queen Mary* and *Queen Elizabeth* (1940). Its use is now commonplace.

VENTILATION

In operating a steam engine, air is required to feed the flames that burn the fuel and was sucked into the boiler rooms through ventilators, which were also employed to introduce fresh air into accommodation on ships. The intake of air was often speeded up by the use of fans. A notable feature on a liner such as *Aquitania* was the forest of cowl ventilators on the upper deck [216]. Once the fuel, whether coal or oil, was burned the smoke had to be got rid of. In coal-fired vessels the smoke was often black and grit-laden, and the design of the liners' funnels was intended to carry it as far as possible from the ship and its passengers.

In addition to their practical role, funnels also played an important part in creating distinct identities for ships and the great shipping companies. Three- and then four-funnelled liners were highly impressive and were believed to create an aura of greater seaworthiness (even though funnels added top-weight, possibly raising the centre of gravity). After the First World War new liners generally had less dominant funnels but those they had were styled to give the ships a distinctive profile. In the last days of liner construction, the unique funnel design for *France* (1962), with its side fins, became a marketing feature reproduced on promotional materials; the Italian liners *Michelangelo* and *Raffaello* (both 1965)

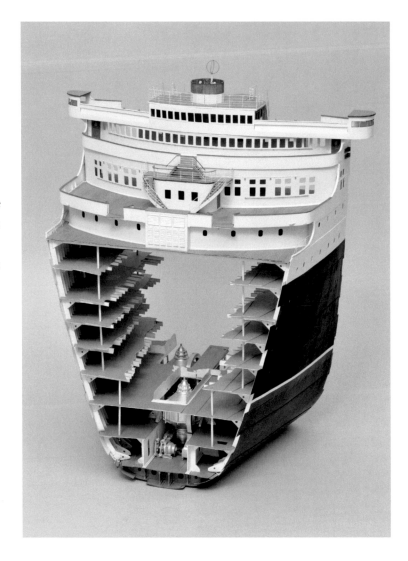

64 ABOVE
Model showing the arrangement of gyro-stabilizers
on *Conte di Savoia*
1930
Metal and wood
PAOLO PICCIONE COLLECTION

65 OPPOSITE
Workmen boarding *Queen Mary* during her fitting
out, 9 November 1935

were also built with aerofoils on top of the funnels, supported on latticework, to carry the smoke well away from the decks [141]. James Gardner (1907–95) designed *Queen Elizabeth 2*'s (1969) elegant funnel and radar mast at a stylish angle, which suggested speed while also helping to carry smoke away.

ELECTRICITY AND TELEGRAPHY

From the 1880s, steam-driven generators were installed, in addition to the main engines, to provide current for electric lighting, not only for passenger and crew accommodation, but also for such spaces as engine and boiler rooms and food-storage areas, which was a tremendous boon. Refrigeration for the preservation of food was introduced at about the same time and was of immense value in dramatically improving travellers' experiences on board, especially on long voyages. When *California* was put in service in 1928 as the first turbo-electric ocean liner, electricity was 'put to work as a willing servant in every department, from the motor room to the navigating bridge', but 'employed exclusively in the ship's extensive freight refrigerating department'.[5]

Guglielmo Marconi (1874–1937) first demonstrated the use of long radio waves in wireless telegraphy in 1895, and by 1902 he could send messages across the Atlantic. The first radio communication system was installed on the American Line's *Philadelphia* (1899) that same year. C.J. Weaver, one of the first operators of this system, noted that this early apparatus 'consisted principally of a ten-inch induction coil with a few Leyden jars and a huge turning coil ... This apparatus was crude and ponderous but we managed to work it'.[6] Early systems had a range of only 70 to 100 miles, but by the 1920s that range increased substantially and liners could communicate from one side of the Atlantic to the other. One of the first applications of this technique was in ship-to-ship and ship-to-shore telegraphy – messages were sent in Morse code, through a service provided by Marconi's Wireless Telegraph & Signal Company. The telegraphy service not only proved very valuable commercially, but also allowed distress signals to be sent. An effective demonstration of this was in 1909 when the White Star liner *Republic* (1903) collided with the Italian Line's *Florida* off the coast of the United States. Five ships, contacted by wireless, came to the rescue, and although more than 700 people were on board the two vessels, only six were killed and two injured. Most famously, ships also used the telegraph during the *Titanic* disaster to ascertain information. The *Olympic* received a message from *Asian* (1898) at 08:36 EST on 15 April 1912, noting 'ICEBERG REPORTED IN LAT 41.50 LONG 50.20 / REGARDS WOOD', the vicinity of the *Titanic*'s last-known location.[7] Eventually, ships fitted with wireless

telegraphy came to offer telegraph services to passengers, which proved a hugely popular feature.

The great liners conveyed thousands of people across often hostile seas, at speeds of more or less 30 mph, and supplied them not only with the necessities of life, but also with comforts and facilities that often exceeded those they experienced on land. These vessels were remarkable achievements that demonstrated the ingenuity and skill of the maritime engineers, designers and the workforces that made them. It is no surprise that they came to be seen as the ultimate symbols of the technological and industrial advancement of a modern nation.

CHAPTER 3

FLOATING PALACES: VICTORIAN AND EDWARDIAN SHIPS

FLOATING PALACES: VICTORIAN AND EDWARDIAN SHIPS

BERNHARD RIEGER

'I SHALL NEVER FORGET the one-fourth serious and three-fourths comical astonishment, with which ... I opened the door of, and put my head into a "state room" on board the *Britannia* [1840] steam packet ... bound for Boston'. It was Charles Dickens (1812–70) who found his sense of humour severely tested as he was setting out in January 1842 from Liverpool to cross the Atlantic for a journalistic assignment that would result in the publication of his *American Notes* (1842). Instead of the 'gorgeous little bower' sketched by a 'masterly hand' in the advertising material the novelist had been shown when he booked his passage, he beheld an 'utterly impractical, thoroughly hopeless, and profoundly preposterous box' of a cabin, which he and his wife would share during a voyage lasting more than two weeks. Wondering how he would cope with this cramped space, he slouched onto 'a kind of horsehair slab or perch' that served as his berth: 'Nothing smaller for sleeping in was ever made except coffins'. His distress was only increased by the 'pretty smart shock' that followed the realization that 'a long narrow apartment, not unlike a gigantic hearse with windows at the side' was in fact the saloon in which the travellers would socialize and take their meals. Even one of Dickens's friends, who had come aboard to see the writer off, was appalled: 'Impossible! It cannot be!' his companion cried – or so Dickens claimed.

By describing his embarkation as a descent into the netherworld, Dickens brought his trademark satirical hyperbole to a highly conventional motif in Western culture. Ships, as most people on either side of the Atlantic would have agreed at the time, possessed deep-seated associations of danger and death, and thus symbolized the precariousness of human existence. Nothing evoked such morbid themes more readily than the image of nutshells struggling on raging seas. The sombre overtone of Dickens's opening paragraphs was thus a nod in the direction of conventional wisdom that, in the middle of the nineteenth century, maritime travel still involved substantial risk and discomfort – as the novelist found out over the course of his 18-day voyage from Liverpool to Boston.

Dickens describes his storm-tossed passage as an extended ordeal that began with a debilitating bout of seasickness. Although he could never shake off a general feeling of queasiness, he recovered sufficiently after a few days to overcome initial speechless apathy and record an 'extraordinary compound of strange smells' that added to his misery, as did the persistent freezing cold in the absence of a proper heating system (in January). Transatlantic travel, Dickens confirmed, remained an unsettled affair in the 1840s.[1]

If Dickens recast well-known motifs by narrating his voyage as a physical and mental trial, his account simultaneously illustrates that maritime travel had begun to change. The novelist may have been disappointed by *Britannia*'s interior architecture and passenger accommodation, but, with a length of 63 m and a beam of 10 m, she was a large ship by contemporary standards, launched by the recently founded Cunard Line in 1840. These proportions allowed her to house 115 passengers in two-berth cabins and operate a dining saloon that served customers a varied diet throughout the trip. Dickens, despite having chosen the most inauspicious time of the year to travel, could be sure to reach Boston in well under three weeks because *Britannia* complemented her sails with steam-powered paddle wheels that propelled her steadily even against powerful headwinds [67]. Indeed, her 18-day trip compared extremely favourably with the 40 to 90 days a westward passage took on a sailing vessel. Irrespective of his suffering, Dickens steamed across the Atlantic in virtually unprecedented style and speed.

Britannia highlights the process that Dickens's contemporaries hailed as the 'conquest of nature'. Throughout the nineteenth century, humankind harnessed new forms of energy, developed a bewildering range of materials and constructed mechanisms small and large that struck contemporaries as mind-boggling 'modern wonders'. Of course, steam technology was the most potent early symbol of the new powers at society's disposal. First used commercially in mining and manufacturing in the eighteenth century, steam began to reinvent travel in the early nineteenth

66 PREVIOUS

First-class embarkation hall on *France*, 1912

67 ABOVE

Steamer Britannia *in a Gale*, by Fitz Henry Lane

Boston, MA, United States, 1842

Oil on canvas

century. At sea, steam promised to advance the 'conquest of nature' through faster and more regular voyages in hostile maritime environments. Over the course of the century, steam became a more effective motive force for ships through the development of powerful, more fuel-efficient compound engines with which vessels were equipped from the late 1850s. While new forms of propulsion such as the screw propeller enhanced the speed and regularity of ocean-going services, these powerful components could only be fitted on vessels constructed from sturdier materials, first iron, then from the 1880s onward, steel. These advances gave rise to larger vessels with more spacious decks after the turn of the century. The quest for size became a particular mark of transatlantic passenger ships. Smaller, yet still substantial, vessels served the colonial routes, which attracted fewer passengers and less cargo traffic. SS *Egypt* (1897), which the Peninsular and Oriental Steam Navigation Company (P&O) operated between Britain and Bombay, was less than two-thirds the size of the largest transatlantic liners around the turn of the century. On the eve of the First World War, Europe's leading shipping lines operated transatlantic services that cut travel times to less than five days. And in conjunction with the opening of the Suez Canal in 1869, the duration of a voyage between Europe and India more than halved to under 14 days.[2] Not even the sinking of *Titanic* in 1912 could dent the conviction among contemporaries that the 'conquest of nature' had made impressive strides.

NATIONS AT SEA

The construction and operation of these large and powerful symbols of humankind's increasing technological confidence required heavy investments that went beyond shipping lines' financial capacities. State subsidies therefore played a crucial role in passenger shipping throughout the nineteenth and into the twentieth century. Governments supported these companies because they considered civilian vessels as part of the national infrastructure. Steamships were ideally suited to provide the reliable lines of communication that proved crucial for the administration of Britain's expanding empire. To ensure a steady flow of mail between metropole and imperial possessions, the Admiralty offered subsidies to liner companies in the form of mail contracts. Upon its foundation in 1837, P&O expanded quickly by relying on several of these financially lucrative agreements. Its steamers served as Britain's 'flagships of imperialism', as one scholar put it.[3] The company that Samuel Cunard founded in 1840 (and which traded under his name from 1879) to operate a transatlantic service also rested on a mail contract. As the world's leading colonial power by a wide margin, Britain pioneered a pattern that other European nations were to adopt. No matter whether one turns to the French, German or Dutch empires at the end of the nineteenth century, shipping lines operating with substantial state subsidies through mail contracts served them all.

By then, intensifying national rivalries in Europe began to lend passenger liners new public and political resonance that led to the construction of the unprecedentedly fast and large transatlantic vessels whose names are recognized to this day. Around 1900, Britain's mid-century claim to be the predominant 'workshop of the world' no longer rang true, because Japan, the United States and Germany had emerged as industrial rivals that matched or even surpassed the United Kingdom. After decades of virtually unchallenged British commercial supremacy, the arrival of competitors spurred concerns that the nation was in 'decline'. Germany fuelled British anxieties after Kaiser Wilhelm II's (1859–1941) ascent to the throne in 1888 by turning its back on Otto von Bismarck's (1815–98) commitment to maintaining international stability. From the mid-1890s, the German government embarked on a series of diplomatic and military forays designed to enhance the Reich's weight in international as well as colonial affairs.

As Wilhelm II grandiloquently put it, Germany aspired to 'a place in the sun'. These policies culminated in a battle-fleet construction programme that challenged Britain's long-standing global naval supremacy. Britain responded by launching its own naval scheme that led to the construction of the Dreadnought class of ships in 1906.

The armaments race between the German and British navies provided the backdrop against which passenger ships gained international political salience. British liners had held the Blue Riband (the unofficial prize for the fastest transatlantic crossing) almost uninterruptedly since the late 1830s, but the Bremen-based Norddeutscher Lloyd Line signalled its global ambitions in 1897 with the steamer *Kaiser Wilhelm der Grosse*. Launched by Wilhelm II and designed to be the largest and fastest ship afloat, the vessel's name paid homage to the emperor's grandfather during whose reign Germany had been unified in 1871. Most German lines previously ordered their flagships from British shipyards, but *Kaiser Wilhelm der Grosse* had been built in Germany, an achievement that underlined the country's expanding industrial strength and maritime presence.[4] In the year of her launch, she became the first German ship to set a transatlantic speed record and captured the Blue Riband for her country.

German vessels also articulated the young nation's maritime ambitions through the artworks displayed on board. Norddeutscher Lloyd's *Kronprinz Wilhelm* (1901) for example, which captured the Blue Riband in 1902, featured an allegorical canvas by Bremen-based academic painter Arthur Heinrich Wilhelm Fitger (1840–1909) as the centrepiece of the smoking room [68]. Entitled *Unsere Zukunft liegt auf dem Wasser* (Our Future Lies Upon the Water), it confidently interpreted a statement by Kaiser Wilhelm II and depicts a muscular youth holding a trident and a German flag ready to conquer the raging seas.

The taking of the Blue Riband by Norddeutscher Lloyd in 1897 predated the start of Germany's battle-fleet construction programme, and although it took the British political establishment by surprise, it was not yet met with anxiety. It did, however, provoke a determined response from Albert Ballin (1857–1918), who oversaw the rise of Norddeutscher Lloyd's rival Hamburg-American Line to global prominence. From a modest Jewish background, Ballin worked his way up in the shipping trade in Hamburg, securing a reputation as an energetic manager with superb tactical and negotiating skills. After Hamburg-American appointed him to its board of directors in 1888, he successfully revived the struggling company's fortunes and became its Director General eleven years later. Through a series of takeovers and deals with competitors to curb potentially ruinous price wars, Ballin succeeded in

establishing Hamburg-American as the world's largest shipping line by 1898. He also placed strong emphasis on passenger comfort and successfully pioneered leisure cruises in the late nineteenth century. Hamburg-American's ambitious Director considered it a matter of national and international prestige to underline his company's ascent with a record-breaking ship. Entering service in 1900, *Deutschland* not only exceeded *Kaiser Wilhelm der Grosse* in terms of size, but also duly won the Blue Riband for Hamburg-American. The race for the fastest voyage across the North Atlantic – which, as we have seen, was previously an exclusively British affair – became a contest between the two German companies until 1907.[5]

At the turn of the century, British observers began to read this development as an assault on the UK's leading international position – and not just because it accompanied the growth of the German navy. Between 1899 and 1902, Britain struggled to suppress a rebellion by white settlers of Dutch descent in South Africa in the Second Boer War. The protracted nature of the campaign against a militarily inferior opponent not only took many Britons by surprise and reinforced concerns about the future of the UK's global pre-eminence, but it also heightened awareness of the strategic importance of passenger ships for military purposes. In return for state subsidies to liner companies, the military had long reserved the right to requisition civilian vessels owned by British companies as troop transports in wartime. Given the global reach of Britain's colonial sphere of influence, such merchant ships were seen as vital for imperial defence. When it emerged that an American shipping trust led by financier John Pierpont Morgan (1837–1913) had seized control of the British White Star Line, the Admiralty conceded that it could no longer employ this line's vessels in a military conflict. The loss of one of Britain's larger shipping companies, the inability to bring the Second Boer War to a speedy conclusion and Germany's naval challenge raised the spectre of a Britain with a diminished capacity to project itself globally.[6]

In 1903, in a political atmosphere that struck some contemporaries as panic, the British government granted Cunard a loan of £2.6 million on favourable terms for the construction of two liners that would surpass recent German vessels in both size and speed. When opposition politicians castigated this subsidy, Secretary to the Admiralty, H.O. Arnold-Foster (1855–1909), reminded them of the dramatic circumstances that required this exceptional step:

69 ABOVE

Postcard of *Imperator*, sailing through Altona,
Hamburg, with an airship, highlighting Germany's
power on the water and in the air, 1913

FLOATING PALACES: VICTORIAN AND EDWARDIAN SHIPS

What would be the position of the Admiralty and of the country, if, in a naval war, no vessel carrying the British flag could cope with merchant cruisers such as those we might find employed against us? The Admiralty had to consider the cheapest and most efficient method of meeting this menace – for menace it must be considered – and they took advantage of the great mercantile lines.[7]

The loan put Cunard in a position to restore Britain's supremacy on the transatlantic route through *Lusitania* and *Mauretania*, which both entered service in 1907. A *Times* correspondent breathed a sigh of relief after inspecting *Lusitania* at the start of her maiden voyage. No German vessel 'could in any way compare' with her.[8] Once the liner had recaptured the Blue Riband, the *Manchester Guardian* was confident that British leadership was secure for years to come:

> The *Lusitania* ... has made a clean sweep of all the Atlantic speed records, and has proved (what, of course, we all knew) that she is the fastest liner on the ocean. She may, and almost certainly will, break her own records from time to time, but until her sister ship, the *Mauretania*, joins her in the service, she can have no possible rival ... We shall thus have a domestic instead of an international competition, and one of much more genuine interest; for, after all, there is no particular glory in beating a German steamer of considerably inferior size and power.[9]

Indeed, *Lusitania* and *Mauretania* kept the record for the fastest transatlantic voyage until Norddeutscher Lloyd's *Bremen* seized it in 1929. Cunard retained the Blue Riband for more than two decades because unforeseen technical difficulties beset subsequent high-speed liners of the early twentieth century and rendered the construction of ever-faster ships impossible. When operated at full steam, *Lusitania* and *Mauretania* suffered from strong vibrations that led to complaints from passengers. Although Cunard sought to control this source of discomfort by reinforcing the ships structurally, both vessels remained prone to the problem. The losses these liners generated added to the management's headaches because operating ships at high speeds involved exorbitant costs. For technological and economic reasons, the quest for prestige on the transatlantic route shifted from speed to size between 1907 and 1914. White Star Line was the first company to challenge Cunard by ordering a set of three ships. *Lusitania* boasted about 31,500 gross tons, while White Star's *Olympic* (1911), *Titanic* (1912) and *Britannic* (which went straight into service as a hospital ship during the First World War and was lost in 1916) measured 45,000 gross tons. Acutely sensitive to status issues, Hamburg-American's Albert Ballin promptly countered White Star's initiative by ordering another trio of liners, each with a tonnage between 52,000 and 54,000. Passenger numbers reflected this increase in size, too. *Lusitania* could accommodate 2,165 passengers, of whom 563 travelled in first-class, 464 in second-class and 1,138 in steerage. Hamburg-American's new vessels were designed to house about 4,600 passengers. Around 970 people found space in first and second-class respectively and a further 2,700 in steerage.[10]

The launch of the first new giant Hamburg-American flagship in May 1912 turned into 'an exceptionally impressive event'. In his christening speech, Hamburg's mayor Johann Heinrich Borchard (1852–1912) praised the new liner as the culmination of the 'glorious development [of] our navy and our merchant marine', whose growth had been fuelled by the emperor's enthusiasm and Germany's 'flourishing, self-confident middle class'. After the local notable's address, Kaiser Wilhelm II, who attended the launch with the Secretary of State for the Navy, Alfred von Tirpitz (1849–1930), stepped forward and released the obligatory bottle of champagne with the words: 'I hereby christen you *Imperator*'. It was a fitting name for a 280-m-long vessel that would establish a commanding presence on the maritime scene.[11]

By the time the First World War broke out, passenger liners counted among the most prominent national symbols that staked out claims of power and prestige.

As much as these ships were tied up with nationalism, they would not have come into existence without the economic globalization that characterized the nineteenth century. Before the First World War, international commercial interaction reached levels that the world achieved again only in the 1980s. Contemporary observers placed passenger vessels in this growing global interdependence, praising ships for literally connecting mankind by establishing new links between faraway places and enhancing commerce. Irrespective of the state subsidies they received, shipping lines could build these expensive artefacts only because they speculated on business opportunities in an expanding global economy. Between 1800 and 1913, the volume of world trade increased 25-fold. Three quarters of this growth was concentrated in commodity exchanges between North America, Western Europe and Australia/New Zealand, turning the North Atlantic into the prime commercial trade route of the second half of the nineteenth century. International commodity trade did not directly prompt the construction of large passenger ships because bulk goods including cotton, wheat and meat were transported on cargo vessels. Yet, it bolstered shipping lines' balance sheets and put them in a position to undertake the heavy investment required for liner construction.

In addition to growing international trade, the cross-border movement of people shaped nineteenth-century globalization and directly underpinned the construction of increasingly sizeable passenger vessels. Between 1850 and 1914, 40 to 45 million Europeans emigrated overseas, primarily to North and South America. At the same time, 11 million Indians, Chinese and Japanese left their birthplace to work as contract labourers in Africa, Asia, the Caribbean and North America.[12] For shipping lines, international migration became a highly profitable business because, for much of the nineteenth century, most global migrants were prepared to travel under spartan, if not downright degrading, conditions in overcrowded, badly ventilated and unsanitary steerage compartments. Until the outbreak of the First World War, emigrants remained a crucial source of revenue for shipping lines, a circumstance reflected in *Imperator*'s 2,700 steerage passengers. To prevent potentially ruinous price wars, Cunard, White Star, Hamburg-American, Norddeutscher Lloyd and other lines formed a cartel that set annual quotas and prices for steerage passengers travelling from Europe between 1892 and 1914.[13] The emigrant trade was less significant for colonial lines such as P&O because destinations in the European empire attracted considerably fewer settlers than the Americas.

While most passengers crossing the Atlantic booked a passage in the hope of beginning a new life, liner companies profited from a shift in the social composition of their clientele towards the end of the nineteenth century. A recent study of passenger lists has shown that the proportion of travellers booking steerage voyages on German liners fell from almost 90 per cent to 70 per cent between 1880 and 1897. Next to those seeking to escape poverty, passenger ships attracted more customers who were sufficiently prosperous to book themselves into a cabin. Traders, shopkeepers and farmers were the largest groups of this new class of traveller. Although the share of emigrants among better-off travellers remains unclear, since some of them were likely to return to Europe after an extended visit of North America for business reasons or as seasonal workers, their increasing prominence among voyagers reflects the expansion of the European middle class in the second half of the nineteenth century.[14] At the same time, Americans with a desire to visit Europe also swelled the passenger pool. Students, artists, businessmen, engineers and other members of the middle class traversed the Atlantic eastward, seeking intellectual, professional and commercial contacts in Europe. The most prominent American voyagers were, however, the Astors, Rockefellers, Vanderbilts and Guggenheims – plutocrats, in short, who were amassing enormous fortunes in the late nineteenth-century boom that Mark Twain labelled the 'Gilded Age'.[15]

STYLE ON BOARD

Luring these diverse groups aboard amounted to a substantial challenge for shipping companies in the late nineteenth century. Irrespective of liners' enhanced size and speed as well as their ascent to national icons, operators needed to design and present new vessels in ways that overcame the overwhelmingly negative associations of ocean travel. To counter deep-rooted scepticism, shipping lines emphasized the splendour, luxury and comfort that travellers would encounter on board. The industry insisted that passenger ships had turned from spaces of danger and disease into 'floating palaces'. This label had come into fashion for vessels with improved passenger facilities as early as the 1820s, but many voyagers – including Charles Dickens – found a gap as vast as the Atlantic Ocean between promise and experience once they boarded.[16] This discrepancy began to recede only with the adoption of steel in the 1880s, which put companies in a position to construct ships with expanded decks for communal and private facilities. Companies staked the huge investments necessary for steel vessels on attracting prosperous travellers who promised higher financial returns than steerage passengers. Above all, liner operators had

71 ABOVE

Design for interior elevation of a cabin with portholes,
decorated in a Neoclassical style with gilded pilasters and
trophy panels, by Alfred Rogg
France, c.1900–10
Pencil, ink and watercolour, heightened with Chinese white
V&A: E.1403–1989

FLOATING PALACES: VICTORIAN AND EDWARDIAN SHIPS

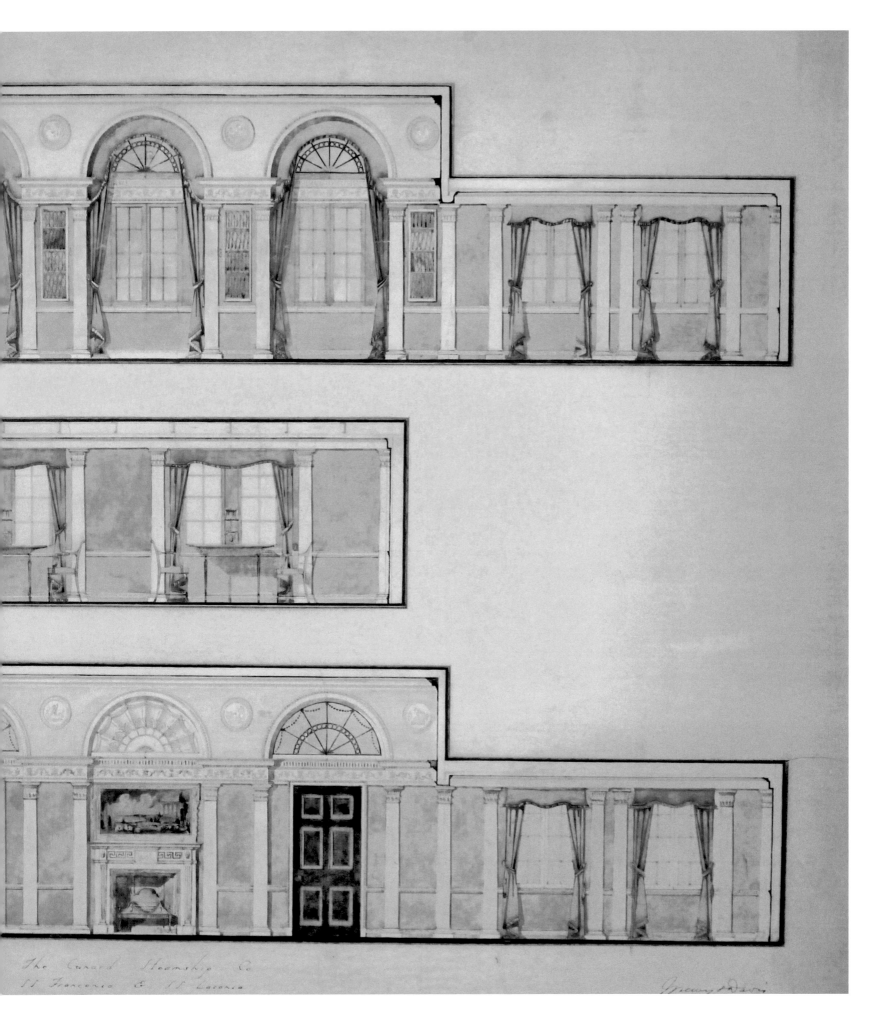

The Cunard Steamship Co
SS Franconia & SS Laconia

Mewes Davis

their eye on the upper classes because attracting the rich promised prestige and profit.

Shipping lines recognized that they required professional expertise if they wished to replicate the tastes and service standards that upper-class travellers expected. Having previously relied on skilled tradespeople and artisans to furnish and embellish interior spaces, shipping companies approached academically trained architects to develop and oversee interior-design schemes in the late nineteenth century. From 1880, P&O collaborated repeatedly with Arts and Crafts architects J.J. Stevenson (1831–1908) and Thomas Edward Collcutt (1840–1924). Collcutt's reputation had received a boost from his extension of the Savoy Hotel in 1889 and the upmarket Holborn Restaurant in 1894. The most influential architecture firm for liner design, however, was headed by the French architect Charles-Frédéric Mewès (1860–1914) who had trained at the École des Beaux-Arts in Paris, which gave its name to the eponymous classical style of architecture. Mewès's designs were inspired by the highly fashionable French seventeenth- and eighteenth-century Louis styles, the craze for which was illustrated by the avid collecting of French eighteenth-century art and decorative arts. He made his name by designing the Ritz Hotel in Paris before remodelling the Carlton Hotel in London and designing the Ritz in London with his British junior partner, Arthur Joseph Davis (1878–1951) all in the Beaux-Arts style.

Albert Ballin was profoundly impressed by Mewès's hotels and commissioned him to design the first-class public rooms on Hamburg-American's *Amerika* (1905), which proved a success with customers. Their business partnership lasted for almost a decade, culminating in the interior designs for first class on board *Imperator* in 1913, produced together with Mewès's partner Alphonse Bischoff, who was based in Cologne. The spaces they designed included the Tudor smoking room and the grand Pompeian-style swimming pool echoing the one designed by Mewès and Davis for the Royal Automobile Club in London (1908–11). Evoking antique architecture, the pool was surrounded by mosaic-decorated fluted columns that framed a double-height space [73]. Mewès and Davis were also among the architects on whom Hamburg-American's competitor Cunard relied to attract affluent travellers. On the medium-sized *Franconia* (1911) and *Laconia* (1912), which sailed between Liverpool and Boston, they provided the plans for the first-class reading room that sought to convey cultivation through a Neoclassical approach featuring a shallow moulded frieze and delicate semicircular windows [72]. Cunard must have been satisfied with the result, because they hired Davis to oversee the interior designs for first class on their new flagship *Aquitania*, which entered into service in 1914.[17]

Shipping companies hoped to match the exacting standards that wealthy travellers expected on land in terms of both service and style. In this quest, prominent vessels relied on traditional upper-class architecture and innovative trends in high-end consumption. In addition to the gentleman's club and the aristocratic house, grand hotels served as models for first-class liner interiors. In particular, the Ritz hotels in London and Paris became a yardstick for the industry because they proved a resounding success with upper-class customers. The Ritz in London offered more than deluxe rooms furnished in Louis XVI style and Escoffier cuisine. With its long staircase for ostentatious entries into the Grand Hall and its bright, airy Palm Court in which guests took tea under a skylight, this hotel offered a cheerful stage for upper-class social display. Around the turn of the century, the material splendour of ships and the illustrious passengers travelling first class lent the formula of the 'floating palace' a far more convincing ring than in the days of Dickens.

Arthur Davis spelled out in 1914 what he considered the main architectural challenges for a successful liner design: 'It must be remembered that on a ship a number of people are imprisoned together for days, and sometimes for weeks.' Moreover, voyagers could not pursue their usual routines but 'are forced to live a life altogether different from that to which they are accustomed on land'. Even on the most recent liners, Davis conceded, a voyage could 'often [be] tedious'. Some travellers found relief from boredom in idiosyncratic on-board pastimes ranging from bets on the distance covered each day to sporting contests and party games. Others played 'thread the needle', in which male and female participants cooperated to pass a thread through the eye of a needle – an exercise in manual dexterity with added flirtatious charge.[18]

Those for whom these activities held little appeal, Davis knew, were 'compelled to look to the ship herself' to relieve potential ennui. In the early twentieth century, liners boasted amenities that Charles Dickens, who had spent most of his voyage in a cheerless dining saloon, could only dream of. Since mealtimes continued to structure days on board, the first-class dining saloon still counted among the facilities that determined a ship's success and consequently ranked highly among architects' priorities. In the 1860s and '70s, these rooms had a cramped atmosphere deriving from low ceilings and large communal tables with long rows of bolted swivel chairs that would remain in place in heavy seas [74]. After 1900, voyagers entered high-ceilinged rooms stretching over two decks that were lit by domed skylights. Although swivel chairs remained in use after the turn of the century, lines now seated guests frequently on chairs that moved freely around numerous separate tables for dining parties of varying sizes.

73 ABOVE
Swimming pool on *Imperator*, photograph
by Oswald Lübeck, 1913–14

Shipping companies thus invested heavily in comfortable spaces to lend their vessels an aura of sophisticated splendour and attract affluent customers. In an article written for an architecture journal in 1914, Arthur Davis enumerated the facilities for first-class passengers on liners such as *Imperator* and *Aquitania*. 'On the lower decks, we find the great dining saloon ... with an adjoining grill room, foyer, and lounge', while the upper decks boasted a 'ladies' drawing room and writing room ... a hall, lounge, and bathroom, verandah café, smoking room, exhibition gallery' and more.[19] In addition to providing ample public rooms for socializing, shipping lines lavished care on the cabins. On the White Star liner *Olympic*, first-class travellers had a choice of rooms that sought to offer the same standards as luxury hotels on land, featuring comfortable beds (not bunks), porcelain washbasins with cold and hot running water and en-suite facilities.[20]

To ensure economic success, most shipping lines chose a conventional aesthetic repertoire that was familiar to the upper classes in Europe and North America. Given the popularity of period styles in representative architecture around the turn of the century, it comes as no surprise that the majority of liner designs adopted a historicizing aesthetic [71]. Period styles indirectly underlined humankind's advancing control of nature. After all, the taming of nature was a precondition for transferring artistic sophistication to otherwise inhospitable surroundings, or so the argument ran. Indeed, liner companies celebrated this very theme in artworks on their ships including a carved clock panel on the White Star vessel *Olympic*. First-class passengers passed it while descending the 18-m-high and 5-m-wide staircase that connected the promenade deck with the reception and dining room. Entitled *Honour and Glory Crowning Time*, it invoked ancient artistic motifs in an accessible manner [77]. Chastely draped in flowing gowns, Honour and Glory appear as angels of virtue that frame Time in the shape of a clock. Honour attentively keeps a record, her foot casually placed on a globe, while Glory's elbow rests on the clock, her hand extending a palm branch symbolic of victory over Honour's head. Honour, this emblem suggests, records mankind's virtuous triumph over time and space, a theme further underlined by a laurel wreath – another victory symbol – that leans against the clock pedestal.

Above all, period styles bestowed cultural prestige on liners and invested them with an air of sumptuous, aristocratic luxury. When Norddeutscher Lloyd began its quest for global prominence at the end of the nineteenth century, it adopted lavish neo-Baroque interior design schemes by Bremen architect Johann Georg Poppe (1837–1915) as displayed in the smoking cabin on board the *Kaiser*

74 ABOVE
P&O saloon chair with reversible seat
*c.*1900
Mahogany on a cast-iron base
LAISTER COLLECTION

75 ABOVE

Bed from *Mauretania*, made at Swan Hunter
& Wigham Richardson shipyard, Wallsend
Tyne and Wear
United Kingdom, *c*.1906–7
Possibly English oak

COLLECTION OF JONATHAN QUAYLE

76 ABOVE

The grand staircase on *Olympic*, with the
Honour and Glory Crowning Time panel *in situ*,
c.1911

Wilhelm der Grosse [79]. Arthur Davis probably had these ships in mind when he warned against the 'temptation' to 'overcrowd a room with heavy ornament and meretricious decoration' that resulted in 'tawdry magnificence and over-elaboration'. Instead, he continued, architects should restrain their decorative instincts and aim for a calm 'air of repose and comfort in the appearance of the different rooms'. To avoid 'monotony' and minimize the risk of boredom among travellers, he favoured ships that derived aesthetic 'variety' from a series of public rooms, each of which embraced a specific style.[21]

In the early twentieth century, many liner companies strove to lend their flagships aesthetic distinctiveness through combinations of period styles. On board *Olympic*, for instance, travellers encountered rooms designed in styles including Louis XIV, Louis XV, Louis XVI, Empire, Italian Renaissance, Queen Anne and 'old Dutch'.[22] Like most liners, *Olympic* and her ill-fated sister vessel *Titanic* contained a spacious first-class lounge, in which passengers could congregate. Decorated with ornate, carved panels in Louis XV style, travellers entered into this saloon through an arch embellished with a curved panel depicting musical scrolls and instruments – highly appropriate motifs for a space that, among other things, served for musical performances [80]. Cunard, meanwhile, employed richly produced promotional material to market its new flagship vessel *Aquitania* as 'The Ship Beautiful'. Her luxurious public rooms referenced British themes, drawing on Jacobean and Georgian styles complemented by copies of artworks from the National Gallery in London. The first-class lounge was inspired by Baroque styles and paid homage to Christopher Wren (1632–1723), an effect reinforced by a plush carpet whose floral patterns were set against a wine-red background [81].[23] *France*, which the Compagnie Générale Transatlantique operated on the route between Europe and North America from 1912, also employed style as a commercial weapon with particular success. Although she was much smaller than the leading British and German ships, she proved highly popular with affluent travellers because of her luxurious interior designs, which invoked France's aristocratic past. Boasting Louis XIV, Empire and orientalizing Moorish revival styles, her suite of public spaces, which were linked by corridors decorated with carved-wood panels with gilded ornaments and classicist columns in bas relief, extended across the whole 150-m boat deck to allow travellers to promenade and people-watch.[24]

Efforts to offer refined surroundings were by no means restricted to vessels serving transatlantic routes. Travellers booking a P&O passage to the British Empire could look forward to sumptuous, stately rooms paying stylistic homage to the British

past. In keeping with their purpose, these vessels' decorative schemes included colonial themes. Several P&O liners featured elaborate tile work by leading Arts and Crafts designer and ceramicist William De Morgan (1839–1917). Between 1882 and 1900, he was commissioned to design schemes and provide tiles for no fewer than 12 P&O ships. De Morgan was strongly influenced by Iznik tiles, polychrome ceramics from the sixteenth-century Ottoman Empire, that he encountered in the South Kensington Museum (now the Victoria and Albert Museum). Among the orientalizing motifs that he designed for P&O liners is a colourful panel depicting an arcade enclosing a mosque and minarets [6]. Although this composition was never fitted on a ship, it lends a good impression of the exotic atmosphere that interiors of ships serving colonial routes sought to invoke. De Morgan was also responsible for the tile with a floral pattern in turquoise, blue and green that graced the saloon of *Sutlej* (1882) [82, 83 & 84].[25] Moreover, P&O liners featured new types of decorative materials that were suitable for on-board use. For instance, Tynecastle canvas – an embossed wallcovering manufactured in Scotland – had much to recommend itself. Not only was it a lightweight flexible material but it also emulated rich, fashionable Spanish leathers, thereby lending public rooms on many a P&O steamer an opulent and exotic air [78]. Ships on imperial routes thus not only underpinned European colonialism but also celebrated it aesthetically.

While historicizing aesthetics prevailed on most international liners in the late nineteenth and early twentieth centuries, this approach to maritime interior design attracted increasing critical scrutiny in Germany after 1900 in more than one respect. Nationally minded commentators vocally questioned the patriotic credentials of German ships on which they detected undue foreign aesthetic influence. Irrespective of its launch by Wilhelm II, *Imperator* caused controversy in patriotic circles for the Louis XIV, Louis XVI and Empire styles that Mewès had chosen for the public rooms. The involvement of foreign architects and the preponderance of French styles on a ship that represented Germany abroad was a thorn in many a nationalist's side. The influential cultural reform periodical *Der Kunstwart* hurled an acerbic charge of aesthetic high treason against Hamburg-American because, on *Imperator*, 'Louis XVI appears to be the real emperor'. This publication considered the vessel a faulty national symbol for failing to showcase distinctly German cultural achievements to the wider world.[26]

These attacks carried a particular punch in Germany because of the alternative designs that emerged after the foundation of the Deutscher Werkbund (German Association of Craftsmen) in

79 ABOVE

Smoking cabin on *Kaiser Wilhelm der Grosse*, designed by Johann Georg Poppe, 1897

80 OPPOSITE ABOVE

Panel fragment from the first-class lounge on *Titanic*, the area where the ship broke in half

*c.*1911

Wood

81 OPPOSITE BELOW

Design sketch for the carpet of the first-class lounge on *Aquitania*, by James Templeton & Co. Glasgow, United Kingdom, *c.*1913

Paint on cartridge paper

1907. Led by a group of architects, designers, entrepreneurs and public intellectuals, this cultural reform organization gained a sizeable following among sections of the German middle class that found the prominence of period styles in contemporary culture anachronistic. Social change and new modes of industrial production, the Werkbund argued, had propelled Germany irreversibly into modern times. Rather than revive the styles of the past, this new age called for distinctly modern forms of expression. Liners, which contemporaries counted among the technological artefacts that literally embodied modernity, exemplified the cultural dilemma of the early twentieth century. Leading Werkbund architect Bruno Paul (1874–1968) observed in 1914 that 'nowhere was the contrast between advanced technological development and ... the inadequacy ... of the decorative arts more palpable than in maritime interiors'. As towering technological achievements, these huge ships possessed a novel 'technological beauty', Paul wrote, that had to find an aesthetic equivalent in interior designs. Embellishing ships with 'a kind of Louis XIV-style with lots of gold' struck him as 'snobbish deprivation'.[27]

To the Werkbund, *Imperator* also appeared as a setback because its members had previously succeeded in securing commissions for maritime interior designs. As early as 1906, Bruno Paul, Joseph Maria Olbrich (1867–1908) and Richard Riemerschmid (1868–1957) were responsible for the decoration of 30 passenger cabins and suites on the Norddeutscher Lloyd vessel *Kronprinzessin Cecilie* (1907), named after the wife of Crown Prince Wilhelm (1882–1951), son of Wilhelm II. Partly inspired by Art Nouveau, their interiors received praise from critics and customers alike. The armchairs Riemerschmid designed for the breakfast room in the 'Imperial Apartment' highlight the Werkbund's approach [85 & 86]. Rather than employing dark carved hardwood and patterned fabrics, he selected wicker to create a light, unadorned chair to enhance the room's bright and airy atmosphere. It avoided historicizing aristocratic forms and instead embodied a simplified aesthetic through which Riemerschmid hoped to replicate the functional

85 ABOVE
Armchair for the breakfast room in the Imperial Apartment on *Kronprinzessin Cecilie*, designed by Richard Riemerschmid, made by Theodor Reimann
Dresden, Germany, *c.*1905
Wicker and pine
MÜNCHNER STADTMUSEUM: M–74/2

86 ABOVE

Salon table for the Imperial Apartment on
Kronprinzessin Cecilie, designed by Richard
Riemerschmid, made by Deutsche Werkstätten
für Handwerkskunst
Dresden, Germany, 1907
Mahogany, inlaid mahogany and bog oak
MÜNCHNER STADTMUSEUM: M−1958/35

beauty of technology. While Norddeutscher Lloyd's management was prepared to experiment with new German designs, Hamburg-American's Albert Ballin was more conservative. Fearing that Werkbund-inspired decorations would clash with the tastes of an international upper-class clientele, he opted for tried-and-tested period styles on liners including *Imperator*.[28]

While the sumptuous surroundings for first-class voyagers established the ocean liner's reputation as a 'floating palace', the presence of thousands of steerage passengers onboard raised the spectre of social tensions between rich and poor. To counter potential image problems and attract the custom of emigrants and less affluent travellers who provided vital revenue, shipping companies tirelessly drew attention to the improved facilities for poorer travellers. Beyond providing better gastronomic services and larger public areas, they began to move away from large dormitories for steerage travellers and replaced them with simple cabins of two, four and six berths. Even the poor could cross the seas in unprecedented comfort, or so public relations material suggested. Furthermore, the management enlarged the second-class and equipped it with more comfortable cabins for customers with sufficient means to avoid travelling in steerage. Above all, shipping companies emphasized measures that enforced social order and prevented conflicts on board. In addition to separating travellers in different classes, operators enforced strict discipline among a workforce filling some of the most dangerous and dirty jobs the Industrial Revolution had created. Boiler rooms were particularly unsafe and physically demanding workplaces, in which trimmers (who wheeled the coal from bunker to furnace) and stokers worked long shifts amid coal dust, smoke and heat [153]. Shipping lines and most newspapers accounts maintained steadfast silence about the harsh working conditions below decks as they did about the low pay that service staff received. The notion of the 'floating palace' was thus predicated on a sanitized image of the ship as a hierarchical social microcosm devoid of the tensions that increasingly characterized class relations on land after the 1890s.[29]

Since the late nineteenth century, 'floating palaces' have embodied seductively beautiful, carefree dreamworlds of consumption and provided an idealized image that has fuelled a lasting fascination with passenger ships and ocean travel. The ever-increasing popularity of cruises as a luxury holiday draws on it to this day. In the 1840s, when Dickens described his Atlantic crossing as a sickening ordeal, the idea of travelling the world's seas had a distinctly unappealing reputation, as P&O found out when it offered the first cruise trips through the Mediterranean in 1844. After only a few years, the line abandoned the experiment for lack of customers.[30] In 1891, however, Hamburg-American undertook a new attempt at Albert Ballin's suggestion, and the initiative was a commercial success that other lines soon emulated – thanks to ships that the interplay of technological innovation, state subsidies, nationalism, globalization and a changing clientele had thoroughly transformed and that now warranted the label of the 'floating palace'.[31]

Norddeutscher
Lloyd · Bremen

Cabine-
de-Luxe
(Bedroom)

Designed by
Professor
Bruno Paul

Furnished
by the
Vereinigte
Werkstätten
für Kunst im
Handwerk

CHAPTER 4

INTER-WAR LINERS:
THE POLITICS OF STYLE

LA RUE PRINCIPALE

INTER-WAR LINERS:
THE POLITICS OF STYLE

GHISLAINE WOOD

THE LAUNCH OF THE NAZI CRUISE LINERS *Wilhelm Gustloff* and
Robert Ley, in 1937 and 1938 respectively, marks the end of a period
in which the design of ships was put to the service of nationalist
political agendas in many countries [90]. The explicit ideological
mission of the Kraft durch Freude (KdF, 'Strength through Joy')
organization was to promote National Socialism through the
enjoyment of leisure activities, while investment in the construction
of these liners also helped German recovery from the effects of the
Depression. As Robert Ley, Head of the Deutsche Arbeitsfront (the
German Labour Front), stated at the launch of the *Wilhelm Gustloff*:

> Today is a momentous day. What appeared yesterday to be
> fantasy and romanticism has now become reality. It is unique
> in the world that a state, a community builds ships for its
> workers. We did not take old relics or junkyards. We created
> 'Kraft durch Freude' knowing that only the best is good
> enough for the German worker.[1]

These ships carried thousands of German workers on holiday
cruises in the first example of mass tourism, embedding 'Strength
through Joy' as an effective tool of the Nazi state. Despite being
emblazoned with KdF insignias – including decorative metalwork
balconies of interlinking swastikas – the largely functional interior
design of *Wilhelm Gustloff* and *Robert Ley* powerfully contrasted
with how many other European countries were projecting a vision
of the modern nation and the ship as an extension of state during
this period [89]. As nations continued to compete for the coveted
Blue Riband (and national subsidies continued to underwrite
their construction) ocean-liner design became a matter of national
prestige and an arena in which the larger dynamics of global
competition and the decline of empire were played out. The period
between the two World Wars was the great age of the ocean liner,
the high point that saw travelling by ship transformed into an
aspirational leisure activity. The iconic ocean liners of this period

– *Bremen* (1929), *Rex* (1932), *Normandie* (1935), *Queen Mary* (1936)
– were regarded as the finest ever created and became symbols of
their nation's cultural, technological and economic achievements.
Moreover, the style in which the interiors of these ships were
executed was much debated, and carried both commercial and
national concerns. Indeed the politics of style needed to be balanced
against commercial imperatives, and each shipping line and
country responded differently.

The First World War, with its catastrophic loss of millions of
lives and the social, political and economic instability it wrought for
the following two decades, also witnessed the destruction of much
of Europe's merchant shipping. After the war, as nations rebuilt,
a programme of shipbuilding helped stoke industrial recovery
in many countries including France, Germany, Italy and Great
Britain. Although interrupted by the Stock Market Crash of 1929,
huge investments were made in the construction of liners during
the 1920s and '30s and the shipping lines amassed vast fortunes
by attracting wealthy passengers to their transatlantic routes.
Intense competition between the European nations for passengers
on routes to both North and South America pushed the design of
liners to ever more extreme heights and helped establish Art Deco
as the pre-eminent style for the liner. The great French ships *Île-
de-France* (1927), *L'Atlantique* (1931) and *Normandie* represent the
pinnacle of French Art Deco style, while the British *Queen Mary*
and *Queen Elizabeth* (1940) presented a more conservative vision
of the modern in Britain. The German ships *Bremen* and *Europa*
(1930) did much to promote Modernist streamlining in liner design
and spurred competition between the European nations. In Italy,
Rex mixed eclectic historical forms while the *Conte di Savoia* (1932)
presented a more progressive approach to mixing old and new
designs. Together these ships helped define for the travelling public
what modern style was, and became for many their first taste of it.

During the 1920s, a number of ships, particularly in France,
explored an eclectic range of visual sources for their decorative

88 PREVIOUS

'Rue de *L'Atlantique*', from presentation brochure,
published by the Compagnie de Navigation Sud-
Atlantique, illustration by Marcel Hemjic and Léon
Benigni
Paris, France, 1931
Printed paper
COLLECTION VILLE DE SAINT-NAZAIRE –
ECOMUSÉE: 999.14.2

89 ABOVE

Salon with paintings showing folk costumes on
Wilhelm Gustloff, designed by Deutsche Werkstätten,
1938

schemes, which, like their late nineteenth-century predecessors, drew inspiration from the imperial destinations they serviced. The Marseilles-based Compagnie des Messageries Maritimes (MM) dominated the Eastern Mediterranean and Indo-China lines during the 1920s, servicing the French colonies of North Africa and the Far East (historically the rich British India trade had been and continued to be the domain of the Peninsular and Oriental Steam Navigation Company, or P&O).

During the 1920s, MM President Georges Philippar (1883–1959) injected a new vision and energy into the design of the company's fleet that built on earlier traditions of ship decoration by evoking a romantic vision in its furnishings of the destination country to which the ship travelled. Running between Marseilles and Alexandria in Egypt, two ships spectacularly represented this trend. *Champollion* (1925) and *Mariette-Pacha* (1926) embodied the passion for all things Egyptian, spawned by English archaeologist Howard Carter's (1874–1939) discovery of Tutankhamun's tomb in the Valley of the Kings in 1922. Images of the tomb, with its extraordinary cache of objects, were quickly disseminated around the world and created a desire for Egypto-Deco, or the 'Nile style' as it became known, that swept all spheres of design, from fashion and entertainment to interior design and architecture. Egyptian imagery could be seen on everything from biscuit tins to cinemas, but the two MM ships were perhaps the most extraordinary manifestations of the style.

The richly decorated public spaces were complemented with cabins in a sparer, more contemporary modern style.

The halls, dining rooms and salons fused neo-Egyptian motifs with modern elements, creating extraordinary fantasy spaces where the coherence of the Egyptian schemes ran through every aspect of the design from the decorative metalwork of the lift cages to the richly patterned carpets with their interspersed lotus and papyrus pattern. Lotus-form columns (copies of those found in the Great Temple at Tell el-Amarna), Egyptian-style statues and a painting of an ancient Egyptian barque by the Orientalist painter Jean Lefeuvre (1882–1975) adorned the glass-roofed hall on board *Champollion* [91].

Champollion and *Mariette-Pacha* were followed by other ships of the MM line whose decoration was determined by the cultures of their destination countries. *Félix Roussel* (1931), which served the Far Eastern route, was decorated in the Indo-Chinese 'Khmer' style, while *Aramis* (1932) looked to ancient Crete for its decorative inspiration. Importantly, the interiors of these ships moved away from the Beaux-Arts style that had dominated the great pre-war ships such as *France* (1912) where sumptuous gilded woodwork recalled the great French traditions of the past and bore much in common with the design of grand hotels rather than meeting the needs of ocean travel. The MM ships were emblematic of a desire within the wider sphere of French architecture and design to present a grander vision of France and her colonies by fusing Western and 'exotic' forms. This ideology was perhaps most effectively realized in the architecture and displays of the Paris *Exposition Coloniale Internationale* of 1931.[2]

The first Compagnie Générale Transatlantique (CGT) ship to establish the pre-eminence of modern French style was *Paris* (1921).

With this liner, the CGT Chairman, John Dal Piaz (1865–1928), aimed to compete for rich transatlantic passengers by embracing the modern and moving away from historical revival styles. *Paris* marks a key moment in the wider concerted effort to re-establish France as the principal centre for luxury goods consumption. In 1925, the much delayed *Exposition Internationale des Arts Décoratifs et Industriels Modernes* aimed to consolidate French dominance of the luxury-goods markets and *Paris*, which carried many American visitors to the *Exposition*, provided a foretaste of the full-blown modern French style they would witness there. Léon Rosenthal (1870–1932), writing in *Art et Décoration* in 1921, described *Paris* as 'the first liner to have its decor designed by artists working freely, without any pastiche of the past'.[3]

Many leading figures of the early French Art Deco style worked on the interiors and furnishings including Louis Süe (1875–1968), André Mare (1885–1932), Paul Follot (1877–1941) and René Prou

(1889–1947). One outstanding feature of the ship was the two-storey foyer by French architect Richard Bouwens van der Boijen (1863–1939) [183]. Its balconies, by Edgar Brandt (1880–1960), established a fashion for decorative metalwork that would be seen on all later liners. It was also the first ship to be equipped with a cinema, fusing entertainment with Art Deco style, a conflation that would soon appear in the architecture of thousands of cinemas around the world. Rosenthal saw *Paris* as representing the essential characteristics of French design, but, beyond this, he identified how these liners came to symbolize much more, by also embodying French culture: '[the passengers] will be surrounded by discreet luxury, intelligent riches and revel in our best qualities; they will also see the true moral physiognomy of France'.[4] This notion of the attributes of design relating to a nation's ethics was further developed in the narratives of later great ships and characterized much of the discourse on modern national style.

Paris was an extremely popular ship that carried wealthy American passengers as well as European emigrants. However after the First World War the number of emigrants to the United States decreased when the US introduced an immigration quota system, while at the same time travel for leisure was expanding. Most emigrants either embarked from the United Kingdom or Italy, so the CGT targeted first-class passengers and an American clientele. Attracting the wealthiest and most glamorous people became key to profitability and drove competition between the national lines.

The success of *Paris* encouraged the CGT to fully embrace a modern idiom for their next great liner, *Île-de-France*, which entered the New York service in June 1927. Writing on the launch in the

---

92 OPPOSITE
First-class grand staircase on *Île-de-France*, designed by Richard Bouwens van der Boijen, with metalwork by Raymond Subes, 1927

93 ABOVE LEFT
Chair for the grand salon on *Île-de-France*, designed by Louis Süe and André Mare, made by Henri Nelson with upholstery by Maurice Lauer
France, 1924
Mahogany, velvet and metal
COLLECTION VILLE DE SAINT-NAZAIRE — ÉCOMUSÉE: 2000.11.2

94 ABOVE RIGHT
La Nymphe de Fontainebleau (The Nymph of Fontainebleau), sculpture for the first-class mixed salon on *Île-de-France*, by Alfred Janniot, *c.*1927

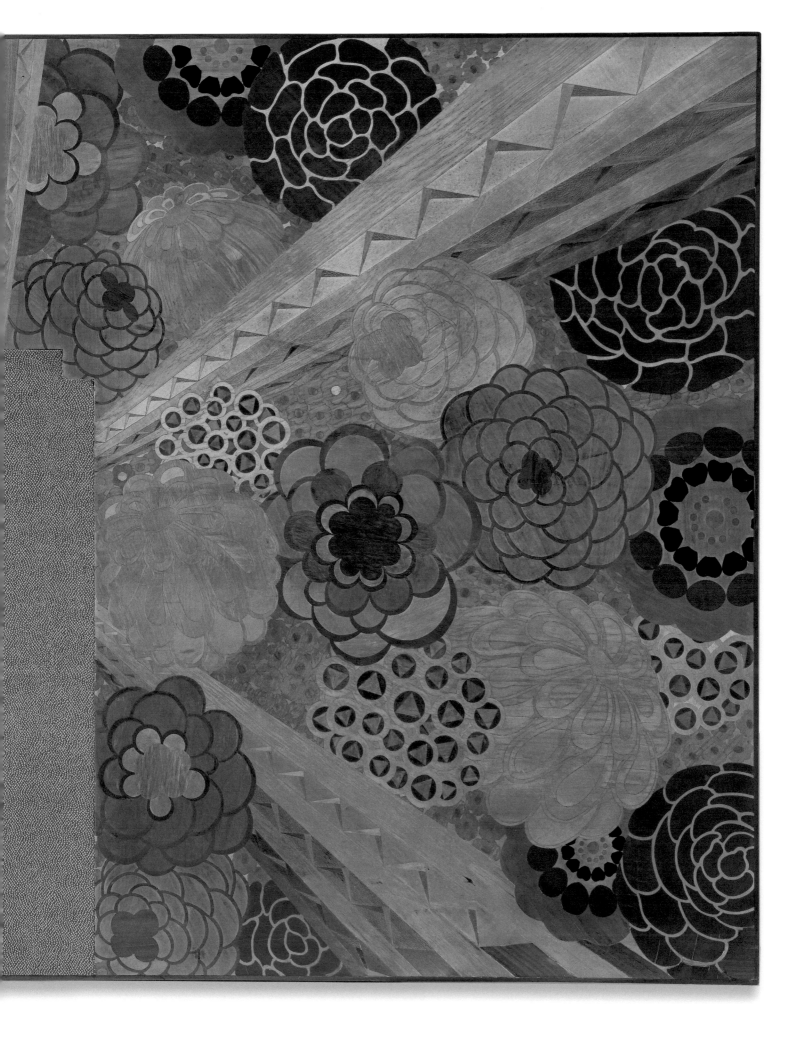

95 PREVIOUS
Wall panel from the Beauvais deluxe suite on
Île-de-France, attributed to Marc Simon
1927
Wood, marquetry
PEABODY ESSEX MUSEUM: M27835

96 LEFT
Passengers sitting in front of the wall panel in the
Beauvais deluxe suite on *Île-de-France*, 16 May 1934

97 BELOW
Salon in luxury apartment no. 22 on *L'Atlantique*,
designed by La Maison Old, manufactured by the
Établissements Marc Simon, with lacquer panel by
Gaston Priou, 1931

British *Studio* magazine, the veteran critic Gabriel Mourey (1865–1943) congratulated the President of the CGT for 'having conceived the whole decoration and furnishing of the new liner *Île-de-France* in an entirely modern spirit'. He went on:

> [the ship's design] was handed over to the architects and decorators imbued with that bold and progressive spirit which was made manifest at the international exhibition of 1925.

> ... The result has surpassed the most optimistic forecasts. French decorative art has risen nobly to the occasion, aided by its simplicity of ornament, its taste in fine materials and its linear sobriety.[5]

Île-de-France was, at the time of its launch, the largest and most luxurious ship on the transatlantic route and its innovative architecture was most apparent in its first-class public spaces such

and see opposite

98 ABOVE

Study for a lacquer panel for luxury apartment no. 22 on *L'Atlantique*, attributed to Gaston Priou
France, *c.*1930
Lacquer mixed with mineral material on plywood panel
COLLECTION VILLE DE SAINT-NAZAIRE —
ÉCOMUSÉE: 2006.19.1

as the spectacular dining room by architect Pierre Patout (1879–1965). The huge three-storey hall designed again by Bouwens van der Boijen elaborated on the grandeur of the hall on board *Paris*. But, whereas the earlier ship had presented a fusion of Art Nouveau and Art Deco, the marble-clad surfaces and elegant double staircase of *Île-de-France* were pure statements of Art Deco [92]. From the hall, with its superb decorative metalwork by Raymond Subes (1891–1970), guests entered the enormous, 432-m² grand salon. The scheme for the salon, executed by Süe and Mare, recalled great French decorative traditions of the past with its Louis Philippe-inspired furniture, floral Aubusson tapestries and sculptural figures personifying the rivers of France [93].

The adjacent mixed salon included important works by Jacques-Émile Ruhlmann (1879–1933), Jean Dunand (1877–1942), Jean Dupas (1882–1964) and the sculptor Alfred Janniot (1889–1969), adding to the rollcall of conservative modern French artists, all of whom had been showcased at the Paris exhibition of 1925 [94]. Patout, Henri Pacon (1882–1946) and Jules Leleu (1883–1961) joined them, taking responsibility for the first-class dining room, smoking room and reading room respectively. The focus on the promotion of a conservative modern style was not lost on Gabriel Mourey who wrote 'The "Ile-de-France", in a word, is a museum of modern French decorative art.'[6] Reinforcing the reputation of French design for luxury and quality was a central aim of the *Île-de-France*'s interiors, and the detailing of every aspect of the furnishings was considered paramount, with extraordinary attention given to detail. For instance, the Beauvais suite utilized beautifully coloured marquetry panels that evoked the floral decoration made popular by designers such as Paul Poiret (1879–1944) and was typical of the Art Deco style in the 1920s [95 & 96]. These interiors promoted the reputation of French luxury goods within the continuing tradition of the high-style French decorative interior. *Île-de-France* was innovative in many ways, but perhaps most significant was the inclusion of the department store Au Bon Marché. After *Île-de-France* the association of French Art Deco and luxury consumption was cemented.

The end of the 1920s saw the entry of two new German ships on the transatlantic route that would inject great impetus to the use of Modernist principles within ship interiors and change the way that all companies approached ship design. Both over 51,000 gross tons, *Bremen* and *Europa* were launched in 1928 by Norddeutscher Lloyd. *Bremen* was to prove particularly influential with her high-speed engines and low, streamlined profile. The new liner captured the Blue Riband from the British pre-war *Mauretania* shortly after its launch and the two German ships were to hold it alternately for the next few years. Importantly, the design of these ships presented a greater formal coherence between interior and exterior, the streamlined profile of the exterior was mirrored within. The desire to arrive at a synthesis between the exterior, technical aspects of a ship's design and its interior architecture was much debated by naval architects and designers during the period. Writing in 1930, the Italian Ugo Ojetti (1871–1946) argued, for example, that the principle should be to 'reveal not to hide the contours of iron and steel structures'.[7] The greater formal unity presented in *Bremen* was widely admired at the time.

A number of eminent German architects were also involved in the design of the two ships including Fritz August Breuhaus de Groot (1883–1960), Rudolf Schröder (1874–1929) and Paul Ludwig Troost (1878–1934). Troost had been affiliated with the Modernist Deutscher Werkbund, and fellow members, such as Richard Riemerschmid (1868–1957) and Bruno Paul (1874–1968), had been involved in designing interiors for Norddeutscher Lloyd before the First World War. *Bremen*'s interior design clearly shows the influence of the Werkbund in the clean lines and shapes of its fittings and furnishings [202]. The streamlined contours and casing of the first-class shopping street, for instance, echoed the engineered forms of the ship's exterior, metaphorically representing its technological modernity. *Bremen* was also the first ship to create a central axis of space – allowing for a series of wide and high rooms – which was to prove very influential. *Bremen* and *Europa* came to symbolize the new Germany and sparked an international competition in the building of large, fast, luxurious ocean liners, which were becoming increasingly symbolic during the growing national tensions of the 1930s. Importantly, these innovative vessels played a key role in accelerating the use of Modernist styles in ship interiors. Sadly, little survives from the interiors of *Bremen* and *Europa*. *Bremen* was bombed and burnt during the war while *Europa* was given to France as reparation. The ship was refitted and relaunched as *Liberté* after the war.

The influence of these German ships in Italy was profound. *Bremen* had been exhibited at the *4th Triennale Exposition* in Monza in 1930 and the architect Gustavo Pulitzer Finali (1887–1967), who executed the interiors of many Italian ships in the inter-war period, was particularly struck when he travelled onboard, commenting: 'in the beauty of the hull and of the external structures [is] the constant presence of a new aesthetic awareness'.[8] This 'new aesthetic awareness', which married interior design with external structures, would govern Pulitzer's approach to ship design for the next 15 years and would be seen in the interiors of *Victoria* built by Lloyd Triestino between 1930 and '31. It was

in marked contrast to the interiors of many Italian ships of the
1920s.

  After the war, Italy re-entered the field with two ships that
had been commissioned by Lloyd Sabaudo of Genoa, *Conte Rosso*
(1922) and *Conte Verde* (1923), which showcased the work of Studio
Coppedè of Florence (consisting of the architect brothers Adolfo,
1871–1951, Gino, 1866–1927, and a third brother, Carlo, 1868–1952,
who was a painter) [100]. The Coppedès's grand eclecticism, would
dominate ship design during the 1920s and foreground an Italian
historicism that was careful to avoid historical styles associated with
either France or Germany. The Coppedè style was characterized by

extreme theatricality and an over-abundance of decoration that can
be seen in the interiors of two further Lloyd Sabaudo ships, *Conte
Biancamano* (1925) and *Conte Grande* (1928) [99].

  In 1927, Benito Mussolini's (1883–1945) new Fascist
government announced the construction of two ships of state to
be built by the Navigazione Generale Italiana (NGI), which shortly
afterwards merged with the Lloyd Sabaudo line. *Rex* and *Conte
di Savoia* were of a similar size to the German ships and were
delivered in 1932, with *Rex* taking the Blue Riband in 1933. The
decoration of *Rex* however, although opulent, was acknowledged to
be outmoded from the start, with one disappointed critic writing:

Here is one of the great prides of our lives as Italians today: the *Rex*. I read with great desire of the *Rex*'s departure from Genoa; a formidable sign and instrument of power, it is one of the great achievements of modernity. It was when I reached the highest levels of enthusiasm then came the cold shower. The *Rex* had been worked on not only by engineers, carpenters, electricians, people with the most suitable instruments in their hands. Otherwise a work of perfect beauty would have resulted. No, decorators and architects also put their hands to it and I do not know why God didn't strike them down.[9]

The elevation of technical skills – 'engineers, carpenters, electricians' – in the artistic service of Modernism was a familiar discourse of the 1920s.

The deeply historicist decoration of the ship was executed by the firm Ducrot of Palermo and picked up on an eclectic range of styles. *Conte di Savoia*, on the other hand, employed a greater mix; the first-class ballroom executed by Adolfo Coppedè perhaps showed the brothers' style at its most dramatic, but many other areas of the ship were executed in a more contemporary idiom. Pulitzer, founder of Trieste's Studio Stuard, was commissioned to do several of the ship's interiors and developed a restrained decorative Modernism that used indirect, suffused cornice lighting to great effect. He went on to design a large number of ship interiors for several Italian lines both before and after the war.

The CGT in France had great success with *Île-de-France* on the transatlantic crossing, and the Compagnie de Navigation Sud-Atlantique hoped to emulate that success on the South America route. During the course of the 1920s, the company had lost ground to British, German and Italian ships and aimed to re-establish its dominance by building a liner that would be the fastest and most luxurious on the route. *L'Atlantique* was built in the Chantiers de Penhoët shipyard in Saint-Nazaire and embarked on her maiden voyage in September 1931. Pierre Patout, Gilbert Raguenet and Camille Maillard won the competition to design her interiors, which were executed in the Art Deco style [97 & 98], but her most innovative feature was in her layout, which, in a further innovation from *Bremen*, split the ventilation shafts to create a suite of large spaces through the middle of the ship, which enabled a succession of rooms on the main axis that provided an uninterrupted gallery.

The 'Rue de *L'Atlantique*', as this space became known, was 137 m long, 5 m wide and 6 m high [88]. Located in the first-class quarters, it emulated a Parisian shopping boulevard with 36 showcases displaying the best French products and services – even a motorcar was presented. Designed by Marc Simon, its white marble walls, enhanced by pillars and mouldings of polished steel, provided a chic shopping spectacle for its captive audience. The notion of *L'Atlantique* representing a floating extension of Paris with all its pleasures and amenities was not lost on René Chavance (1879–1961) who, writing in *Art Décoration* in 1931, described her as 'a floating city', adding 'this expression isn't new, but has never rung so true'.[10] The extraordinary layout, so suggestive of a street, sadly also precipitated her destruction. In 1933, fire ripped through the open space of the hull and the entire ship was lost after only two years in service. After the disaster, much stricter rules regarding the use of fireproof materials on board came into effect. However, the open layout of *L'Atlantique* was developed into an even more striking feature on the next, and greatest, French liner of the inter-war period – *Normandie* [101].

If *Île-de-France* planted the seed that a liner could stand for the patrimony of France then *Normandie* was the full embodiment of that idea. Every aspect of the ship's design reinforced the notion that *Normandie* was a direct expression of French national characteristics, taste and style. The ship was, in effect, an extension of France – a floating fragment of the country. One critic at the time commented:

> the most resplendent attempt to turn ships into floating displays of a nation's artistic genius is represented by the great French liner, *Normandie*. No one who visits her, or who even sees pictures of her, will fail to be impressed with the beauty and sweetness of her external lines and the splendour of her interior accommodation. Architecturally and artistically she is a magnificent achievement, one worthy of the highest French traditions. In fact, she stands pre-eminently for the French outlook on much more than merely ships.[11]

Normandie was planned for 1933, but a number of financial and technical issues had delayed the project, and the ship eventually entered service in 1935 with a vast investment from the French government. Technically innovative in terms of hull and funnel shapes, the Managing Director of the CGT in England outlined the ambitions for the new super-liner: 'We wanted to produce … a ship which would embody the most modern artistic trends and be the exact reflection of the French nation's genius; we had in mind above all cleanness of line and big architectural effects'.[12]

Like *L'Atlantique*, the split up-take allowed for a breathtaking 140-m-long open gallery through the main axis of the ship and this

101 ABOVE
Normandie berthed in front of the Gare Maritime
of Le Havre, by night, *c*.1935–9

INTER-WAR LINERS: THE POLITICS OF STYLE

133

space was divided between two managing architects, Pierre Patout and Henri Pacon. At 80,000 gross tons *Normandie* was almost double the size of *L'Atlantique* and an array of architects, artists, designers and sculptors were involved in her layout, decoration and furnishing.

A grand staircase led down to the fumoir, or smoking room, with its extraordinary scheme of golden lacquer panels by Jean Dunand exploring the theme of 'The Pursuits of Man' [102 & 105]. Dunand was commissioned to produce a number of schemes on *Normandie*, as he had on *L'Atlantique*, since lacquer was deemed an appropriate material for ships being more fire resistant than wood panelling. Double doors led from the fumoir to the grand salon under Dunand's great lacquer composition the *Chariot of Aurora*. The glittering walls of the salon were decorated with verre églomisé panels, designed by Jean Dupas and executed by Jacques-Charles Champigneulle, and dedicated to the theme of navigation [7 & 8]. Seating covered in rich orange Aubusson tapestry, following designs by Émile Gaudissard (1872–1956), complemented them, while columns of light made of glass by Auguste Labouret dramatically articulated the vast space [104]. The salon showcased the very best of French craftsmanship and skill, and the handcrafted nature of the decoration on *Normandie* was an important element of her appeal. The decoration matched or exceeded the very best of France's grand and historical decorative arts traditions, and as such *Normandie* bolstered France's position as the global centre for the production of luxury goods and consumption, an agenda foregrounded at the 1925 *Exposition*.

An important thematic strand of *Normandie*'s decorative schemes presented the art and traditions of the region of Normandy, thereby privileging French culture and positioning *Normandie* herself at the end of an ancient tradition of creativity. The 6-m-tall cast bronze doors leading to the first-class dining room, with their bas-relief medallions depicting the towns of Normandy, helped to reinforce the notion that the ship was part of a long history of architectural beauty and innovation, which included the castle at Alençon and the cathedrals of Caen and

102 LEFT

First-class smoking room and staircase on
Normandie, with lacquer panels by Jean Dunand,
*c.*1935

105 ABOVE

Les Sports, panels for the first-class smoking room
on *Normandie*, by Jean Dunand
France, 1935
Lacquered gold leaf

MUSÉE D'ART MODERNE DE LA VILLE DE PARIS:
AMS 571

106 ABOVE
First-class swimming pool on *Normandie*,
photograph by Byron Company (New York), *c.*1935

107 OPPOSITE
Interior view of the winter garden and aviary on
Normandie, by Roger-Henri Expert
France, 1934
Gouache and watercolour on paper
ACADÉMIE D'ARCHITECUTURE / CITÉ DE
L'ARCHITECTURE ET DU PATRIMOINE /
ARCHIVES D'ARCHITECTURE DU XXE SIÈCLE:
DOC. RHE-DES-014-03-01

PAQUEBOT "NORMANDIE"
JARDIN D'HIVER   10.12.1934

Rouen. Inside the dining room sculptural panels also explored aspects of the region. Raymond Delamarre (1890–1986) and Pierre-Marie Poisson (1876–1953) respectively depicted the themes of 'La Normandie Artistique' and 'La Normandie Maritime', again asserting the propagandistic role of the ship's architecture and decoration [103].

With over 40 per cent of her passengers in first class, *Normandie* presented an extraordinary vision of opulence and grandeur that was unparalleled in the history of ocean liner design.[13] Indeed for the richest of the rich, the liner contained four 'grand luxe' apartments and ten 'de luxe' suites, and the CGT's savvy publicity strategy snapped film stars and celebrities both in the public spaces and the private suites of the ship. One striking image shows Marlene Dietrich (1901–92) in the Rouen suite wearing Elsa Schiaparelli's (1890–1973) 'Zodiac' ensemble of 1938. The extreme exclusivity of this image accentuated the glamour and desirability of life on board. Indeed the publicity departments of the shipping companies were extremely effective at promoting an image of luxury and, importantly, high fashion. The New York photographic company Byron was commissioned to take pictures that, although evidently staged, made powerful statements about the fashionability of life on board. In one photograph models lounge in the latest swimwear around the swimming pool [106]. Indeed the fashionability of Art Deco in the French context is key to understanding both the evolution and wider reception of the style. Figures such as Paul Poiret, Jeanne Lanvin (1867–1946) and Coco Chanel (1883–1971) were not merely fashion designers, but avatars of a new age, leading glamorous lifestyles permeated by Art Deco. They did as much to promote the *moderne* in the way they lived their lives as they did through their innovative design, and it is in the close relationships and co-dependencies between the spheres of fashion, art, architecture and design that we find Art Deco's huge success as a commercial style. *Normandie* provided an extended arena for the performance of fashion, whether in dressing for dinner in the evening or in what was worn in the pool or on deck.

The effectiveness of the French in promoting Art Deco as a modern national style through ship decoration was widely commented upon at the time and spawned much soul-searching particularly in the British context. The conservatism of British ships led one commentator in 1930 to observe that Britain appeared to be offering 'the goods of yesterday, while some of our competitors were selling the goods of today. Does that not apply with distressing truth to the period decoration of big ships? Distressing because a liner is in a sense a national advertisement and is seen by a large number of nationals.'[14] The British responded to the advances of

the French and Germans with *Queen Mary* and *Queen Elizabeth* but, although popular, neither was as effective as *Normandie* in embodying a sense of refined national culture.

Sadly, *Normandie*, like *L'Atlantique*, caught fire and burned in the New York harbour in 1942. The liner was in the process of being refitted as a troopship and so many of the works of art on board had already been removed. These surviving remnants of the super-liner, which include a large section of the Jean Dupas wall from the grand salon, now in the Metropolitan Museum of Art in New York, attest to the unique and extraordinary quality of arguably the greatest French Art Deco 'object' ever created.

By contrast, *Queen Mary* presents Britain's more ambivalent and problematic relationship with modern style. Spurred into action by the launch of *Bremen* and *Europa* in the late 1920s and by the successes of the French CGT ships, the British companies of White Star and Cunard embarked on two new liners at the end of the 1920s. Work on Cunard's hull number 534 started at John Brown's yard at Clydebank in 1930, but almost immediately came to halt as the great depression hit and the workforce was laid off. Cunard was forced to ask the British government for a loan, which was given under the condition that the two companies merge and create the largest shipping company in the world. The loan was sufficient for work to restart on both *Queen Mary* and her sister ship *Queen Elizabeth*, also constructed on the Clyde.

The commissioning process for *Queen Mary*'s interiors – which saw many artworks rejected on the grounds that they were too modern, including works by Ben Nicholson (1894–1982) and Stanley Spencer (1891–1959) – reveals the rather conservative, risk-averse culture of the Cunard company and its deep anxiety over introducing anything that was too contemporary for British audiences and tastes. The decoration of previous British ships had tended to emulate the English country house with historicist panelling and heavy oak furniture, and, although the need for a modern liner that could compete with the French and German ships was understood by the board of Cunard, what form that modern design should take was not clear.

A promotional piece published to coincide with *Queen Mary*'s maiden voyage on 27 May 1936 suggested that the balance between the conservative and the modern had been perfectly struck:

Elegance and architectural lightness are essential points of the design of all the rooms. The decorative themes are modern without any use of the flashiness of a Grand Babylon Hotel, and widespread use has been made of unique woods and timbers with unusual textures and colourings. Period styles

have been discarded in favour of a restrained modernism. The rooms will be perfectly satisfying to the most cosmopolitan conceptions of culture and good taste and at the same time convey the atmosphere of restfulness and comfort associated with the most dignified British country homes ... [15]

Clearly the ship promoted a vision of Britain that was fundamentally rooted in empire and, as increasing anxiety over the future of Britain's overseas territories coloured public debates at home, *Queen Mary* played a role in allaying fears, becoming a showcase for the reach of the British Empire with an extremely pragmatic focus on goods and products. The decoration of the ship utilized woods from British colonies and *Queen Mary* became known for its wide use of marquetry. The booklet *The Ship of Beautiful Woods* (1936) was published to promote this aspect of her design. Rich marquetry panels depicting very British scenes of waterfowl were used in the first-class suites as well as in many of the public areas of the ship. The panels were executed by A. Dunn & Son of Chelmsford who continued fitting out later British ships including producing the panels for *Uganda* (1952) [108].

In the first-class dining room, Philip Connard's (1875–1958) *Merrie England* was the largest artwork commissioned for

108 ABOVE
Detail of *Birds of Africa*, marquetry panel for *Uganda*, designed by Peggy Hodge, made by A. Dunn & Son
United Kingdom, 1952
Various woods
P&O HERITAGE COLLECTION, LONDON:
AC/01549/00

109 ABOVE

Long Gallery on *Queen Mary*, c.1936–9

110 ABOVE

Table from the Long Gallery on *Queen Mary*,
by G.T. Rackstraw Ltd
United Kingdom, *c.*1936
Maple burl veneer, silver bronze, rubber,
baize felt and lacquer over aluminium
COLLECTION OF JONATHAN QUAYLE

111 ABOVE

Armchair from the Long Gallery on *Queen Mary*,
upholstery by Wade Furniture Group
Long Eaton, United Kingdom, *c.*1936
COLLECTION OF JONATHAN QUAYLE

patterns, the cut velvet, plush and chintz, the "salon", the boobles, and the vaguely Louis cutlery'.[19] O'Rorke used simple grain woods and materials such as chromium and Bakelite within Modernist-inspired interiors that contrasted with contemporary ships. Indeed *The Architectural Review* described *Orion* 'as a landmark in the evolution of the modern liner'.[20] O'Rorke did away with decoration, relying instead on unadorned finishes and clean lines while also developing flexible interiors that employed movable walls to create flow between interior and exterior space [114]. *Orion* became the first British ship to truly adopt Modernist principles and attempt to create a style of design appropriate to ocean travel and the demands of tropical seas; it was the first British ship to use air conditioning. The popularity of *Orion*, with her single funnel and corn-coloured hull (the colour chosen by Anderson), led to the commissioning of a sister ship, *Orcades* (II), which was delivered in 1937. On this, and later Orient Line ships, Anderson and O'Rorke worked together employing many of Britain's leading artists and designers associated with the Modernist movement, including Marion Dorn (1896–1964) [115], Robert Goodden (1909–2002) and Robert Welch (1929–2000). In the British context perhaps these ships achieved

the greatest cohesion between Modernist design and maritime architecture, creating an integrated approach to modern ship design When cruising, these ships had to appeal to all classes. In the politics of style of the 1930s, Modernism was the style that most readily showed itself able to traverse class distinctions.

Promoted through a golden age of advertising that witnessed leading graphic designers such as A.M. Cassandre (1901–68) and Edward McKnight Kauffer (1890–1954) create some of the most alluring and striking images of the century, the attraction of the inter-war liners often lay in their conflation of glamour, luxury, entertainment and consumption. Above all they provided the ultimate fantasy spaces where dreams could be realized; as one contemporary critic observed:

> when, after my imagination has been fired and my will broken by those wickedly seductive posters and pamphlets issued by the shipping companies, I decide to make a voyage, what is it that I, as a passenger, am after? Surely, fresh fields, novel experiences, something new, adventurous and exciting? The shipping companies realise this.[21]

INTER-WAR LINERS: THE POLITICS OF STYLE

Queen Mary and, like many of the works onboard, presented a bucolic, pastoral vision that reinforced the notion of Britain as the centre of her empire in a rather different formulation of colonialism to that of the French notion of '*la Plus Grande France*', where France's territories became a direct extension of French culture [112].[16] The very British and mostly rural subject matters of the artworks underlined the conservatism of much of the decorative scheme on board. For instance, the illustrator A. Duncan Carse's (1876–1938) two paintings on the theme of birds of the old and new worlds for the first-class dining room evoked an eighteenth-century style of country house decoration with its silver background and overtones of Chinoiserie.

The sisters Doris (1898–1991) and Anna Zinkeisen (1901–1976), who were commissioned to decorate several spaces onboard,

worked in a more contemporary if highly decorative style. The Verandah Grill, whose murals were executed by Doris, was a restaurant and nightclub and the decorative scheme was dedicated to the theme of entertainment, depicting stars such as Josephine Baker (1906–75) and Mae West (1893–1980) [113]. Writing in *Vogue* in 1936, Cecil Beaton (1904–80) described the Verandah Grill as 'By far the prettiest room on any ship – becomingly lit, gay in colour and obviously so successful that it would be crowded if twice its present size'.[17] The Verandah Grill's murals and colour scheme, which included a chic black floor and pale pink and white walls and linen, chimed perfectly with the more decorative approach to the interior design of the ship and proved hugely popular.

Much of the decoration and particularly the lighting on board *Queen Mary* was typically Art Deco. If not as dramatic and grand as

112 ABOVE

First-class dining room of Queen Mary, by Herbert
Davis Richter
United Kingdom, c.1936
Oil on canvas
GIFT FROM THE LIVERPOOL OFFICE, CUNARD LINE,
1971
WILLIAMSON ART GALLERY AND MUSEUM,
BIRKENHEAD: BIKGM: 4387

113 OPPOSITE

Sketch for the Verandah Grill mural, depicting
pantomime, theatre and circus characters, for
Queen Mary, by Doris Zinkeisen
United Kingdom, c.1934
Oil on canvas
COLLECTION OF STEPHEN S. LASH

Normandie, it was certainly perceived as being welcoming. One of the most successful and loved spaces onboard was the Observation Lounge. With its streamlined zinc bar, originally topped with red Formica and lit by red up-lighters, it presented the streamlined forms that characterized much of the design on board, particularly in the public spaces such as the tourist-class cocktail bar with its clear association with American 'Jazz' styling. Hundreds of small companies and craftsmen from around Britain contributed to the fitting out of *Queen Mary*, including Morris & Co. of Glasgow, Poole Pottery, G.T. Rackstraw of Worcestershire and Waring & Gillow to name just a few. *Queen Mary* proved to be one of the greatest achievements of the British shipbuilding industry, although her sister ship, *Queen Elizabeth*, was larger, faster and technically superior. *Queen Elizabeth* did not serve as a liner until 1946 but went immediately into service as a troopship in 1940, and sailed from the Clyde without having completed sea trials to avoid enemy attack. Her restrained *moderne* interiors were executed by the highly regarded architect George Grey Wornum (1888–1957) who also designed the headquarters of the Royal Institute of British Architects in London.

While competition on the transatlantic route pushed shipping companies to design vessels with ever bigger and better first-class accommodation, with reputations dependent on excellence in first-class provision, an analogous process characterized changes on ships on the Eastern routes through the Mediterranean to the Antipodes. The Orient Line had emerged from the First World War with just five ships and so in 1922 embarked on a construction programme to increase the fleet and enable the company to run a regular service to Australia. Orders were placed for three new liners, two with Vickers in Barrow-in-Furness, which did much to revive the fortunes of the yard during the '20s. These ships were designed to carry 600 first-class and 1,200 third-class emigrants to Australia. However, during the 1930s, as a consequence of the recession, emigration to Australia dropped and the Orient Line was forced to remodel the ships in order to reduce the amount of third-class accommodation.[18] For the line's new ship, ordered in 1933, accommodation was adjusted to carry 486 first-class and 653 'tourist'-class passengers alongside 466 crew and, while the ship was used for cruising, it accommodated 600 passengers in a single class. *Orion* came into service in 1935 and her design coincided with an important change in the management of the Orient Line.

Colin Skelton Anderson (1904–80), son of the owner Alan Garrett Anderson, had taken over responsibility for the Orient Line's design department and had implemented a programme of change, modernizing the interior and exterior design of ships to create greater formal coherence between the two. He employed New Zealander Brian O'Rorke (1901–74) to produce designs for *Orion*, later commenting: 'we were fighting the baroque figuration of veneered panelling and insisting that straight and uneventful grain was what we must have. We were rejecting all the damask

patterns, the cut velvet, plush and chintz, the "salon", the boobles, and the vaguely Louis cutlery'.[19] O'Rorke used simple grain woods and materials such as chromium and Bakelite within Modernist-inspired interiors that contrasted with contemporary ships. Indeed *The Architectural Review* described *Orion* 'as a landmark in the evolution of the modern liner'.[20] O'Rorke did away with decoration, relying instead on unadorned finishes and clean lines while also developing flexible interiors that employed movable walls to create flow between interior and exterior space [114]. *Orion* became the first British ship to truly adopt Modernist principles and attempt to create a style of design appropriate to ocean travel and the demands of tropical seas; it was the first British ship to use air conditioning. The popularity of *Orion*, with her single funnel and corn-coloured hull (the colour chosen by Anderson), led to the commissioning of a sister ship, *Orcades* (II), which was delivered in 1937. On this, and later Orient Line ships, Anderson and O'Rorke worked together employing many of Britain's leading artists and designers associated with the Modernist movement, including Marion Dorn (1896–1964) [115], Robert Goodden (1909–2002) and Robert Welch (1929–2000). In the British context perhaps these ships achieved

the greatest cohesion between Modernist design and maritime architecture, creating an integrated approach to modern ship design When cruising, these ships had to appeal to all classes. In the politics of style of the 1930s, Modernism was the style that most readily showed itself able to traverse class distinctions.

Promoted through a golden age of advertising that witnessed leading graphic designers such as A.M. Cassandre (1901–68) and Edward McKnight Kauffer (1890–1954) create some of the most alluring and striking images of the century, the attraction of the inter-war liners often lay in their conflation of glamour, luxury, entertainment and consumption. Above all they provided the ultimate fantasy spaces where dreams could be realized; as one contemporary critic observed:

> when, after my imagination has been fired and my will broken by those wickedly seductive posters and pamphlets issued by the shipping companies, I decide to make a voyage, what is it that I, as a passenger, am after? Surely, fresh fields, novel experiences, something new, adventurous and exciting? The shipping companies realise this.[21]

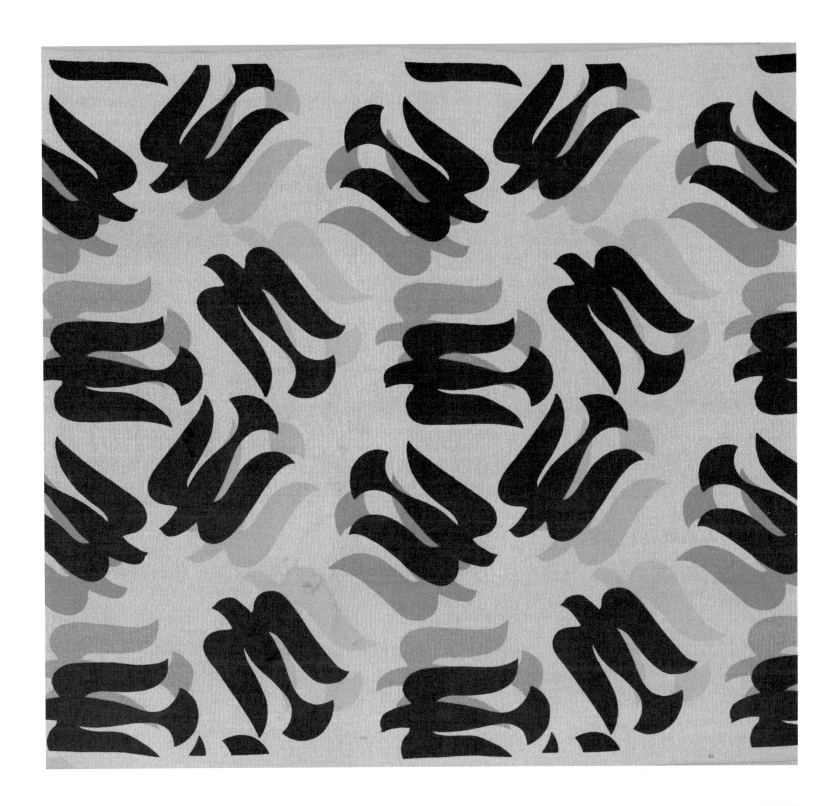

114 OPPOSITE

Design for a dance floor or ballroom on *Orion*,

by Brian O'Rorke

London, United Kingdom, 1934

Pencil and gouache on board

RIBA LIBRARY, DRAWINGS AND ARCHIVES

COLLECTION: PA828/2(2)

115 ABOVE

'Aircraft', furnishing fabric used on *Orcades* (II),

designed by Marion Dorn, made by Old Bleach

Linen Company Ltd

Northern Ireland, United Kingdom, 1938

Screen-printed linen and rayon

V&A: CIRC.241–1939

LINERS AT WAR

MEREDITH MORE

When SS *United States* was launched in 1952 its engineers claimed it could carry 2,000 passengers in comfort, or 15,000 troops if converted for use in a war. It was the fastest ship ever built, capable of transporting an army division from the United States to Europe in only three days. The state-subsidized military readiness of SS *United States*, which was after all primarily a commercial ocean liner, demonstrated to the world America's rise to dominance in the post-war period. America's drive to design such a ship was influenced by the crucial role played by requisitioned liners in the First and Second World Wars. These global conflicts, that required the rapid transport of huge numbers of troops and supplies over long distances, proved that liners were essential military assets.

As political tension mounted in the build-up to the First World War, the British government invested in merchant shipping to ensure the availability of naval auxiliaries should war break out. In 1903, the government agreed to subsidize the construction of two Cunard liners, *Lusitania* (1907) and *Mauretania* (1907), with the provision that they could be requisitioned in the event of a war

and that they were specially designed for rapid conversion into armed merchant cruisers. For protection against mines, torpedoes and gunfire, watertight compartments for coal ran along each side of both ships and the steam plant, engines and steering gear were located below the waterline.[1] Gun emplacements were also installed on deck to allow for 12 6-inch guns to be brought on board if necessary [116]. Ultimately liners of this size were not used as armed merchant cruisers because of their enormous fuel consumption. Instead, their size and speed, which far exceeded that of navy ships, made them invaluable as troopships and hospital ships. *Mauretania* served in these capacities in the First World War, but a German submarine off the coast of Ireland torpedoed the *Lusitania* in May 1915, with almost 1,200 passengers and crew losing their lives. The demise of this much-loved ship was capitalized upon in army recruitment posters in Britain and the United States, and many believe spurred America's entry into the war.

Germany's unrestricted submarine warfare policy meant that all ships travelling in the warzone were at constant risk of

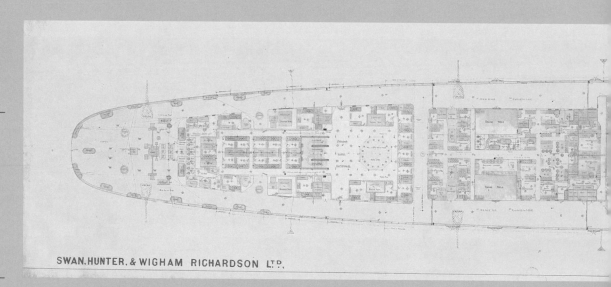

116 RIGHT

C deck plan of *Mauretania*, showing details for gun mountings, by Swan Hunter & Wigham Richardson Ltd

United Kingdom, 1907

Colour-washed paper dyeline

NATIONAL MARITIME MUSEUM, ROYAL MUSEUMS GREENWICH: NPB6679

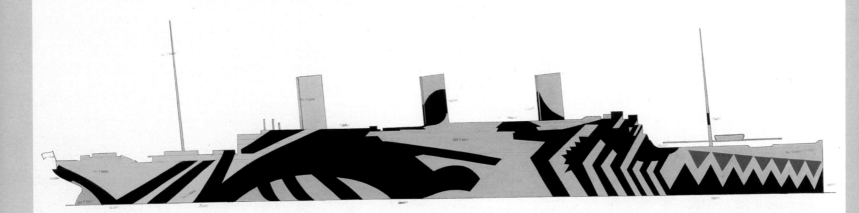

S.S. LEVIATHAN.

117 ABOVE
Order No. 285, SS *Leviathan*: schematic drawing for dazzle camouflage, Ministry of Shipping Transport Department
United Kingdom, 1917
Gouache and ink on paper
IMPERIAL WAR MUSEUM: ART.IWM DAZ 0189 1

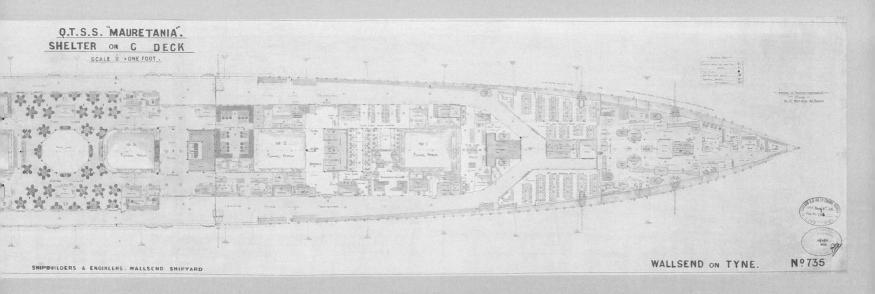

Q.T.S.S. "MAURETANIA".
SHELTER OR C DECK
SCALE ⅛" = ONE FOOT.

SHIPBUILDERS & ENGINEERS, WALLSEND SHIPYARD

WALLSEND ON TYNE.   Nº 735

submarine attack, with an average of 23 British ships a week sunk by German submarines between March and December 1917.[2] To help counteract this, British artist Norman Wilkinson's (1878–1971) dazzle camouflage scheme was implemented, with the aim of producing 'an effect (by paint) in such a way that all accepted forms of a ship are broken up by masses of strongly contrasted colour, consequently making it a matter of difficulty for a submarine to decide on the exact course of the vessel to be attacked'.[3] Wilkinson and his team designed the colourful, abstract patterns that were then painted onto small ship models and tested by viewing them from all angles on a rotating table against a background simulating different weather conditions. The successful designs were transferred onto ship plans and sent to merchant ports to be applied to the ships. For example, the design for the American ship *Leviathan* by Frederick Judd Waugh (1861–1940) was transferred onto the ship when it was docked in Liverpool in 1918 [117]. The plans reveal that each dazzle scheme was unique, with a different design for either side of the ship.[4]

Leviathan started her career as *Vaterland* (1914), the pride of Germany's Hamburg-American Line, but was interned by the American government at the outbreak of the First World War. Germany's liners were mostly used against them in the war, with the newly named *Leviathan* employed to transport almost 200,000 people on the Allied side to and from Europe. More than a hundred German ships were seized by the Americans and later

divided among the Allies as reparations after the war.[5] Some, such as *Leviathan* and *Berengaria*, (previously Hamburg-American's *Imperator*, 1913), even became flagships for the victorious nations.

Britain's *Aquitania* (1914), *Mauretania* and *Queen Elizabeth* (1940), Holland's *Nieuw Amsterdam* (1938), France's *Île-de-France* (1927) and the United States' *America* (1940) all played crucial roles as troopships in the Second World War, but perhaps the most effective troopship of all time was *Queen Mary*. During the war she transported 765,429 military personnel across the world, and on one Atlantic journey set the record for the most passengers ever transported on one ship (16,683) [118]. Her camouflaged appearance and ability to sail faster than enemy torpedoes made her known as the 'Grey Ghost'. She also sailed on a zigzag course and was installed with sonar detection devices for extra protection. The relentless demand for troops meant conditions on board steadily deteriorated, with soldiers sleeping in shifts on berths stacked seven high, while others slept on deck. The constant refitting meant a first-class cabin on board *Queen Mary*, originally designed for two passengers, was later able to hold over 20 soldiers.[6]

After the Second World War, aircraft generally took over as troop transports, but as late as 1982 *Queen Elizabeth 2* (1969) and *Canberra* (1961) were requisitioned to carry British troops to war in the Falklands Islands. In fact, in this instance, liners were the British government's only option to carry the requisite quantities of troops and equipment to the remote warzone.

Accompanying the troops on board the *QE2* was official war artist Linda Kitson (b.1945), whose drawings capture the strangeness of a luxury liner when populated with soldiers and weapons. The ship's conversion was so rapid that alterations were still being made when she boarded: 'I remember stumbling on the deck … and all [the] luxury fittings coming out; huge mirrors, rolls of carpets, fittings of bars with their lights and all [the] mountains of cosmetic stuff for passengers, and then seeing the military kit going on'.[7] All the public spaces, including those designed for shopping and entertainment, were required for training and headquarters. The incompatibility of these settings and their new purposes is particularly evident in Kitson's drawings. One shows soldiers setting up an anti-aircraft gun outside the perfume boutique, while in another the once-glamorous Double Room, with its dance floor and iconic spiral staircase, is transformed into a different type of multipurpose space where everything from rifle training to desk work and slide lectures had become the norm [119].

The *QE2* was widely viewed as a national symbol of British design and engineering, so reports and photographs of the ship carrying troops to and from this controversial war had the power to evoke feelings of patriotism and nostalgia in the British public. Ocean liners had also fulfilled this symbolic role during the World Wars, as evidenced by the international outrage caused by the *Lusitania* disaster and the exultant crowds that gathered to watch *Queen Mary* embark and return with soldiers. Conversely, the seizing and splitting up of the German fleet as war reparations shows how the possession of liners was important for establishing the new balance of power. Subsidized by the state and specially designed with conversion in mind, ocean liners were essential military assets throughout the twentieth century, as well as potent symbols of victory and defeat.

CHAPTER 5

POST-WAR LINERS:
1945 – 1975

POST-WAR LINERS: 1945–1975

BRUCE PETER

THE DESTRUCTION WROUGHT BY THE Second World War both decimated Europe's merchant fleets and disabled its economies. At the start of the conflict, Britain's merchantmen had dominated the world's sealanes – but torpedoes, bombardment and sabotage had destroyed numerous vessels, and the post-war priority, for all shipping nations, was to build afresh.

Britain's Cunard Line came out of the war in a relatively strong position with both the popular *Queen Mary* (1936) and *Queen Elizabeth* – which since completion in 1939 had been used solely as a troop transporter – finally able to provide the two-ship service with weekly departures that had first been envisaged in the late 1920s. No other transatlantic liner company at the time was in a position to emulate the style or capacity of Cunard's Southampton–New York route, but this situation would soon change.

The interior design of the new generation of liners commissioned in the 1950s and '60s sought to encapsulate ideas of the modern nation in an increasingly cosmopolitan age. The differing visions of their various owners were represented through a blend of national schools and styles, with elements of international Modernism, the latter becoming increasingly apparent as time progressed and liner operators grew more adventurous in their design commissions.

In 1951, the industry journal *Shipbuilding and Shipping Record* sent its 'design' correspondent, a fine artist by the name of Gordon Graham, to the Festival of Britain in London to report on the possibilities offered by this showcase of up-to-date British design, but he evidently found little of practical use, dismissing all the furniture launched there as being too flimsy for shipboard use. He did, however, write in more positive terms about furnishing fabrics and carpets with repetitive 'atomic' designs produced by the Festival Pattern Group (which consisted of designers of wallpapers, fabrics and tableware in patterns inspired by scientific research). These soon began to appear in British ships, albeit mostly only in the context of 1930s-style *moderne* polished woodwork and light fittings.

For its new Liverpool–Montreal liner *Saxonia*, delivered in 1954, Cunard attempted an entire lounge with the Festival's 'atomic' look, although the result was sadly lacking much of the exhibition's sense of lightness. *The Architectural Review* was scathing, stating that the space appeared to have been attacked by mice (on account of the many small round holes, presumably intended to represent atoms, all over the bulkheads and ceilings).[1] Subsequently, Cunard and other British shipping lines opted for a whimsical reinterpretation of English 'tradition' instead, as seen at the Festival Pleasure Gardens installed in Battersea Park and in the official Coronation decorations. Indeed, the revival of a neo-Regency style, allegedly suitable for a 'new Elizabethan age', is an aspect of British post-war design that is often overlooked. Cunard's subsequent UK–Canada liner *Sylvania* (1957) [121] was decorated in this manner, the first-class dining saloon even reused chairs from the recently-withdrawn, Edwardian-era 'floating palace', *Aquitania* (1914). Both Cunard and the UK–South Africa liner company Union Castle subsequently employed the London-based, 'society' interior decorator, Jean Monro (1916–2013), to lend their newest vessels an English country house aesthetic with extensive draperies, ornate chintz-upholstered sofas and Monro's favoured coral pink and leaf green colour palette.

Of British liner companies, only the Orient Line, under the consciously progressive chairmanship of Sir Colin Skelton Anderson (1904–80), fully embraced the modern. Following the critical acclaim of *Orion* in the mid-1930s, the company went on to commission a succession of significant post-war liners – *Orcades*, *Oronsay* and *Orsova* (1947–53). On these vessels, Anderson's favoured architect, Brian O'Rorke (1901–74), was responsible for the majority of the interior design, as well as advising on the selection of artworks, bespoke designs of tableware and even menu covers from a number of significant British art and design practitioners. Orient Line's design-conscious patronage of the arts led to a very high degree of visual integration, illustrated by Edward Bawden's (1903–89) decorations of ceramics, a painted

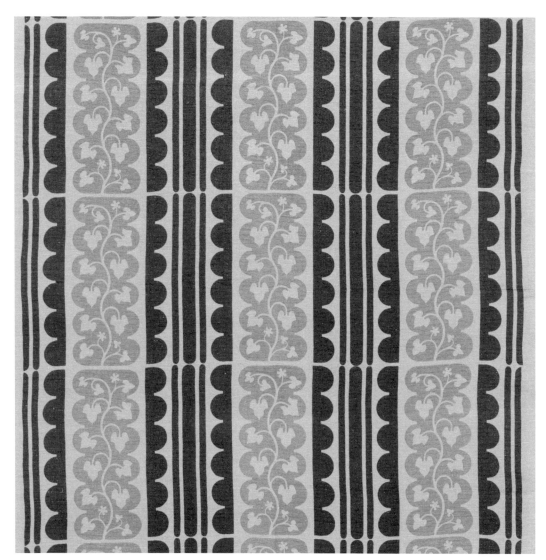

122 LEFT

'Oronsay', furnishing fabric, designed by
Edward Bawden for Gerald Holtom
United Kingdom, 1954
Screen-printed linen
V&A: CIRC.195–1955

123 BELOW

Ceramics with 'Heartsease' pattern, designed by
Edward Bawden, made by Josiah Wedgwood and
Sons Ltd for the Orient Line
Stoke on Trent, United Kingdom, 1952
Bone china, lithographic transfer-printed decoration
GIVEN BY JOSIAH WEDGWOOD & SONS LTD,
V&A: CIRC.417&A–1959, CIRC.416–1959
GIVEN BY THE ORIENT LINE,
V&A: CIRC.327&A–1955, CIRC.329–1955

124 OPPOSITE

The English Pub, mural for *Oronsay*, by Edward
Bawden, assisted by E.W. Fenton and M. Hoddell
1949–51
Oil on panels
PRIVATE COLLECTION COURTESY OF JENNINGS
FINE ART AND LISS LLEWELLYN FINE ART

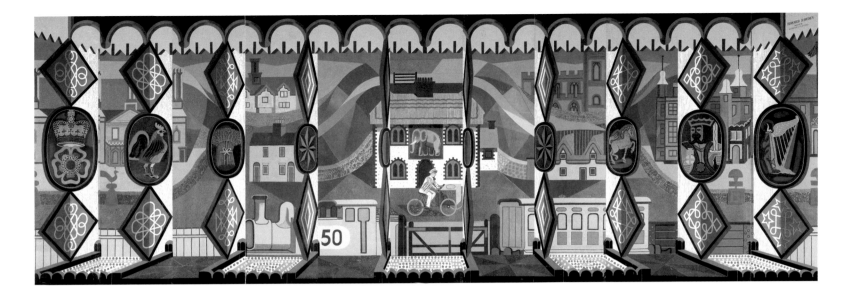

panel and textile designs [122, 123 & 124]. Although both Anderson and O'Rorke wished Orient Line's vessels to convey an up-to-date image, nonetheless, they sought to avoid anything too visually challenging, preferring instead the relatively gentle and inclusive approaches associated with the Festival of Britain.

In the post-war era, it was from countries whose ships benefited from generous government subsidies covering building and operational costs – most notably Italy, America and a newcomer, Israel – that the most glamorous and innovative interior designs appeared.

Only a small number of the state-owned Italia di Navigazione's (often known outside Italy as the Italian Line) fleet had survived the Second World War in Allied service. Thereafter, the 1920s steamships *Conte Biancamano* (1925) and *Conte Grande* (1928), and the motor vessels *Saturnia* (1927) and *Vulcania* (1928) were returned to Italy in decrepit condition.[2] The two steamships were stripped back to bare steel and refitted with new interiors by a group of like-minded Modernist architects and designers of whom the key members were Gio Ponti (1891–1979), Giovanni 'Nino' Zoncada (1898–1988), Gustavo Pulitzer Finali (1887–1967) and Matteo Longoni (1913–84); they went on to design the interiors of a large part of the post-war Italian passenger fleet. Other architects involved in the design of individual spaces were Umberto Nordio (1891– 1971), Aldo Cervi-Hirsch (1901–72), Vittorio Frandoli (1902–78), Romano Boico (1910–85) and Alessandro Psacaropulo (1915–2000), all of whom were from Trieste. The Milanese Ponti, a vocal polemicist, became internationally famous and his vision of a world in which 'good' design should be available to all was promulgated under his editorship of the influential journal *Domus*. As far as ship design was concerned, he believed:

Italian ships should be dedicated to ... the honour of Italy, in two ways. One is figurative, represented in the decorations, pictures and ornaments, and it is the restatement of the ... legendary Italy of art and history ... The other way of honouring Italy is to make Italian ships superior to all the foreign ones, even if we conceive of a ship only as a 'functional means of transport' and not as propaganda. Do you not want to achieve the maximum elegance and decisive unity?[3]

Conte Biancamano and *Conte Grande* emerged from their rebuilds completely transformed: ornate saloons in period styles were replaced by calm spaces with contemporary furniture [147], indirect lighting and abstract murals by various Italian artists – such as Paolo De Poli's (1905–96) enamel panels in the *Conte Grande*'s first-class ballroom, depicting Italy's agricultural abundance [125 & 126]. The majority of artworks on these and subsequent Italian liners, however, reinterpreted imagery from Italy's classical and Renaissance past in a modern romantic idiom. This was fully in line with Ponti's stated aims regarding how these vessels' interiors were expected to communicate an attractive, modern, yet historically rooted 'image' of Italy to their American passengers.

Italy's first post-war transatlantic liners, the motor ships *Giulio Cesare* (1951) and *Augustus* (1952), were built at Trieste and Monfalcone respectively for service to the east coast of South America.[4] Modernity was signalled externally by raked bows, curved-fronted superstructures, single masts and very large centrally placed funnels, while their interiors were similar in style to the rebuilt steamships. There was full airconditioning and each ship boasted three swimming pools and four cinemas. On the *Giulio*

125 ABOVE LEFT

First-class ballroom on *Conte Grande*, designed by
Gio Ponti and Nino Zoncada, with enamel panels
by Paolo De Poli, *c.*1948

126 ABOVE RIGHT

Panel from the first-class ballroom on *Conte Grande*,
by Paolo De Poli
Italy, 1948
Enamel and paint

127 OPPOSITE

Augustus, docked in Genoa.

Cesare, Ponti and Zoncada were responsible for the first-class areas, with Pulitzer designing the dining room. Spaces on board *Augustus* were mainly by Nordio, Cervi-Hirsch, Frandoli and Boico, with Pulitzer again responsible for the first-class dining saloon.[5] Their approaches were remarkably similar, utilizing three-dimensional ceiling treatments (consisting of layers of panelling, illuminated troughs and floating panels), plate-glass partitions, shiny vulcanized rubber flooring and distinctive Cassina-manufactured furniture upholstered in velour with slim legs for stability in rough seas. Artworks were often installed so as to appear to float in front of background panels; this reflected an increasing distance between modern art and interior design as the former sought greater autonomy from government and commercial forces in the wake of the Second World War. Wall-mounted figurative sculptures by Marcello Mascherini (1906–83) from various Italian liners of the 1950s and '60s clearly demonstrate this approach [128]. Italy's new and rebuilt liners were, however, widely praised as superbly well-integrated 'showcases' for the country's engineering, design and artistic talents.

In 1930s' America, professional industrial designers had been employed to increase the attractiveness of consumer goods to stimulate demand in the wake of the Great Depression. Just before the Second World War, the most prominent of these men, Raymond Loewy (1893–1986), had collaborated with the naval architect George G. Sharp to design three passenger and cargo liners for the Panama Line, operating from New York to the Panama Canal. In most conventional accounts of their work ashore, Loewy and his counterparts are considered merely as stylists, enclosing existing engineering in fashionable-looking, stream-formed packaging. Loewy's work on the *Panama*, *Ancon* and *Cristobal* (all 1939), however, was extensive and, through his close collaboration with Sharp, it was possible to harmonize their external silhouettes, livery, signage and interior design. This highly cohesive approach provided a successful precedent for a majority of post-war American liners. On these vessels, the decorative arts were eschewed in favour of technology and servicing similar to those found ashore in the newest Statler and Hilton hotels – such as air conditioning, private bathrooms, bedside telephones and

fitted carpets. To conceal complex wiring, plumbing and ventilation ducts, tiled suspended ceilings were installed beneath the deckheads, reflecting light from fluorescent tubes concealed around the perimeter. Furthermore, after a disastrous fire in 1934 on the American coastal liner *Morro Castle* (1930), the US government had mandated that all American-flagged liners would be of fireproof construction. The so-called 'Method 1' safety standard demanded that internal spaces were segregated into fireproof compartments with steel bulkheads and the use of only very thin decorative veneers on asbestos backing. Rather than the showy polished woodwork so typical of European vessels, fire-retardant laminate came to be favoured and, in the 1950s, this became available in a broad range of patterns and colours.

The *Independence* and *Constitution* were built in 1951 for the American Export Lines' service from New York to Mediterranean ports. The company employed the industrial designer Henry Dreyfuss (1904–72) 'to provide distinctive interiors that represent the best features in Modern American Living. We wanted to make sure that our passengers will be able to enjoy the comfort and convenience that the best skills and ingenuity of American industry can provide for years to come'.[6] Dreyfuss's belief was that everything connected with a company should reflect a consistent 'look' and, in so doing, create an immediately identifiable

'lifestyle' to which the prospective customer could aspire [129 & 130]. Elaborate mock-ups were constructed to refine the deck arrangements, the relationships between cabin groups, corridors and services, colour schemes, locations of furniture, lighting and ventilators. The British travel writer C.M. Squarey was impressed by the fact that:

> Every basin has hot, cold, and iced water, all from the same tap. Room temperature is at your own control over a range of 60–80 deg. F. Port-holes are permanently sealed, but fitted with a polarised lens, the object of this ingenious device being to banish glare. Bed lamps are the same as those used over aeroplane seats.[7]

Soon America was commissioning a 'ship of state' to usurp Britain's *Queen Mary* and *Queen Elizabeth*. As the liner historian Peter C. Kohler has observed, however, the *United States* was 'less the creation of a nation than of a man' – the naval architect William Francis Gibbs (1886–1967). As Kohler states: 'Having nurtured the idea of building the ultimate ocean liner for most of his 40-year career, Gibbs succeeded magnificently'.[8] In July 1952, the *United States* sailed eastbound in only three days, 10 hours and 40 minutes at an average speed of 35.59 knots (41 mph) – the

128 OPPOSITE

Danzatrice con tre gabbiani (Dancer with three seagulls), sculpture by Marcello Mascherini, originally shown on *Franca C.* with two seagulls, then later installed with three seagulls on *Eugenio C.*
Italy, 1959
Bronze
COLLECTION OF COSTA CRUISES, GENOA, ITALY

129 RIGHT

Lounge on *Independence*, designed by Henry Dreyfuss, *c.*1950

130 BELOW

Independence at sea, *c.*1950

fastest-ever Atlantic crossing by a large liner – and its subsequent westbound crossing was achieved in three days, 12 hours and 12 minutes [131]. Should war have broken out with the Soviet Union, the *United States* could quickly convert into a troop transport, capable of conveying an entire army division to Europe in three days. The liner's complete lack of woodwork, coupled with its well-publicized secondary military role, led some potential passengers and employees of rival companies to describe it as a 'troopship in disguise' in hope of denting its prestige.

Unlike his fellow naval architect George G. Sharp, who was very conscious of the benefits of collaborating with industrial designers, Gibbs considered his task solely within the terms of engineering. Only once he was satisfied that his technical brief was fulfilled (by which time the deck layout was a *fait accompli*) could the 'hotel' elements be 'decorated' by others. This work was given over to Dorothy Marckwald (1898–1986) of Smyth, Urquhart & Marckwald, who had previously designed the interiors of United States Lines' *America*, which had entered service in 1940. Although Marckwald was forced to work with a narrow range of Gibbs-approved fireproof materials – such as stainless steel, aluminium and plate glass – she was able to achieve an atmosphere of contemporary modernity and relative comfort through the judicious use of bright, saturated colours, set against soft pastel shades and witty details, such as cocktail tables in the form of ship's propellers [173]. And yet, despite the interiors' appearance of modernity, Kohler notes:

> *United States* was an oddly formal, class-conscious ship inside, especially for an American one – but Gibbs had practically dictated to United States Lines that its flagship would be laid out along traditional lines with three classes, not two – and the ship owner apparently had little choice but to agree with its forceful naval architect.[9]

In 1952, when the *United States* entered service, the first jet airliner, *Comet 1*, was also introduced and so, despite its technological brilliance, the liner arguably represented the beginning of the end of the northern North Atlantic express passenger service. The more southerly route from New York to Mediterranean ports was too lengthy for serious airline competition as yet and, due to its warmer weather for a greater part of the year, lent itself to more of a leisure-orientated, cruise-style service approach.

Italy followed the lead of American Export Lines' *Independence* and *Constitution* by commissioning a new transatlantic flagship, *Andrea Doria*, which was introduced in 1953. Next, the same Ansaldo shipyard in Genoa completed a sister ship, *Cristoforo Colombo*, which entered service in 1954. Both owed much in general design to the recent *Augustus* and *Giulio Cesare*. Ponti, Zoncada, Cassi, Rossi and Parenti, among others, designed *Andrea Doria*'s interiors, while the *Cristoforo Colombo* was largely Pulitzer's work.[10] Of the two, *Andrea Doria* was the more glamorous ship, outfitted with mirrored walls, three-dimensional ceilings, contemporary sculpture and murals alluding to Italy's classical and Renaissance history [132]. Ponti's first-class 'Zodiac Suite' in blue and cream had a surreal, dreamlike quality, with every surface decorated with astrological signs by Piero Fornasetti [227]. By contrast, Pulitzer's treatment of the *Cristoforo Colombo* was demure, with gentle colours and indirect lighting. Tragically, after just five years' service, *Andrea Doria* sank off Nantucket Island after colliding with the Swedish motor ship *Stockholm* (1948).[11]

For the new state of Israel, passenger ship interior design became an important way of signalling its cultural ambitions to the world. Surrounded by hostile neighbours, the nation was effectively an 'island' as its international airport and one deep-sea harbour at Haifa were its only links to the outside world. Against this background of war and isolation, the Zim Israel Navigation Company developed a fleet initially consisting of second-hand ships to bring thousands of Jewish refugees and immigrants to Israel. When, in September 1951, Germany announced it would make financial reparations for the Holocaust, the possibility emerged to expand the Zim fleet.

Between 1953 and 1955, Zim ordered four new passenger liners from German shipyards, including *Israel*, *Zion*, *Theodor Herzl* and

---

131 OPPOSITE ABOVE
SS *United States* at sea, 1952–69

132 OPPOSITE BELOW
First-class grand salon on *Andrea Doria*, with painted decoration by Salvatore Fiume, 1950s

133 ABOVE

'The Synagogue' from a brochure for *Shalom*,

photograph by Sadeh, printed by United Artists Ltd,

Tel Aviv, Israel, *c.*1964–7

Jerusalem, which were built by Howaldtswerke-Deutsche Werft in Hamburg. Zim chose two well-known Israeli architecture firms for the ships' interiors: the partnership of Al Mansfeld (1912–2004) and Munio Weinraub (1909–70) in Haifa,[12] and the husband and wife team of Dora (1912–2003) and Yeheskel Gad (1911–58) of Tel Aviv. Mansfeld had studied architecture in Berlin and Paris,[13] Weinraub had attended the Bauhaus at Dessau, where Ludwig Mies van der Rohe's (1886–1969) approach to architecture was latterly influential, and Dora Gad had been educated in Vienna.

The interiors of the new Zim liners reflected their architects' affinity with the modern movement, which was considered appropriate for a young Mediterranean nation with (at that time) internationalist ideals. Colour schemes of turquoise, purple, olive and tan supposedly reflected the Israeli coast and landscape, while frameless glass doors and suspended staircases with open risers enhanced the feeling of space. Indirect ceiling lighting was complemented by wall and table lamps, designed by the architects and manufactured by Louis Poulsen & Co. in Copenhagen, and – as on recent Italian liners – there were extensive and well-integrated displays of contemporary art, including works by Ben Shahn (1898–1969), Yaacov Agam (b.1928) and other Jewish artists, several of whom subsequently found international fame. Zim's new passenger fleet was widely admired and the Scandinavian influences upon the interior design were in line with wider design trends in the 1950s [133].

By the late 1950s, the threat of increasing airline competition divided opinion among transatlantic liner operators as to whether the year-round passenger trade had a long-term future. On the one hand, air was obviously the faster and more convenient mode for the wealthy but time-poor; on the other hand, the fact that a liner could offer the unique benefits of space, luxury and economy of scale led many liner company managers to hope that there would always be a market for sea travel. For government-owned liner companies, providing continuity of employment in shipbuilding and for the crew were important political considerations. What turned out to be the 'final generation' of transatlantic liners, introduced in the 1959–69 period, was split between two distinct approaches to layout and service provision. Those of the state-owned and subsidized Compagnie Générale Transatlantique and Italia di Navigazione continued to reflect traditional requirements, as first codified in the twentieth century's earlier decades. In contrast, new vessels commissioned by more commercially oriented liner companies were designed as dual-purpose, liner-cum-cruise ships, the idea being that they would offer two-class Atlantic crossings in the calmer summer months and one-class luxury cruises in winter. Dutch, Scandinavian and British liner operators would all soon adopt this approach.

Holland-America Line's *Rotterdam* (1959) represented a significant departure from established liner deck layouts. Hitherto, first-class passengers had occupied an exclusive 'island' amidships where there was less sea motion, the remaining accommodations being split fore and aft. On the *Rotterdam*, by contrast, first and tourist-class spaces were divided horizontally on alternate decks. This meant that each class had a complete run of public rooms from end to end of the superstructure and cabin decks extended fully fore and aft. A key feature of this approach was the liner's unique 'scissors' arrangement of double interleaved stairways. Concealed sliding panels could be closed on each deck lobby to segregate the two sets of stairs during Atlantic crossings. With the panels opened for cruises, all passengers had the complete run of the ship.[14] Furthermore, the *Rotterdam*'s machinery was located about three-quarters aft, rather than amidships, so as to allow for a greater amount of open space throughout the passenger accommodation.

Rotterdam's interior design reflected the contemporary architecture and outlook of its namesake city, which pre-war had been the home of the avant-garde De Stijl art, design and architecture movement. By the 1950s, Rotterdam's harbour, at the mouth of the Rhine, was being marketed as 'Europort' and by 1960 was overlooked by the 'Euromast'. By designing a 'European' ship, Holland-America would be able to offer potential passengers the best of everything – from French cuisine served on Delft porcelain to an Italian ice cream parlour, all arranged within an abstract Modernist framework. Whereas the interiors of the company's pre-war flagship, *Nieuw Amsterdam* (1938), were richly decorated in a streamlined Art Deco idiom, *Rotterdam*'s – using similar materials such as hardwoods, leather and Delft ceramics – were characterized by trapezium shapes, zigzags and patterns of atoms. Comparable forms adorned the new façades of the post-war city of Rotterdam.

Both as a transatlantic liner and as a cruise ship, *Rotterdam* was a great success and aspects of the 'dual-purpose' design approach were emulated on the Israeli *Shalom*, the Norwegian *Sagafjord* and the Swedish *Kungsholm*, all of which were completed in the mid-1960s. In contrast, Italy's *Leonardo da Vinci* (1960) – which was built to replace the lost *Andrea Doria* – and the new Compagnie Générale Transatlantique super-liner *France* (1962) were conceived primarily for express liner service.

Leonardo da Vinci was built by the Ansaldo shipyard, and safety was a high priority in its construction. To give a high degree of resilience in the event of damage, there were two separate engine rooms, an unusual and costly solution for a vessel of moderate size. Passengers were accommodated in three classes with vertical subdivisions, forward and aft of amidships. The deck layout was designed for open-air activities, including a swimming pool for each of the three classes. While the first and second classes attracted a leisured clientele, young people travelling on smaller budgets and migrants found third class still to be the cheapest way of crossing between Europe and the United States.

Designs by Pulitzer, Longoni, Gottardi, Zoncada and the prominent Rome-based architects Vincenzo Monaco (1911–69) and Amedeo Luccichenti (1907–63) were selected for the interiors. But stylish though *Leonardo da Vinci* undoubtedly was, passengers in each class constantly encountered dead-end corridors, giving a frustratingly restrictive impression in comparison with the spacious *Rotterdam*.

The new super-liner *France* was constructed at the Chantiers de l'Atlantique shipyard, where *Normandie* (1935) had been built just over two decades earlier, and comparisons between the two liners were thus inevitable. To prevent any repeat of the fire that destroyed *Normandie*, open-planning and axial internal vistas were avoided on the new ship and, wherever possible, non-combustible internal finishes were specified – aluminium and other metals, fire-retardant synthetics and plastic laminates with only sparing use of specially treated wood veneers.

Externally, the *France*'s modernity was signalled by fins extending from the aerofoil-shaped funnels, which – ironically – were obviously inspired by aircraft wings [134].[15] As on *Rotterdam*, only two classes of accommodation were offered using a similar 'sandwiched' deck layout. Tourist class was called 'Rive Gauche', reflecting the bohemian fashionability of Paris's University Quarter.

The Société des Artistes Décorateurs was consulted to select designers and artists for the liner's interiors; they included the architect Guillaume Gillet (1912–87), the artist Roger Chapelain-Midy (1904–92) and the art critic Pierre Mazars (1921–85), who chose artworks to adorn the vessel's interiors. Gillet was working concurrently on the French Pavilion for the 1958 Brussels World's Fair, a situation reflecting Jacques-Emile Ruhlmann's (1879–1933) work at the 1925 *Exposition Internationale des Arts Décoratifs et Industriels Modernes* shortly before he designed interiors for *Île-de-France* (1927).

France's decoration was grand in scale, luxurious in finish and quirkily chic in style. Its double-height first-class dining room was entered through frameless plate-glass doors, down a flight of wide red-carpeted stairs. Beneath a shallow circular dome, brass panelling warmly reflected light and movement below, but also echoed any noise into a loud background din. The overall form of

the space was rather akin to that of the United Nations' General Assembly chamber in New York. Also of double height, the first-class fumoir was reminiscent of *Normandie*'s interiors, yet the decorative scheme by André Arbus (1903–69) was understated, the space being animated instead by a vibrant tapestry on the forward bulkhead by Jean Picart Le Doux (1902–82) depicting 'The Phases of Time' [135].[16]

Micheline Willemetz, meanwhile, decorated the fumoir in Rive Gauche in rich, saturated colours. A mural by the noted stage designer Jean-Denis Malclès (1912–2002), showing a night scene of dancing Harlequin figures set against a Parisian skyline, formed a suitable backdrop for couples on the adjacent dance floor [136]. The seating plan was informally asymmetrical with decorative dividing panels to create a sense of intimacy. Yet, as with the *United States*, the bespoke aluminium-framed furniture often appeared to have been designed primarily for safety or hygiene rather than comfort (as the Rive Gauche armchair by Jacques Dumond [1906–88], demonstrates). Also for use by Rive Gauche passengers was a swimming pool and gymnasium located towards the stern, protected from the elements by a Perspex dome. There were even occasional opportunities for the two classes to mix, such as at the teenagers' soda fountain and gaming arcade, which became a popular late-night social space. With facilities such as these, it was unsurprising that travelling Rive Gauche on board *France* became a favourite way for prosperous American students to visit Europe in style. Thus, the liner very briefly captured and reflected aspects of the youthful, progressive spirit of its era.

In Britain, *Queen Mary* and *Queen Elizabeth* continued to attract a large and loyal clientele on the Southampton–New York route, so any new British liner commissioned in the early 1960s was for use elsewhere. The Union Castle Line, serving South Africa, introduced the large and well-appointed *Windsor Castle* (1960) and the one-class *Transvaal Castle* (1962), while Canadian Pacific took delivery of the *Empress of Canada* (1961) for the Liverpool–Montreal service and the Shaw Savill Line added the *Northern Star* (1962, a near-sister of the seven-year-old *Southern Cross*, 1955) for its round-the-world route via New Zealand. All these new vessels offered unprecedentedly spacious, fully air-conditioned accommodation – although, in terms of layout and style, they differed little from each line's existing fleet. Much more innovative in these regards were the Orient Line's *Oriana* and P&O's *Canberra* – two large, new liners commissioned for a joint service to Australia, New Zealand and onwards to the Pacific Rim.

134 RIGHT

Funnel and illuminated lettering on *France*, c.1962

135 BELOW

First-class smoking room on *France*, designed by
André Arbus, with a tapestry by Jean Picart Le Doux,
c.1962

While the collapse of the British Empire had brought a decline in P&O's traditional passenger trade to the Indian subcontinent, demand for passage to Australia appeared insatiable and, with two bigger, faster liners, P&O and Orient Line would both benefit from improved economies of scale while being able to shorten voyage times by two weeks. Both vessels measured over 40,000 gross tons and had up to a 27.5-knot (31.6 mph) service speed, but they were designed and built almost entirely independently.

Oriana was the ultimate expression of Orient Line's progressive design trajectory begun in the mid-1930s with *Orion* and continued post-war with *Oronsay*, *Orcades* and *Orsova*. By contrast, P&O – a much larger shipping company than Orient Line and chaired by Sir Donald Anderson (1906–73), brother of Orient Line's own Chairman, Sir Colin Skelton Anderson) – had a reputation for design conservatism. Yet, with *Canberra*, it too adopted a forward-thinking approach, reflecting the modernity of Australia's capital for which it was named. Built by Harland & Wolff in Belfast, *Canberra* followed the example of Shaw Savill's *Southern Cross* with the machinery located fully aft. The layout was chosen by P&O's naval architect, John West, and inspired by recent oil tankers for another

division of the fleet. It enabled uninterrupted suites of public rooms in the superstructure and expanses of open-air recreation space above.

Former Festival of Britain co-ordinators took on the design of passenger accommodation on both *Oriana* and *Canberra*. Misha Black (1910–77) took charge of *Oriana* and Sir Hugh Casson (1910–99) handled *Canberra* with his architectural partner, Neville Conder (1922–2003). Since 1951, both Black and Casson had become major figures in British architecture and design, the latter having worked on interiors for the royal yacht *Britannia* (1954) and on rooms in Buckingham Palace. As far as the ruling classes were concerned, they represented the acceptable face of British Modernism.

Black's company, Design Research Unit, worked with Orient Line's regular architect Brian O'Rorke on most of the first-class public rooms on board *Oriana*. He also collaborated with Russell, Hodgson & Leigh on the first-class dining saloon and cabins, and with Ward & Austin on some of the tourist-class public rooms.[17] As with Orient Line's other recent vessels, *Oriana* was generously adorned with specially commissioned contemporary artworks. In line with Britain's growing enthusiasm for Modernism, these

136 OPPOSITE

Tourist-class smoking room on *France*,
designed by Micheline Willemetz, with a mural
by Jean-Denis Malclès, *c.*1962

137 RIGHT

Canberra at sea, after 1962

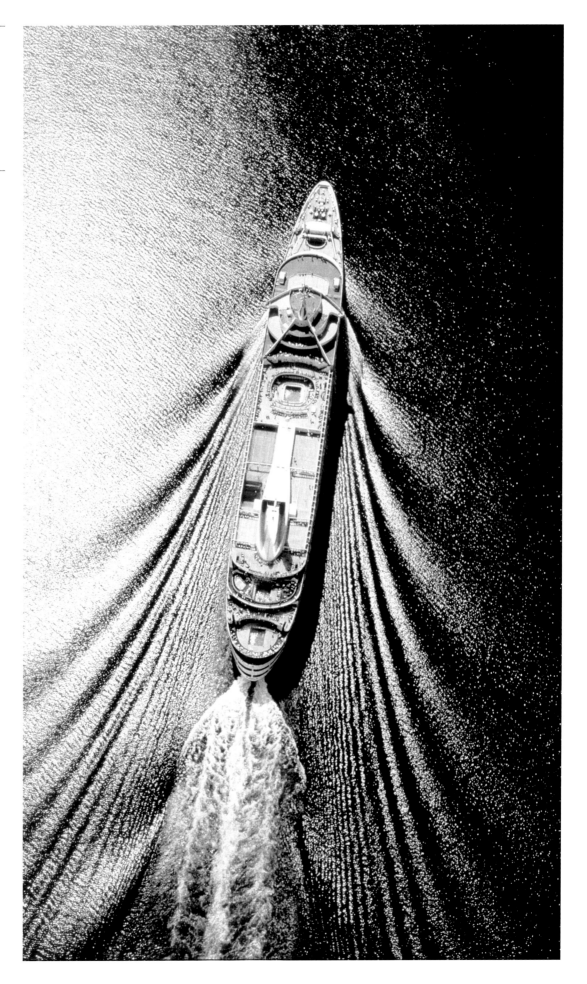

138 ABOVE

Tourist-class Peacock Room on *Canberra*, designed
by John Wright, photograph by Stewart Bale Ltd,
1961

139 ABOVE

Maquette for one of six full-size relief sculptures
from the series *Tidal Movements* for the first-class
staircases on *Oriana*, by Mary Martin
United Kingdom, *c.*1960
Plywood panels with solid timber blocks and painted
decoration
P&O HERITAGE COLLECTION, LONDON:
AC/03574/00

140 ABOVE

Neptune chair (lounger) for *Canberra*, designed
by Ernest Race
United Kingdom, 1960s
Laminated woods, webbing, Tygan seat pad
COLLECTION, THE TARGET GALLERY, LONDON

Europa New York Canada Brasile Uruguay Argentina Venezuela
Curaçao Colombia Panama Ecuador Perú Cile Crociere

tended to be more confidently abstract than on previous vessels – a good example of this approach being Mary Martin's (1907–69) 'Tidal Movements' compositions, installed in the main first-class stairwell [139].

For *Canberra*, Casson Conder not only designed the interiors, but also styled the liner's distinctive and critically acclaimed silhouette. The first-class public rooms were accessed via a white marble spiral staircase inside a cylinder of dark Indian laurel wood. This rose through four decks from the Meridian Room to the Crow's Nest observation lounge. The only source of illumination was from fluorescent tubes concealed inside the aluminium-clad balustrades.[18] Above, the Bonito Club had a glazed aft bulkhead that could be hydraulically lowered to the floor, seamlessly bringing its large teak dance floor together with the adjacent lido area, planked in the same wood. Terraces on either side linked the space to the open-air deck above.[19] For the first time on a P&O liner, an attempt was made to emulate Orient Line's highly integrative approach to shipboard art and design. Ernest Race's (1913–64) new plywood deck-chair was used on the ship [140], while Casson's firm designed many different types of furniture and Margaret Casson (1913–99) devised bespoke tableware.

The architects John Wright and Barbara Oakley designed *Canberra*'s tourist-class public rooms and cabins. These were remarkably informal by P&O's historic standards, being aimed at a younger clientele on assisted passages to Australia, rather than the typical mix in colonial service. The Cricketer's Tavern was a cosy, sports-themed pub with banquettes upholstered in leather and cricketing memorabilia displayed on the walls and in vitrines. The walls of the teenagers' coffee bar, the Pop Inn, initially featured Pop Art 'graffiti' murals burnt into the veneer by David Hockney (b.1937), at that time still a student at London's Royal College of Art [157].[20]

On four-week passages to Australia, cabins were of great importance and on both vessels similar design solutions were found. For *Canberra*, a 'court cabin' layout was selected (this was derived from the 'air light' approach initially promoted in the mid-1920s by the American naval architect George G. Sharp and first featured on the Italian liner *Saturnia*). Cabins were grouped around transverse corridors that widened progressively, each pair of rooms on either side having windows facing onto a small 'courtyard' with windows in the ship's side, thereby enabling even cabins located deep within the hull to have some daylight.

In the mid-1960s, Italia di Navigazione went on a final spending spree, and ordered two new flagship vessels for the transatlantic route from Genoa to New York. Completed in 1965, *Michelangelo* and *Raffaello* soon proved to be among the most spectacular white elephants in the history of passenger shipping. The Sestri Ponente shipyard in Genoa built the former and Cantiere San Marco in Trieste the latter. In outward appearance, they were visually impressive. Smoke-dispersal research by the Turin Polytechnic proposed unusual lattice-work funnel casings, surmounted by smoke-deflecting fins [141]. This solution would allow air to blow beneath and so prevent downward suction of soot particles onto the lido decks.[21]

The interiors perpetuated Italia di Navigazione's inflexible, vertical separation of the passenger accommodation into three classes. Few cabins had portholes in case they were smashed in winter storms, meaning that even those adjacent to the shell plating were mostly 'inside' rooms. On *Michelangelo*, Vincenzo Monaco and Amedeo Luccichenti planned the glamorous first-class accommodation in collaboration with Nino Zoncada. The ballroom and cocktail bar had a double-height central area illuminated by three very large Lucite chandeliers.[22] Throughout, strong colours and sharp angular forms were used. Gustavo Pulitzer Finali was responsible for the first-class dining room and hallways, while Giulio Minoletti (1910–81) designed the tourist-class public areas. The outdoor lido spaces in all three classes were by Matteo Longoni featuring irregularly shaped, mosaic-clad swimming pool surrounds, diving platforms and cocktail bars – similar features to those of the era's new tropical hotel resorts onshore.[23] Whereas a majority of artworks on the earlier post-war Italian liners were either semi-abstract or figurative, on *Michelangelo* several entirely non-representational pieces were installed, including a wool tapestry by Giuseppe Capogrossi (1900–72), which covered an end bulkhead in the first-class ballroom [120].

Alas, despite *Michelangelo* and *Raffaello*'s expense and first-class opulence, they ran in transatlantic service for less than a decade. After a period in lay-up, they were sold in 1976 to the Imperial Iranian navy for use as barracks ships in Bandar Abbas and Bushehr respectively. *Raffaello* was destroyed by aerial bombardment during the Iran–Iraq war, and *Michelangelo* was sold to Pakistan for scrap in 1991.[24] *Leonardo da Vinci* faired little better, being withdrawn in 1978 and gutted by a fire two years later.[25]

SS *United States* had been withdrawn in 1969 and *France* in 1974. These liners' fates were prematurely sealed by the advent of the wide-bodied Boeing 747 'jumbo jet', the 1973 Oil Crisis and – in the case of *France* – by a government decision to shift subsidies to the supersonic Concorde airliner.

Had Cunard realized its early-1960s plans for a new Southampton–New York liner, a project code-named 'Q3', the outcome might have been similar but, most fortunately, more advanced thinking prevailed with regard to how best to serve a sea-travel market facing profound and rapid change.

In 1964, Cunard superseded the Q3 project with a smaller liner-cum-cruise ship, code-named 'Q4' and subsequently completed in 1969 by Upper Clyde Shipbuilders as the *Queen Elizabeth 2*. Shortly after the 'Q4' project was announced, the company's Chairman, Sir John Brocklebank (1915–74), resigned because of poor health. His replacement, Sir Basil Smallpeice (1906–92), was the former Managing Director of British Overseas Airline Corporation (BOAC), where he had played a key role in introducing the de Havilland Comet and Vickers-Armstrong VC10 jets. Cunard's operations were familiar to him because of a transatlantic co-operation between the two companies, which had formed Cunard-BOAC to offer combined air-and-sea travel packages.

Smallpeice's aim – as far as was possible – was to bring Cunard's image and service approach into the jet age.[26] Onshore, as the 'baby boom' generation came of age, a cultural revolution occurred throughout the Western World, bringing with it a new 'pop' culture. Cunard would therefore not only need to please their existing passengers, but also reflect the latest fashions of Swinging London. An early move was to discard the company's traditional three-class stratification in favour of a two-class arrangement that could easily be dissolved for cruising.

Cunard retained the industrial design consultant James Gardner (1907–95), who had recently developed external styling suggestions for the unrealized Q3, working in close co-operation with the company's chief naval architect, Daniel Wallace (1916–79). Gardner was – like Misha Black and Hugh Casson – a veteran

142 OPPOSITE
QE2 at sea, 1977

of the Festival of Britain, for which he had designed the Festival Pleasure Gardens in Battersea Park, which mixed neo-Regency, eccentric Victoriana and decorative modern elements. An imaginative and resourceful designer, he was equally accomplished with jet- and space-age aesthetics.[27]

As a cruise ship, *QE2* would need to fit the Panama Canal's locks, but to incorporate the broad range of leisure facilities imagined by Cunard and their designers, the vessel would need a relatively tall superstructure in comparison with transatlantic liners of the past. Inspired by *Oriana*'s example, the solution was to make very advanced and extensive use of lightweight aluminium.[28] In designing the exterior, not only did Gardner achieve a notable sense of visual integration, but also a subtle suggestion of science-fiction fantasy [142]. Rather than the broad, barrel-shaped funnels of past Cunard vessels, research by the National Physical Laboratory had shown that a tall, slender stove-pipe would be most efficient in carrying exhaust gases high above the ship. A scoop at its base used the airflow over the superstructure to add an extra updraft. The bridge was dramatically sculptural, its windows recessed in a horizontal slot creating the illusion of it pulling the remainder of the upper works in its wake. Above, the 'space needle'-like mast – containing a galley flue – echoed the funnel's slender vertical form. In place of Cunard's black, red and white livery, a charcoal grey and white scheme was introduced with 'Cunard' emblazoned in red on the forward superstructure, much like the corporate graphics of a jetliner.

A number of prominent interior architects and designers were inherited from the Q3 project, including Dennis Lennon (1918–91) and the society interior designers Michael Inchbald (1920–2013) and David Hicks (1929–98), plus the Australian émigré, Jon Bannenberg (1929–2002). Gardner recommended to Smallpeice a greater role for Lennon, who was promoted to overall co-ordinator. Recently, he had designed critically well-received interiors for J. Lyon & Co.'s Albany hotel chain and a similar approach was adopted for Cunard. In his autobiography, Gardner observed that:

143 OPPOSITE
Tourist-class Double Room on *QE2*, designed by Jon Bannenberg, 1969

Most designers I could think of would slip either 'Scandinavian' or 'Bauhaus' – and this wouldn't appeal to Cunard's American customers. If Lennon slipped I guessed it would be in the safer direction towards international Hilton (the best international Hilton). In practice he didn't slip at all, so we will never know.[29]

In addition, because the liner was partly financed through a government loan, the Council of Industrial Design intervened, advising Smallpeice that the interior design team should be augmented by Misha Black, Gaby Schreiber (1916–91, another BOAC designer) and the design team Crosby, Fletcher, Forbes.

Of the QE2's many diverse public rooms, several were of notably striking design. The circular embarkation lobby continued the space-age theme of the exterior with extensive use of moulded white fibreglass for a central 'trumpet' column and the ceiling, which radiated as a series of concentric rings – indeed, the liner was promoted as 'The Space Ship' and 'the most exciting thing to be launched since Apollo 1' in Cunard's publicity material.[30] In first class, the Queen's Room lounge and ballroom, by Inchbald, likewise made extensive and imaginative use of fibreglass for furniture and to encase columns, the futuristic sense of lightness and 'uplift' being heightened by a white lattice ceiling. Its tourist class equivalent in transatlantic service was the two-deck-high Double Room by Bannenberg, who wanted QE2 to be a 'fantastically exciting ship' [143].[31] He linked its levels with a dramatic, spiral staircase with red carpeting and smoke-tinted glazed balustrades,

which continued around the upper level. Brushed aluminium bulkhead and ceiling finishes contrasted with red William Plunkett (1928–2013) lounge chairs. Using similar finishes, Dennis Lennon's Grill Room restaurant was entered by a curved staircase similar to those accessing the Boeing 747 jetliner's upper deck. The first-class Columbia and tourist-class Britannia restaurants – also by Lennon – were decorated respectively in shades of brown leather and in the bright colours of the Union Flag; both featured specially designed chairs by Robert Heritage (1927–2010) [144]. An innovation for Cunard was that every cabin was en suite – an approach pointing ahead to the forthcoming generation of purpose-built, full-time cruise ships.

Although the QE2's entry into service was beset with mechanical problems, resulting in a dispute between owner and builder, in the long run the liner proved an enduring success. If its underlying planning was mostly prescient, the interior design was less enduring and, from the early-1970s onwards, progressive changes were instituted that gradually fragmented the initial sense of aesthetic cohesion. By the mid-1970s, the liner was the last in its trade flagged in a Western country (though smaller, considerably less well-appointed Soviet and Polish examples continued for a while longer). QE2 thus appeared to represent the end of an era – but, as a cruise ship, it presaged the start of a new one. From representing an apotheosis of modern British design in the late-1960s, the vessel subsequently took on a 'retro' look, nostalgically evoking Cunarders of the Edwardian and inter-war eras. The cruise industry was to follow with similarly postmodern design strategies.

144 OPPOSITE
QE2 Britannia restaurant chair, designed by Robert
Heritage, made by Race Furniture Ltd
United Kingdom, 1968
Upholstered plywood shell laminated with Formica
on an aluminium base
GIVEN BY RACE FURNITURE LTD
V&A: CIRC.711–1969

GIO PONTI

PAOLO PICCIONE

In 1928, the Italian architect and designer Gio Ponti (1891–1979) launched the magazine *Domus* in his native city of Milan with the specific intention of stimulating new thinking about architecture and the applied arts among the Italian bourgeoisie. Distancing himself from the avant-garde, Ponti used the magazine to present examples of interior and exterior design in the modern style, which married European trends with the work of Italian artists and craftsmen. In the same year, an architectural competition was announced for the design of the interiors for *Victoria* (1931), a liner built in Trieste for the Lloyd Triestino shipping company and intended for the Alexandria route. The competition was won by the architect Gustavo Pulitzer Finali (1887–1967), a contributor to *Domus*, and *Victoria* is celebrated as the first Italian ship to be entirely fitted out and furnished in a contemporary style, free from outdated furnishing styles of the past and the architectural eclecticism famously championed in Italy by the Florentine architect brothers, Gino (1866–1927) and Adolfo Coppedè (1871–1951). Ponti was also involved in some of *Victoria*'s decor, designing the ceramic tiles that lined the walls of the first-class dining room and the second-class bar.

Ponti devoted the entire October 1931 issue of *Domus* to the *Victoria*, and the March 1933 edition to the great ocean liner *Conte di Savoia* (1932) – the interiors of which were also designed by Pulitzer in the 'Novecento' style, the Italian version of international Art Deco.

After the Second World War and Italy's return to democracy, the government set out to rebuild its fleet of passenger ships with funding from the European Recovery Program (an American initiative established to provide financial aid to Western Europe, known widely as the Marshall Plan). A great number of ships were built in a period of five years: two ocean liners for the Latin American route (*Giulio Cesare* and *Augustus*), two for the North American route (*Andrea Doria* and *Cristoforo Colombo*) and seven ships for routes to Australia (*Australia*, *Oceania* and *Neptunia*), Africa (*Africa* and *Europa*) and the Far East (*Victoria* and *Asia*), as well as many smaller ships for Mediterranean routes. The competition for the design of the new fleet's interiors was won by a small group of architects including Pulitzer, Nino Zoncada, Matteo Longoni, Giulio Minoletti and the group from Trieste, comprising Umberto Nordio, Aldo Cervi, Vittorio Frandoli and Romano Boico.

Gio Ponti also became involved through his association with the interior designer Zoncada (1898–1988), with whom he designed the first-class interiors of the *Conte Grande* [146 & 147] and various interior spaces for the *Conte Biancamano* in 1948 – two ocean liners built in the 1920s and refitted after being used by the United States as military transport during the war. The Venetian designer and the Milanese architect also won the brief for designing the first-class grand salons of *Giulio Cesare* (1951) and *Andrea Doria* (1953) as well as some interiors for the *Oceania* (1951), *Neptunia* (1951) and *Africa*

---

145 OPPOSITE ABOVE
First-class ballroom on *Giulio Cesare*, designed by Gio Ponti and Nino Zoncada, *c.*1951

146 OPPOSITE BELOW LEFT
First-class dining room on *Conte Grande*, designed by Gio Ponti and Nino Zoncada, 1949

147 OPPOSITE BELOW RIGHT
Chair for the first-class dining room on *Conte Grande*, by Gio Ponti, made by Cassina (model 504) Meda and Milan, Italy, 1948
Wood, brass and velour
PAOLO PICCIONE COLLECTION

(1952). With their modern, elegant interiors, these ships helped to establish the high standing of 1950s Italian design in the United States, alongside Pininfarina automobile design, fashion labels such as Schubert, Fontana, Antonelli and Pucci, Ferragamo shoes and Gucci leather goods.

The *Conte Grande* marked the beginning of a new era in the art of naval interior design and presented the results of Italian research and development on the international stage. Ponti wanted to promote the image of a new Italy and, seeing ships as 'ambassadors' of Italian visual and architectural culture, he commissioned artists and craftsmen who he had featured in *Domus*: ceramicists such as Guido Gambone, Pietro Melandri, Luigi Zortea and Leoncillo Leonardi; notable artists including Fausto Melotti and Lucio Fontana; painters such as Massimo Campigli, Salvatore Fiume and Edina Altara; interior decorators such as Piero Fornasetti; and enamel and glass artists such as Paolo De Poli and Paolo Venini to name just a few. The elements preferred by Ponti tended to be formal and made of lighter materials: anodized aluminium, gold or silver, tempered glass and light-coloured wood – ash, walnut, oak, silver birch and cherry.

Ponti and Zoncada went on to design the first-class salons of the new ocean liner *Giulio Cesare*, whose maiden voyage in October 1951 took her from Genoa to Rio de Janeiro and Buenos Aires. Their salons were coherently conceived, starting with a chromatic palette and employing specific materials and artworks to complement it. The ballroom's colour scheme was golden yellow and incorporated a painting by Massimo Campigli [145]; the lounge was red and featured a painting by Salvatore Fiume covering one wall; the bar was light blue with enamels by Paolo De Poli; and the casino was green with decorations by Piero Fornasetti. For *Andrea Doria*, whose maiden voyage in January 1953 was on the Genoa–New York route, Ponti highlighted his visual philosophy by having the walls

of the first-class grand salon entirely painted with a mural called *La leggenda d'Italia* by Fiume [132]. It depicted an imaginary town square displaying artworks by the greatest Italian masters, Roman and fifteenth-century statues and examples of Roman and Tuscan architecture – all the masterpieces of Italian art history presented in a contemporary spirit. Another interior that exemplified Ponti's style was the Zodiac Suite, luxury accommodation that again availed itself of the graphic imagination of Fornasetti. Here the decorative motifs were based on the signs of the zodiac, and the zoomorphic symbols of the constellations pervaded every surface – from walls and curtains to armchairs, sofas and bedspreads – while images of stars and planets decorated the furniture [227].

Andrea Doria, however, was the last ship to boast interiors designed by Ponti. Disappointed by the impossibility of designing a ship in its entirety rather than just its individual spaces, Ponti began to devote himself to other design projects in the late 1950s, this time on land. In his absence, it was Zoncada who came to be the most prolific Italian ship interior designer, his efforts including such iconic ships as *Ausonia* (1957) and the last Italian ocean liner, *Eugenio C.* (1966).

The era of Ponti's and Zoncada's ships lasted little more than two decades, but during it Italian passenger vessels asserted their own distinct characteristics. Free at last from mimicking the architecture of hotels and palaces (and having not yet turned into the floating tourist villages of today), post-war Italian passenger ships were a true manifestation of industrial design, in which technical and nautical constraints, passenger requirements and distribution systems all shared common aesthetic qualities. The coherence between the ship's body, its superstructures and interiors, the understanding of its structural beauty and its direct relationship with the marine environment were the key factors of Ponti's and Zoncada's work and reputation.

148 OPPOSITE
Easy chair for the first-class ballroom on *Eugenio C.*,
by Nino Zoncada, made by Cassina
Meda and Milan, Italy, 1966
Wood and velour
PAOLO PICCIONE COLLECTION

CHAPTER 6

THE IDEALIZED SOCIETY OF THE OCEAN LINER

THE IDEALIZED SOCIETY
OF THE OCEAN LINER

DANIEL FINAMORE

Don't wait until you get to the other side to begin your vacation. Make traveling there a holiday![1]

SEAFARER ROLE-PLAY

In 1928, a young anthropologist named Cora Du Bois (1903–91) travelled to Europe on board *Colombo* (built 1917). Embracing the role of budding ethnologist, she wrote in her diary about how the curious transitional space of mid-ocean – away from home and far at sea – allowed fellow passengers who would normally be constrained by social mores to break the rules of proper deportment. During a July 4th celebration, she witnessed what she described as 'Legalized license—anthropologists call it in primitive society. The immodest behavior of the American Anglo-Saxons quite shocked the Italian *demi-mondaines*. Fancy living so cramped an existence that one feels the necessity of organized non-restraint.'[2]

Du Bois had no doubt studied the work of Arnold van Gennep (1873–1957) whose book *Les Rites de Passage* (The Rites of Passage, 1909) explored the transitional, or liminal, zone between social spaces.[3] Though usually applied to transitions between states such as childhood/adulthood or unmarried/married, Du Bois saw the physical ocean passage – with its isolation from one's social surroundings on land and abiding sense of community with others on board – as a form of liminality as well. She understood that the immodest behaviour she witnessed within this community of shipmates would end upon arrival in port, whereupon the norms of terrestrial society would be reinstated. Alan Dale (1861–1928), a frequent transatlantic business traveller, satirized the behaviour his fellow passengers exhibited while at sea, creating new personae for themselves (as playboys, heirs, big spenders and so on) that bore no relation to their lives on land. He noted: 'at sea you can be as rich as you say you are. Moreover, you tell so many fibs on the ocean, that one more or less can make no difference.'[4]

Liner companies eagerly fostered the alternate identities and temporary community embraced by travellers in the liminal zone of the sea to enhance the specialness of travel on their ship or line. For example, a sometimes brutal hazing ritual called 'Crossing the Line' had for centuries been acted out on ships when traversing the equator, in which new recruits were indoctrinated into the brotherhood of professional mariners through play-acting, humiliation and enforced fighting.[5] By the twentieth century, paying passengers participated in a safe and light-hearted version that had been devised as casual entertainment, thereby enacting the sailor life in a rite of passage that allowed for social reinvention [150].

For the professional mariner, physically isolated from family and mainstream society, every facet of life remains insular. Once away, all needs – from equipment and food to medical treatment – are supplied on board.[6] The structure of ship society, with its clearly defined occupational and social hierarchy, creates a sense of camaraderie through interdependence and shared experience.

In contrast, the performance of a voyage for ocean-liner passengers often involved luxuries that were comparable or even finer than those available at home. Among them was residing within a physical space that reflected and projected dominant conventions of social class in microcosm. The highly structured social experience on board offered passengers opportunities to live out idealized visions of cosmopolitan social order, an idea rooted in the late nineteenth century, but which remained prevalent through the inter-war period. The convenient package of first-class travel, combined with the close confines of easily observed behaviour, allowed people to put their connoisseurship – of elegant surroundings, fine clothing and haute cuisine – on display and, for the adventurous traveller with extra money, even to transgress class boundaries and try out a more fashionable life. As social attitudes (and passenger demands) changed with time, liners were adapted to offer a reduction in emphasis on the class division of the ship, and an increasingly diverse array of specialized activity spaces.

149 PREVIOUS

Deck activities on *Augustus*, detail from *Augustus*
Navigazione Generale Italiana, brochure, printed
by Richter & C.

Naples, Italy, 1927

Printed paper

HOWARD GALVIN STEAMSHIP EPHEMERA COLLECTION

PHILLIPS LIBRARY, PEABODY ESSEX MUSEUM

THE IDEALIZED SOCIETY OF THE OCEAN LINER

AN IDEALIZED SOCIAL ORDER

To assist physical navigation through a ship, passengers were provided with deck plans that presented the vessel in lateral slices, but illustrating only those portions that were appropriate for each class of traveller to visit. In effect, passengers travelled with conceptual maps of their vessel that reflected only the class they had purchased into. The deck plan substantiated each class as a discrete social unit, with shared activities and boundaries that were different from those of passengers in other classes. Between and after the World Wars, the number of classes on many ships was reduced and, in some cases, brought down to one. The experience of the spaces on those ships expanded and became more uniform among all travellers.

A longitudinal cutaway model of Cunard's *Berengaria*, with a hand-painted cross-section of spaces and activities, offers a visual representation of the physical and social geography of a ship of the 1920s [151]. The explicit structuring of the worlds of passenger and crew is demarcated by the discrete apportionment of spaces according to class, activity and labour role, from upper deck to engine room and from bow to stern. The ship was originally built as *Imperator* for the Hamburg-American Line and when launched in 1912 she was the largest liner afloat. By 1921, when refitted and renamed as *Berengaria*, some of her formal arrangements had been modified to accommodate the demands of the modern traveller.

The first-class passenger spaces extended for seven decks amidships, from the bridge to past the aft funnel. The men's

smoking room and gymnasium were on A (the uppermost) deck,
with a double-height social hall, palm court and à la carte restaurant
extending up from B deck.[7] C and D decks featured suites and
deluxe apartments amidships with staterooms (single first-class
rooms as opposed to suites) forward on D, E and F decks. The
main dining room, with its domed ceiling and sweeping staircase,
could be entered from E or F deck, while the Pompeian-columned
swimming pool on F and G deck was nearly 3 m deep. Second-class
spaces, including similar but less grand dimensions and decor,
were directly aft of first class. What had been the third-class areas
on *Imperator* (towards the stern) were renamed 'tourist class', while
steerage (in the bow) was renamed 'third class'. Service areas were
largely on the lowest decks, including automobile and baggage

storage near the bow, and food storage near the stern. Converting
the power plant from coal to oil reduced the number of engine
room crew, allowing them to have larger accommodations.

151 ABOVE

Berengaria, 1:192 sectional model, attributed to Bassett-Lowke
Ltd, with painted interior by Montague Birrell Black
United Kingdom, *c*.1920
Wood, metal, brass and watercolour
GIFT OF CUNARD WHITE STAR LINE
MARINERS' MUSEUM AND PARK, NEWPORT NEWS,
VA: MD31

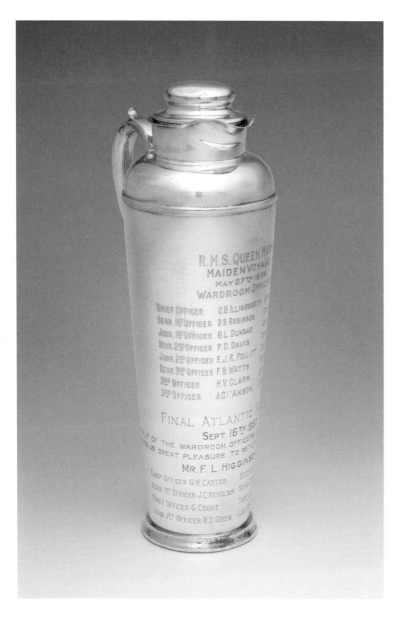

152 ABOVE

Engraved cocktail shaker presented to the Ward
Room officers on *Queen Mary* during her maiden
voyage, made by Gorham Manufacturing Company
Rhode Island, United States, c.1936
Silver
GIFT OF FRANCIS LEE HIGGINSON, 1980
PEABODY ESSEX MUSEUM: M18692

Berengaria was relaunched just as the United States was enacting further serious restrictions to immigration. Old-style steerage – with bunks for more than one hundred passengers, limited privacy and no cleaning services – had been improved many years earlier, but an even more restrictive act in 1924 brought the end of immigration as a source of income for the lines. Pre-war ships that had been designed with large steerage spaces were reconfigured and rebranded to appeal to American middle-class tourists as a form of comfortable budget travel called 'Tourist Third Cabin'. The idea of voluntarily choosing the budget option ran counter to prevailing notions about Americans, whose 'class-distinction complex' would always inspire them to purchase the highest class of service they could afford. As one traveller noted, 'most people on board ship like you to think of them with the richest thoughts possible. It is one of the oddities of ocean travel'.[8] This new class of passage was described as appropriate for the 'educational or otherwise intellectual type ... possessed of an outlook on life that has enabled them to banish class consciousness on shipboard'. More than 40,000 people travelled round-trip transatlantic in this newly defined class in 1925. With no social hierarchy and comfort without elegance, these ships appealed to those who wanted to travel 'with no class above them'.[9]

Although passenger class structure evolved, the distinctions and boundaries among crew remained vital elements for delineating the hierarchy of service to ship and passenger. The visually distinctive uniforms further defined and categorized service roles for the benefit of travellers. Crew positions were often assigned by common heritage to foster internal community. Ethnicity also reflected job status, and those deemed to be of the lowest standing were assigned to the most rigorous and sequestered jobs. Stokers and their arduous labour were recognized as essential to a ship's performance and almost as part of the behemoth engines they fed, but passengers rarely saw them. Publicity images – like that which appeared in the Peninsular and Oriental Steam Navigation Company (P&O) publication *P&O Pencillings* (1892) showing south Asians with glistening skin illuminated by glowing engine fires – reinforced the romanticized aspect of their work in the hellish nether portions of the ship. *P&O Pencillings* was produced by the company as a keepsake for purchase by passengers, but the gradual introduction in the interwar era of oil instead of coal soon eliminated the need for the 'stokers in the black depths below' [153].[10]

One nautical tradition saw passengers presenting crewmembers with a gift of engraved silver to formally recognize their contribution, as well as ritualizing the position of passenger within

P. & O. PENCILLINGS.

"SEEDIE BOYS" FIREMEN AT WORK.

THE STOKEHOLE

153 ABOVE

'The Stokehole', plate from *P&O Pencillings*, by W.W.
Lloyd, published for the Peninsular and Oriental
Steam Navigation Co. by Day & Son
London, United Kingdom, 1892
Chromolithograph

PHILLIPS LIBRARY, PEABODY ESSEX MUSEUM

154 LEFT

Torah ark from the synagogue on *Queen Mary*,
by Cecil Jacob Eprile
United Kingdom, 1930–7
Wood, wrought iron, paint and textile

JUDAH L. MAGNES MUSEUM PURCHASE
THE MAGNES COLLECTION OF JEWISH ART AND
LIFE, UNIVERSITY OF CALIFORNIA, BERKELEY:
92.24 A–B

155 OPPOSITE

Madonna of the Atlantic, altarpiece used when the
first-class drawing room on *Queen Mary* was
converted into a chapel, by Kenneth Shoesmith
c.1934
Oil paint on gold-leaf background

QUEEN MARY HOTEL, LONG BEACH, CA

the seafaring community. One such passenger was 29-year-old Francis Lee Higginson who, during *Queen Mary*'s 1936 maiden voyage, presented the officers with a silver Gorham cocktail shaker engraved with each of their names [152]. Higginson participated in more than 60 transatlantic crossings, and the well-used shaker was later returned to him 31 years later, re-engraved with a dedication of thanks.[11]

RELIGIOUS WORSHIP

Rarely did ships carry full-time clergy but, following nautical tradition, a ship's officer sometimes gathered the crew and passengers in a space that was temporarily converted for religious services. Norddeutscher Lloyd's *Kronprinzessin Cecilie* (1907) maintained a small chapel in a niche in the library. White Star's *Olympic* (1911) had a pipe organ in the main saloon and Hamburg-American's *Imperator* (1913) carried a fully equipped chapel. On *Majestic* (1922) in the 1920s, Catholic Mass was celebrated on Sundays in the first-class library. The ship librarian served as sacristan, and any priest among the passengers performed the service and preached a short sermon. Mass (without sermon) was said in second and third class if there were 'sufficient priests on board'. Episcopal services were less elaborate, being held in the lounge by one of the ship's officers, while services for other faiths were held 'by special arrangement'.[12]

In response to passenger interest, many ships launched between the wars included dedicated religious spaces with distinctive and nationalistic decor. A brochure for *Normandie* (1935) described the chapel as 'an old-world cathedral in miniature' that offered 'the utmost seclusion', stating that 'where the appointments are of the finest, meditation and sanctuary are at hand'.[13] Religious spaces on *Queen Mary* were more prominent than on earlier British ships. Kenneth D. Shoesmith (1890–1939), a graphic artist who executed much commercial work for Cunard, created paintings for the cabin-class (first-class) and second-class chapels. Shoesmith's work was particularly attuned to the desires of Cunard and he had six paintings accepted without hesitation, unlike works proposed by other artists that were either rejected by or modified at the demand of the Cunard Director, who insisted that the ship's decor should not confront passengers with 'rampant modernity'.[14]

The first-class drawing room was converted into a Catholic chapel on Sundays. During the week, a four-panel folding screen bearing a placid Mediterranean harbour scene by Shoesmith obscured the altar recess. The harbour is crowded with small workboats and flooded with sunlight, highlighting the colours of canvas and wood that complemented the famous veneers

of *Queen Mary*. Behind the screen was a near life-size painting of the Madonna and Child in high Gothic style, with an array of nautical instruments, anchors and a globe showing the North Atlantic Ocean around her feet [155]. She stands before a bright, gilt background that bears a mariner's compass, centring the scene on their faces. Although nautical imagery commonly appears in religious art, in this context the symbolism is particularly overt.

In response to the increasing number of Jewish-American transatlantic travellers, as well as refugees and immigrants departing Europe, a salon on board the Gdynia America liner *Kościuszko* was formally consecrated as a synagogue in 1934. Billed as the only 'floating synagogue' on the Atlantic, the space was used for this purpose on Saturdays, with Christian Mass being held there on Sundays.[15] The ship's captain downplayed concerns about the propriety of celebrating Mass in a space displaying a Torah and likened the situation to army posts where such spaces were often shared.

As *Queen Mary* departed Southampton for the first time in 1936, a service was held in a small and simple room dedicated exclusively as a synagogue. The room was intended to hold 40 passengers, but twice that many participants filled the space.[16] British architect Cecil Jacob Eprile (1897–1982), who had previously designed synagogues in London, devised the room and lined it with wood from Palestine.[17] It also featured a spectacularly modern, Art Deco Torah ark with hammered gilt metalwork and the signature *Queen Mary* veneers [154]. The outline of the ark simulates a Hamsa hand, or *hamesh*, which is a symbol of blessing and protection.[18] The synagogue was located on the third-class deck and was accessible to all passengers for services. It was, however, locked when not in use to avoid the risk of desecration.[19]

CHILDREN'S SPACES

One book of advice for travellers stated: 'if children must be taken across the ocean, force them to amuse themselves quietly and reasonably until they get to the other side'.[20] But as the appeal of transoceanic and European travel as a family activity grew, ideas about children on board changed from shutting them away to thinking about them as part of the paying clientele. Offering children special experiences would please the paying parent as much as the child. Beyond mere distraction, societal attitudes regarding the role and significance of children's play also developed during the late nineteenth century. With new ideas about fostering social morality through youthful peer-group interaction, play spaces for children proliferated. Norddeutscher Lloyd's *George Washington* (1909) included a children's room with juvenile murals adorning the walls, but with adult-sized furnishings. By the inter-war years, flagship liners offered extensive play facilities that steeped children in nautically inspired fantasies replete with miniature ship's wheels and bridge telegraphs. *Queen Mary* had a playroom for each of the three classes (the first-class area had separate ends for boys and girls, as well as a built-in slide with pirate caves beneath). The playroom on board Holland America's *Nieuw Amsterdam* (1938) similarly featured a mast with crow's nest. The notion of an ocean passage as a recreational indulgence increased following the wars. On P&O's *Canberra* (1961), Edward Ardizzone (1900–79), a children's book author and illustrator who had also served as an official war artist, decorated the walls of the first-class playroom with the help of his son Philip (b.1931) [156]. His murals of life-size nursery rhyme characters were painted in watercolour and covered with melamine for resistance to the marine environment and easy cleaning.

Canberra also identified teenagers as a category of traveller in need of their own space. Seeking a youthful style that would appeal to them, the Chairman of P&O turned to his brother, the provost of the Royal College of Art, for ideas. The resulting room, called the Pop Inn, had a coffee bar, jukebox and tables made of Perspex with internal fluorescent lighting [157]. The job of decorating the walls was given to 24-year-old David Hockney (b.1937), then a student at the RCA who was paid £100 for ten days' work singeing words and images into the walls with a wood-burning tool. His idea was that young passengers could contribute by adding images and statements of their own, an experiment that met with too much success as the walls were soon covered with graffiti, much of it obscene. By 1963, Hockney's reputation was in ascendance and RCA professor Sir Hugh Casson (1910–99) urged P&O to preserve the work, but the walls had already been covered over due to these additions, and the Pop Inn converted into a camera shop.[21]

THE DECK

Throughout the nineteenth century, passenger activity space remained primarily indoors. Passengers who stepped out onto the deck of an early liner found themselves in the functional area of the ship, surrounded by guy wires, ventilators and other equipment that was necessary for operations. In an 1868 painting by Robert Charles Dudley (1826–1909) of *Great Eastern* (1859) on a mild day at sea, passengers have invaded this area, walking and lounging around the ship's skylights, rail and cannons, while others have carried interior furniture outside to relax upon [159].

As exterior space became more popular for exercise and the social activity of promenading, ships were designed with larger, uncluttered decks. Many who wanted comfortable seating outdoors frequently brought their own steamer chair (and if they were returning home via the same line the steward would store it for them during their trip). By 1900, ships stocked hundreds of chairs that could be rented for an entire voyage. Ordered in bulk by the shipping lines, the classic steamer chair became an iconic manifestation of ocean leisure, while variations within the design became signatures of individual lines [160 & 161]. The location of one's chair in a sunny and protected part of the ship, and in proximity to the 'right' passengers, became a mark of the seasoned traveller.

PHYSICAL FITNESS

Formal exercise facilities were initially focused within the ship, including apparatus that was typical of gymnasia on shore. A featured attraction of larger ships was the 'trotter', a mechanical horse for 'ocean travellers who must have a horse-back ride before breakfast'.[22] On board Cunard's *Franconia* (1911), riders could even choose from Western, English and side-saddle designs. The gymnasium, pool and squash courts formed a complex of 460 m² called the 'Sports Arena', which Cunard promoted as ideal

156 ABOVE

Nursery Rhyme Characters, mural for the first-class
playroom on *Canberra*, by Edward Ardizzone,
assisted by his son Philip
United Kingdom, *c*.1961
Watercolour on melamine-impregnated paper
processed into melamine-faced Perstorp laminate

P&O HERITAGE COLLECTION, LONDON:
AC/01010/01

THE IDEALIZED SOCIETY OF THE OCEAN LINER

for transporting professional athletes to international competitions, branding their ships as ambassadors of physical culture.[23] Outdoor sports were adapted to the limited space of liner decks, with some becoming integrally associated with the ocean passage experience. Tennis was played on a smaller court surrounded by netting. Shuffleboard originated as a casual game with a steward drawing the board onto the deck in chalk when a game was requested. Ideally suited to the shape of spaces available on ship decks and playable by warmly clad passengers in North Atlantic waters, it quickly emerged as the quintessential shipboard pastime.[24]

The earliest ships with swimming pools placed them indoors, with adjacent Turkish baths, steam, hot, temperate, shampooing and cooling rooms, emphasizing health over recreation [162]. Men and women were allotted separate times for swimming. By the later 1920s, with the new demand for less formal travel, even more of the ship's deck was turned over to social space. Outdoor pools and umbrella-lined sports decks anchored the recreational centre of on-

board exercise. *Augustus* (1927), an Italian ship that offered a more southerly route to Europe, had an upper deck that was likened to 'a miniature Lido, with every facility for leading the Lido life – with its cult of the sun' [149]. One passenger noted that a person could travel with little more than a bathing suit, pyjamas and a dinner jacket, since it was still necessary to dress for dinner.[25]

Indoors, Neoclassical-columned swimming pools were replaced with modern designs and an enhanced social dimension where men and women swam together. *Normandie*'s pool featured Sèvres tile friezes and a gilded bronze semi-circular bar. The multi-levelled sloping bottom evoked the famed beaches of southern France, inviting lounging rather than swimming.[26] Seventeen years later the pool onboard the *United States* (1952) synthesized post-war pride and nautical symbolism with a festive display of enamelled flags on six metal halyards, each denoting a word of the phrase 'Come on in, the water's fine' using the International Code of Signals [163]. A seventh halyard bore a single flag indicating that the message is

157 OPPOSITE

The Pop Inn on *Canberra*, a dedicated space for teenagers decorated by David Hockney, c.1961

158 ABOVE

Children's chair from the first-class playroom on *Normandie*, designed by Marc Simon and Jacqueline Duché
France, c.1934
Painted wood

159 ABOVE

From Sheerness to Valentia: A Deck Scene on the
Great Eastern, by Robert Charles Dudley
1868
Oil on canvas

160 OPPOSITE ABOVE

Deck-chair from *Titanic*, made by R. Holman & Co.
Boston, MA, United States, c.1912
Mahogany and other hardwood

161 OPPOSITE

Deck-chair from SS *United States*,
by Troy Sunshade Company
Troy, OH, United States, c.1952
Aluminium, Bakelite and nylon

understood. Though probably not deciphered by most swimmers, the flags enforced the aura of patriotism and maritime prowess that unified the ship's decor.

PROVISIONS

Provisioning ships with adequate stores for crew and passengers has always been a key factor in the success of a voyage. The same tenets applied to the transatlantic lines, which vied for passengers with heavy investments in culinary offerings. Shipboard cuisine became a key feature that distinguished different classes of travel, and expectations of quality and diversity increased over time. Food service management became more sophisticated than at any hotel or restaurant on land, and head chefs became influential to the marketing of a ship. As larger vessels were launched, the quantity of necessary provisions increased, while sourcing reliable supplies on both ends of a route and matching it with passenger demand became more complex.

Companies promoted their ability to source, store and prepare huge quantities of food as equivalent to feeding a floating city,

thus emphasizing their efficiency at organization and leadership in the progress of modern life. A poster for the Norddeutscher Lloyd Line advertises the quantities and diversity of food carried by *Bremen* (1929) on a single transatlantic round-trip voyage, including 6,300 kg of fish, 4,200 kg of veal, 12,000 kg of beef, 85,000 eggs, 9,500 kg of poultry, 19,500 kg of fresh vegetables, 12,300 kg of fruit, 250 kg of caviar, 1,300 kg of lobster, as well as mutton, pork, beer, sausages, ice, flour and other products [164]. The balance of provisions on Cunard's *Aquitania* (1914) reflects the different tastes that were catered to on a British vessel, such as 2,300 kg more beef, as well as 2,700 kg of bacon, 500 sheep kidneys, 500 sweetbreads, 400 ox tails, 680 kg of ox liver, 800 tongues and large quantities of frog legs.[27]

DINING

The social meaning of first-class dining evolved over time. In a nineteenth-century lithograph portraying dinner on a P&O ship, well-dressed passengers sit at long tables in a ship's saloon, but their faces display a touch of anxiety. The ship's motion is evidently

---

162 ABOVE
Swimming pool on *Saturnia*, photograph
by Byron Company (New York), 1928

163 ABOVE
Swimming pool on SS *United States*, with signal
code flags designed by Lewis E. York and made
by John Scott Williams, 1950s

the concern, as tableware lies askew and a man reaches for a bottle that is falling over. One woman grips the wooden fiddles that run along the edge of the table and separate each setting to reduce the slipping of plates. Meanwhile, service staff, who are used to the motion, carry out their duties capably. The traditional liner dining room contained a number of long tables with rows of seats bolted to the floor. The steward posted seat assignments once the ship was under way, and passengers sat adjacent to the same family or strangers for the entire voyage.

Dinner in the first-class saloon was the principal social moment of any day at sea. The performance of commensality – the social act of eating and drinking that bound the ship's elite players as a group – was augmented through haute cuisine, formal attire, dining rooms with central staircases that enabled dramatic entrances and mezzanines offering sight lines to other 'important' diners [165].

In 1905, dining took an overtly luxurious turn, when Hamburg-American Line's *Amerika* (1905) and her sister ship *Kaiserin Auguste Victoria* (1906) began offering à la carte restaurant service, a new standard for ocean liner dining. For an extra charge, first-class passengers could enjoy a meal that was cooked to order from an extensive menu and sit at smaller tables with their own parties. French architect Charles Mewès (1860–1914) designed an interior that emulated those he had created for Europe's Ritz hotels, and chef Auguste Escoffier (1846–1935) was seconded from London's Carlton Hotel to oversee a kitchen and restaurant staff that was separate from the first-class operation.

Most first-class travellers of the day were American, and Hamburg-American realized that they were tapping only half the potential market. The à la carte experience, co-marketed by the Carlton Hotel, was therefore intended to entice Europeans to visit America, claiming that 'all tastes are consulted' and that 'the Englishman will find he can get a grill luncheon or dinner only to be excelled, if excelled at all, by the Carlton Hotel in London'. The appeal for the German was 'the delicatessen peculiar to his Fatherland', while for the Parisian 'it is sufficient for him to know that M. Escoffier or some of his principal assistants are in the kitchen'.[28] Feeding curiosity for internationally diverse cuisine, however, was not to appear until after the First World War.

The overwhelming success of à la carte necessitated that up to 40 passengers a night were turned away during crossings for lack of space, and one traveller described how other first-class passengers peered through the restaurant windows at diners in their finery, seated before gold table settings. One diner was overheard saying that the restaurant was expensive, but that 'the price keeps the rabble out'.[29] Once this new standard had been set associating

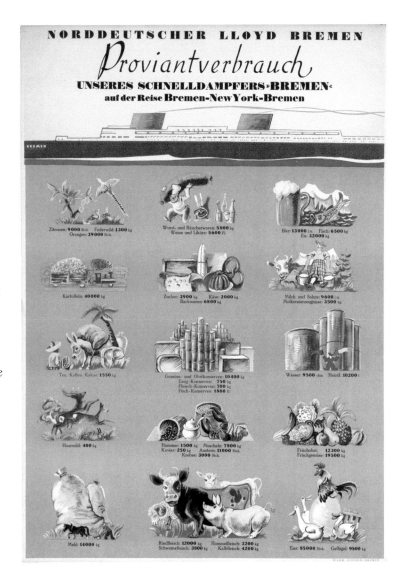

164 ABOVE

'Proviantverbrauch, Unseres Schnelldampfers, Bremen, auf der Reise Bremen-New York-Bremen', (Consumption of travelling provisions on our express liner *Bremen* on the Bremen-New York-Bremen trip) poster for Norddeutscher Lloyd, designed by Wilhelm Jöntzen

c.1933

Colour lithograph

COLLECTION OF STEPHEN S. LASH

ocean travel with luxury dining, à la carte service soon became the norm, and the conspicuous consumption and leisure manifested in exclusive spaces was replicated and expanded upon throughout the industry, a prime example being the luxurious Verandah Grill on board *Queen Mary* [166].

Among the social rituals that occurred during a day at sea were bugle calls announcing meals, with an additional dress call half an hour before dinner that built anticipation for what was to come.[30] Decorated and embossed menus presented an extensive selection of dishes over multiple courses and became treasured souvenirs. Beyond flavour and novelty, notions of what constitutes luxury dining can involve associations with tradition, difficulty of access to a product and specialized labour in its preparation. The idea of *caviar givré du Volga* or celery-fed Nantaise duckling is much more luxurious when consumed while far at sea, where the supply and preparation are at their most challenging. Whether a passenger found a ten-course meal (and the etiquette it required) to be the norm or completely novel, the transitory surroundings of the ocean crossing encouraged experimentation in social mobility. For a short period, then, an ocean crossing offered an opportunity for travellers to cast off the rigid boundaries of social position at home and try on the trappings of a more appealing lifestyle, or at least a lifestyle as expressed in popular culture via advertising and feature films. Whether the dominant taste referenced aristocratic tradition or swank modernity, first class offered more of it than second or third.

The table service of the four Appartements de Grand Luxe on board *Normandie* are likely the consummate manifestation of festive luxury on a liner. Products that were especially created by prominent French designers for the ship included cutlery by Puiforcat; many forms of Lalique glassware for specific uses; Haviland dishes; multiple specialized sizes and forms of serving dish, platter and tureen, along with a silver and rosewood carving station by Christofle [167 & 170].

Food service in the less-expensive classes offered fewer options, but the border decoration for a 1922 third-class menu card from Cunard's *Scythia* (1921) included a statement assuring: 'It is the Cunard Company's wish that passengers should have an ample supply of food. Anyone not receiving this should report the matter at once'.[31] The focus was on supplying enough food, probably in response to the legacy of complaints about conditions on earlier immigrant vessels. By the early 1950s, SS *United States'* daily schedule included six meal services. The preparation and quality of food in each class was the same, but the number of options varied and first class offered a wine list of over 37 champagnes.[32]

The ocean liner could provide carefully managed exposure to the manners, art and food of a nation. The novelty of international cuisine began to appeal to Americans between the wars and became a major feature of Cunard's advertising scheme following the Second World War. As with a ship's decor, a touch of the exotic may have been appealing, but companies knew they would lose market share if the timid traveller felt overly challenged. In 1916, the Japanese line Nippon Yusen Kaisha (NYK) established a school in Yokohama to train their staff under a French cordon-bleu chef. The emphasis was on American and European dishes, with each menu offering a single traditional Japanese '*plat du jour*' such as sushi or tempura. By the 1930s, NYK advertised that their ships provided a 'happy blending of east and west' where, over the course of a Pacific crossing, passengers were gradually introduced to the use of chopsticks, Japanese soups, rice and bamboo shoots. Shortly before arrival, this culminated in a full sukiyaki dinner with passengers seated around iron pots on braziers on tatami mats laid out on the promenade deck.[33]

On an eastbound Atlantic crossing in November 1933, three up-and-coming Hollywood actors hosted a private dinner for seven guests in their suite on board the *Paris* (1921), the printed invitation announcing: 'Three Licentious Old Men from Hollywood Invite Youse to Dinner'. A 29-year-old Cary Grant (1904–86) was enjoying his recent superstardom after appearing in *Blonde Venus* (1932) and *She Done Him Wrong* (1933). He was sharing his first-class suite, containing a grand piano, with fellow actors David Manners (1900–98) and Randolph Scott (1898–1987). Paramount Pictures underwrote the suite so that Grant could appear at a London premiere.[34] The dinner – which included caviar, turtle soup, sole and partridge – was commemorated with a printed menu that also listed the attendees, mostly literary, financial and theatrical figures. The diners annotated Grant's copy with witticisms such as 'a ship what did carry Grant is a happy ship'.

One item in particular on that menu undoubtedly imparted a special significance for the diners. *Tortue claire au sherry*, or turtle soup, is a clear consommé served with cubes of meat and a dash of sherry. The best soups were created from fresh green sea turtle meat, taken from large animals that were so named because of 'the fat – the lovely green fat – that is so highly prized by epicures'.[35] Chiefly captured in Caribbean waters and transported live, the larger animals were more desirable because they carried more fat. The difficulty of preparing the soup in small quantities rendered this dish fit primarily for large groups only, and the labour involved in butchering the animal with its heavy shell contributed to conceptions of the soup as a 'symbol of opulence' that was 'de rigueur in the rarefied salons of fine dining'.[36]

165 RIGHT

Promotional image of the first-class dining room on
Lusitania, c.1907

166 BELOW

Culinary display in the Verandah Grill on *Queen
Mary*

Turtle soup was almost ubiquitous on first-class ocean liner menus from the 1880s to the early 1970s. Further, it was inextricably associated with maritime life. For centuries, turtles were the primary fresh meat available to sailors operating in warm waters. Turtle hunters supplied them in large numbers for crews to eat when lading their ships and during return passages to Europe, as they could survive for months before being slaughtered for consumption.[37] For sailors who brought the creatures to Europe, it was a basic provision, but once back home turtle meat took on an aura of luxury. When consumed on board an ocean liner, the soup turned diners into seafaring role-players, fostering a sense of celebratory cohesion among shipmates and bonding the isolated community upon the liminal zone of the sea. Menu cards indicate that the soup was served as late as December 1972, but the following year international protection acts for threatened and endangered species were initiated in various countries, and commerce in green turtle – along with the nautical and culinary tradition – abruptly ended.[38]

Yet the gastronomic indulgence that had come to define the typical ocean crossing found expression in many additional forms. On board *Liberté* (1950), a triumphant dessert centrepiece, baked to emulate the ship itself, was displayed amid a festive cornucopia of confections [171]. With it, the ship's dining room became more than a site of physical consumption – a microcosmic laboratory of idealized social production, reified as a floating container that provided all manner of luxury to the closed society on board.

167 OPPOSITE ABOVE
Service for the four luxury apartments on *Normandie*, including ceramics designed by Suzanne Lalique, made by Haviland & Co.; ceramics by Limoges; glassware by Lalique; cutlery by Puiforcat; silver designed by Luc Lanel, made by Christofle; vase by Edgar Brandt
France, c.1935
Porcelain, glass, silver
MIOTTEL MUSEUM, BERKELEY, CA

168 & 169 OPPOSITE LEFT
First-class plate and third-class soup bowl for use on Red Star Line passenger ships
United Kingdom, 1890s–1920s
Earthenware
LAISTER COLLECTION

170 OPPOSITE RIGHT
Carving station from *Normandie*, by Christofle
France, c.1935
Wood, silver
MIOTTEL MUSEUM, BERKELEY, CA

171 ABOVE
Cake tin in the shape of *Liberté*
After 1950
Zinc
COLLECTION VILLE DE SAINT-NAZAIRE –
ÉCOMUSÉE: 2000.18.3

SS UNITED STATES

DANIEL FINAMORE AND SARAH N. CHASSE

THE FIRM OF GIBBS & COX worked primarily for the US navy, but architect William Francis Gibbs (1886–1967) had a lifelong interest in ocean liners. Between the wars the firm directed the conversion of the German *Vaterland* (1914) into the American *Leviathan* (1923), and designed a series of American ships for Matson and Grace Lines, as well as the larger *America* (1940)

for the United States Lines. Following the Second World War, Gibbs proposed a jointly funded ship to serve both defence and commercial needs – a modern, luxury passenger liner, which would be easily convertible to a fast troop transport. The design conformed to navy regulations for safety, with compartmentalized engine rooms and many bulkheads, and the complete elimination of wood to secure against fire. The government funding meant that nothing could be perceived as unnecessarily opulent or lavish, a functionalist imperative that played into the Modernist aesthetic of the times. Extensive use of aluminium on the low superstructure (the decks above the hull) allowed the ship to have a fine, narrow hull, which made her very light compared to her steel predecessors. The result was a ship nearly 300 m long that could still carry as many passengers as prior liners. Ample use of aluminium made her lighter than all-steel ships, while fewer decks but a long hull yielded a lower ship that could carry as many passengers as her predecessors.

Construction orders were spread over 800 suppliers in 168 US cities.[1] The ship's hull shape was a closely guarded secret, designed to match the speed anticipated from her highly efficient turbine engines. Elaine Kaplan (1923–96), the firm's top propulsion engineer, designed a combination of four- and five-bladed propellers, a major factor enabling the ship's unparalleled speed and fuel efficiency.[2]

---

172 ABOVE
Anne Urquhart and Dorothy Marckwald with interior and exterior models of SS *United States*, 1952

173 OPPOSITE ABOVE
Ballroom on SS *United States*, with engraved glass panels and propeller tables, 1950s

174 OPPOSITE
Set of glass panels from the first-class ballroom on SS *United States*, by Charles Gilbert (photographed against a black background)
United States, 1952
Etched glass and gilding
GIFT OF RICHARD H. HADLEY
MARINERS' MUSEUM AND PARK, NEWPORT NEWS, VA: 1992.33.01B-E

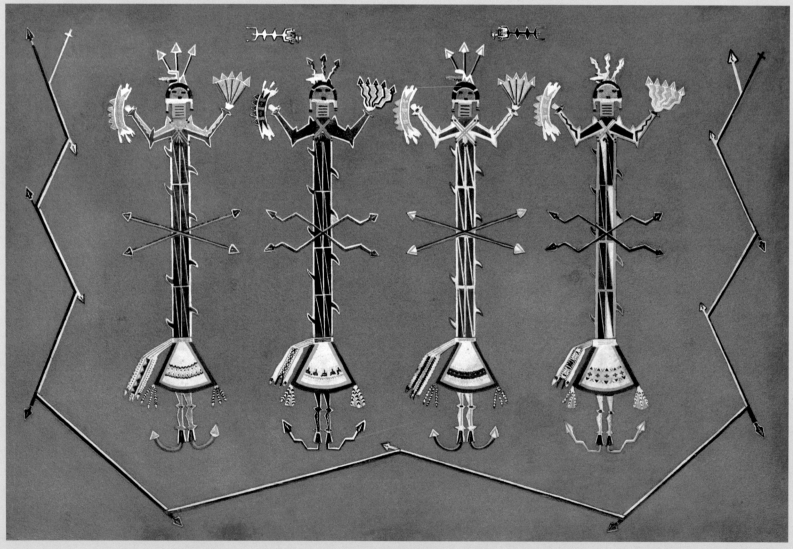

The ship was given a narrow bow and stern below the waterline, with a raked prow and small bulb to create less drag at high speed.

The all-female firm of Smyth, Urquhart & Marckwald, which had worked on many prior liners, was hired to design the interiors of the new ship [172]. Dorothy Marckwald (1898–1986) said that her aim was to provide 'a spirit of gaiety, harmony and tranquility', avoiding muddy colours for passengers 'inclined to seasickness'.[3] The firm designed 23 public rooms, 395 staterooms and 14 first-class suites – using textiles, curtains, upholstery and carpets that were entirely fireproof – as well as all the furniture on the ship, which was manufactured by the General Fireproofing Company of Youngstown, Ohio.[4] Marckwald explained: 'We would draw a picture of the chair and they had to make it work and, of course, it all had to be completely fireproof.'[5] Sample staterooms were mocked up even before the keel was laid and the result was a ship with 'a very American cut to it ... in the easy modernity of the furnishings'.[6]

Hildreth Meière (1892–1961) and Austin M. Purves (1900–77) led a team of 14 American artists to create works that focused on the themes of Americana, oceanography and the space age. Purves created a series of over 200 bas-relief sculptures in aluminium depicting state birds and flowers, along with larger eagles emulating the Great Seal of the United States that were situated on the main stairway landings.

The key feature of the first-class ballroom was a semi-circle composed of 19 etched-glass panels by Charles Gilbert (1899–1970) [173 & 174]. The floor-to-ceiling panels, arranged around the central lounge and dance floor, were ornamented with coral-reef scenes. Each panel was highlighted in gold leaf and painted colours, and lit along the edges to illuminate the imagery. Club chairs upholstered in deep pink surrounded brass-coloured cocktail tables in the shape of propellers with glass tops.

For the intimate, midnight-blue private restaurant, Charles Lin Tissot (1904–94) created large aluminium wall panels inset with cut-glass rods and lenses forming star patterns that were illuminated from behind [175]. Stars of varying sizes gave the illusion of celestial distances.

The Navajo Lounge was a quintessentially 'American' space, featuring 12 enamel panels by Peter W. Ostuni (1908–92) that replicated ritual sand paintings of Diné (Navajo) artists [177].[7] On an additional larger panel, Ostuni presented his own interpretation of these works. He had spent time in the desert southwest studying Navajo sand-painting methods and was exacting in having his enamel technique capture the feeling of these ephemeral pictures.[8]

The Observation Lounge, with its expansive ocean views, was carpeted in dark green with blue upholstery and curtains with aluminium threads woven throughout. Aluminium murals depicted North Atlantic winds and currents, and Mira Jedwabnik (b.1929) was hired to create 14 enamelled cocktail tables [176]. 'The theme was something that they [Smyth, Urquhart & Marckwald] dictated. They said they wanted stars in the sky reflected in the water ... In order to be precise, I got myself a book on stars and constellations ... Each table top had a different set of constellations.' The design connected space with the sea, unifying the ship's transatlantic mandate and America's nautical heritage with a space-age future. Jedwabnik was the youngest artist commissioned for the project, and she had travelled from Poland on board *Batory* in September 1939. 'To me ships meant a great deal, they saved my life. ...We were all Americans working for an American ship and being proud of that. ... After all it was a ship going to Europe and the Europeans going on it would realize that it was authentic American'.[9]

CHAPTER 7

FLOATING IN A DREAMLAND: FASHION AND SPECTACLE ON BOARD

FLOATING IN A DREAMLAND:
FASHION AND SPECTACLE ON BOARD

MICHELLE TOLINI FINAMORE

'THE FEELING OF FLOATING IN A DREAMLAND', is how the French novelist Émile Henriot (1889–1961) romantically described his ocean liner experience in American *Vogue* in 1926. His letter to a fictional '*Chère Zelie*' presented his voyage as an alternative reality, 'primarily because the sense of time disappears – there are no telephones, no telegrams, no letters – one can truly escape real life back at home'. Like fashion, liner travel could operate as a medium between one's dreams and reality. It was an ephemeral space where one experienced the freedom to 'dance as nowhere else'.[1] As a modern mode of transport and communication, the ocean liner was also a significant transmitter of fashion information between the style centres of Europe and American cities. The spectacle of fashion was mediated via the ocean liner from three perspectives – that of the spectator, the wearer and the designer.

SPECTATOR: 'ALL EYES WERE ON ME WHEN I BOARDED THE STEAMER'

The ocean liner was established as a site for fashionable display by the turn of the century, even before marketing campaigns began specifically associating transatlantic travel with high fashion. A postcard from around 1900 satirizes the faux self-consciousness of a woman as she boards, her overemphasized Art Nouveau curves sheathed in a yellow, white and blue dress and wearing a fashionably outsized hat [179]. It is clear from the caption – 'All eyes were on me when I boarded the steamer' – that spectatorship was

an integral part of her experience. The subject's self-assured glance back over her shoulder communicates that she expects to command attention from the crush of people on the dock during departure. Here the gangplank is a runway, a constricted space that effectively focused attention on those embarking and disembarking. And the gangplank was only the first of many arenas for exhibition, to be followed by the upper deck, the grand staircase, the dining rooms and a host of other leisure and entertainment spaces.

The arrival and departure of the major ocean liners were the most visible, accessible and highly publicized events at which people of all classes intermingled to watch the spectacle of transatlantic travel. One might observe 'famous personages ... a noted diplomat, ambassador, a lion of the art world, a gracious scion of royalty, a luminary of international society, or an enchanting bit of feminine charm from the Comédie-Française'.[2] In the 1890s, *Vogue*'s *Society Supplement* noted all the 'Sailings and Arrivals' of prominent travellers, and its celebrity coverage, which intensified into the early twentieth century, contributed to the idea of the terminal as a glamorous space. Theatre companies promoted the arrival and departure of their stage actors travelling between New York and London, and journalists and the public would crowd the docks to see their favourite stars.[3] In later years, newspaper listings of notable passengers encouraged the pageantry, helped in no small part by the Hollywood marketing machine, which presented the comings and goings of film stars such as

---

178 PREVIOUS

Bound for Hawaii, photograph by Edward Steichen
for *Vogue*
1934
Gelatin silver print
CONDÉ NAST COLLECTION: CN00018611

179 OPPOSITE

'All eyes were on me when I boarded the steamer',
postcard, *c.*1900

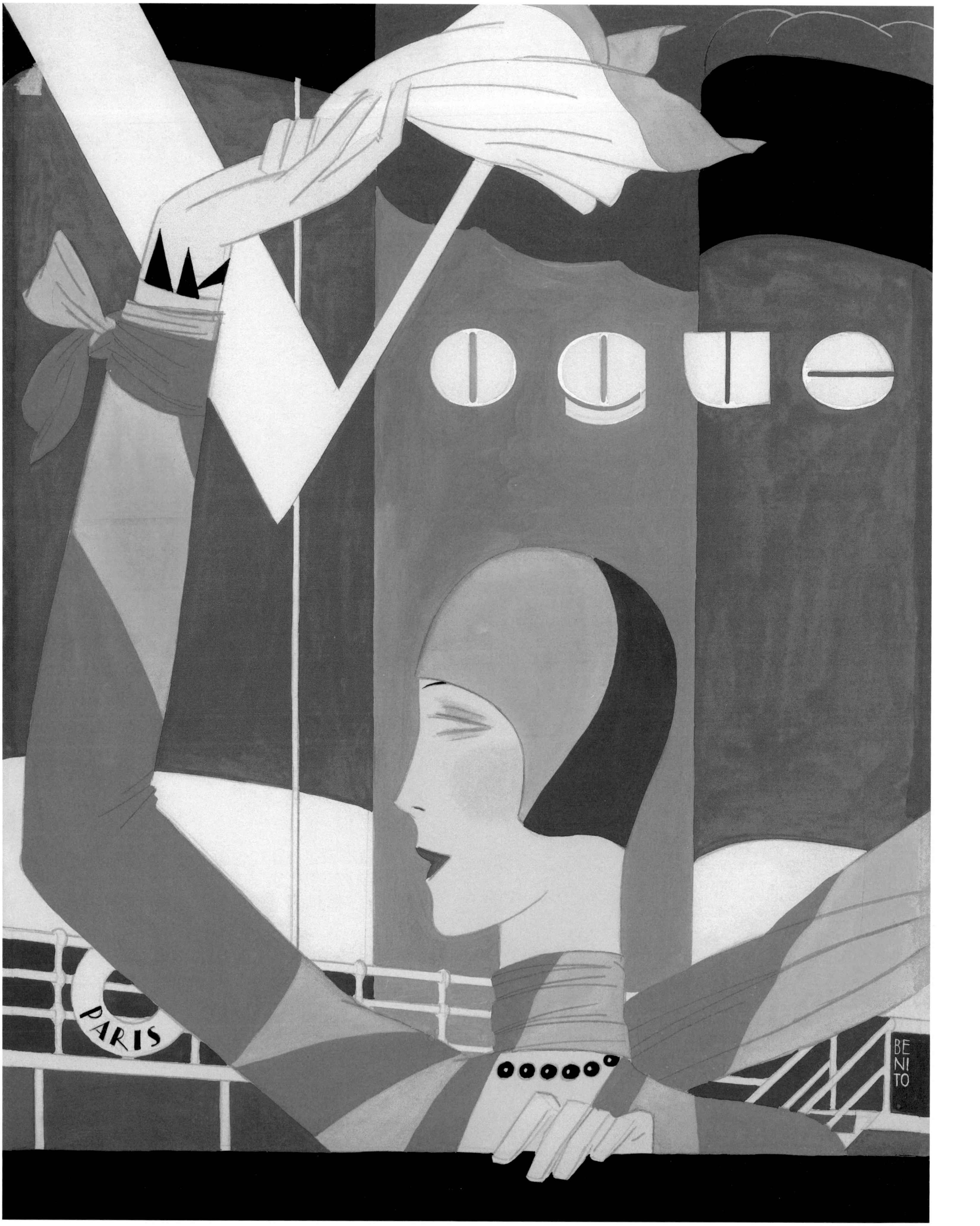
Vogue
PARIS
BENITO

Marlene Dietrich, Gloria Swanson, Cary Grant and Elizabeth Taylor fashionably posed, and of course, impeccably dressed.[4]

Once on board, spaces to be seen in varied according to class, but the idea that a passenger might catch a glimpse of, and even intermingle with, the rich and famous held great appeal. In the 1933 film *Luxury Liner*, third-class passenger Milli Stern (played by Alice White, 1904–83) spends the entire movie trying to attract men who will provide her with an entrée into the upper-class entertainment spaces, and also buy her appropriately fashionable ensembles so that she might blend in with the wealthy crowd.

By the time of *Normandie*'s maiden voyage in 1935, the level of luxury provided even in the lower-class spaces is evident in a *Vogue* article entitled 'And So I Went Tourist' by the writer 'C.P.' who travelled in the newly designated third class. Spectacularly designed liners such as *Normandie* provided a hyper-modern setting for the fashionable figure, clearly important to C.P., who wrote: 'The only regrettable thing about going out on the first sailing of the *Normandie* was that I couldn't see myself sail ... I should like to have stood on the brand new yellow Havre pier ... and watched myself pull out with pomp and excitement.' C.P. continues to explore the ship to choose a dinner setting that would best coordinate with her evening ensemble. On entering a dining room, she 'could not decide whether my type of beauty would be better off by a background of black glass in a dim light or natural wood in broad daylight'. She eventually chose the latter and throughout her story she marvels at the opulence of the lower-class dining room.[5] It was fairly common for these liner spaces to be more sumptuous than those one had at home, which in turn encouraged and necessitated good dressing.

The outdoor spaces and decks also offered an arena for showcasing fashion. As the ultimate expression of speed, style and modernity, fashion photographers and illustrators found the industrial framework of the ocean liner a compelling setting for editorial coverage. The graphic simplicity of the steamship funnel and the linear rail set against a sweep of open sky complemented the streamlined, Modernist body of the late 1920s and '30s.

A cover of *Vogue* from 1927 by Eduardo Garcia Benito (1891–1981) depicts a model set against Cubist planes of colour [180]. The shape of her arm echoes the shape of the funnel, and a tightly fitted cloche turns her head into a sphere; the lines between the body, the ocean liner and the background all converge on one flat plane. Fashion magazines of the period were replete with images by Edward Steichen (1879–1973), Toni Frissell (1907–88), Martin Munkácsi (1896–1963) and Cecil Beaton (1904–80) set on liners. In Steichen's photograph *Bound for Hawaii* (1934), the graphic composition of the ship's rails and sky are the backdrop for two models in Ransohoff sports togs [178]. As in the Benito cover, the visual elements join together to form an image that is appropriately modern for these fashion-forward sports clothes. The riveted metal and massive white shells of liner exteriors proved to be popular for fashion newsreels as well, and countless films made on board – from the 1935 film *For Daughters in Search of the Sun* to a 1961 fashion show on board *Queen Elizabeth* (1940) – highlighted sports attire and bathing suits.[6]

The potential of the ocean liner as an attractive, and lucrative, venue for both formal and informal fashion shows was not lost on business-savvy designers in the early twentieth century. Much like the racecourses or the promenades of oceanfront resorts, ships had a contained, captive and well-heeled audience, and a number of designers emulated the *succès de scandale* of Paul Poiret's (1879–1944) *jupe-pantalons* (or harem pants) at the Auteuil racecourses and started 'planting' women modelling their latest fashions on deck to alleviate the 'interminable afternoon'.[7] Some even set up a system for passengers to order the entire ensemble via the wireless and have it waiting for them when they arrived in Paris.[8]

The most conspicuous space to be seen, however, was the *grande descente* – 'designed for one reason: to allow for the breath-taking entrance of beautifully gowned *femmes*'.[9] The grand staircase was incorporated into the architecture of many large-scale liners by the 1910s. Much like the department stores of the late nineteenth century, the sweeping staircases and viewing platforms encouraged voyeurism, an undercurrent made apparent by the two fashionably

180 OPPOSITE
Cover of *Vogue* (US edition), illustration by Eduardo Garcia Benito (15 October 1927)

dressed women taking in the view in the left foreground of Richard Bouwens van der Boijen's view of the grand staircase and main hall on *Paris* [183]. This watercolour shows stylish passengers walking up and down the grand staircase, rendered in soft brushwork and bathed in a golden hue that heightens the picture's dreamlike atmosphere. The language used to describe the experience is also evocative. Passengers 'drift' up and down the stairway, seeing themselves and others 'against that background of its exquisite decorations ... a world where the social graces hold sway: where life moves with savoir faire and fascinating amiability'.[10] In such an otherworldly atmosphere, both the spectators and the wearers of fashion participated in a dazzling spectacle. The grand staircase was such an important part of ship architecture that Cecil Beaton bemoaned the lack of such platforms on board *Queen Mary* (1936): 'When constructing a boat, even a luxury liner, the English do not consider their women very carefully. There are hardly any large mirrors in the general rooms, no great flight of stairs for the ladies to make an entrance.'[11]

TRAVELLER: THE ACID TEST OF TRUE CHIC

The ocean-liner voyage offered ample opportunity to see and be seen, but how did the prospective traveller decide what to pack? What was appropriate and fashionable travel attire? As noted in *Vogue* in 1926: 'Travel by land and sea often proves to be the acid test of true chic.'[12] From the style of one's luggage to the ensembles within, the traveller's choices communicated socio-economic status and sartorial panache. Fashion magazines, travel guides, the steamship lines' promotional magazines (*The Cunarder*, for example) and special 'travel' departments in stores such as

Henri Bendel were keen to offer advice.[13] Maintaining style while travelling was, nonetheless, a particular challenge because of space limitations, the vagaries of climate and, by the 1910s and '20s, the great range of garments needed. Although it varied with one's travel class and the style of ship, starting with the departure ensemble, a traveller could potentially need clothing fit for swimming pools, squash and tennis courts, shooting galleries, deck lounging, Turkish baths, cocktail bars, restaurants, smoking rooms and nightclubs.

Throughout the first half of the twentieth century, a woman's departure ensemble usually comprised a smart tailored suit and era-appropriate accessories [184 & 185]. A passenger's luggage was an extension of their ensemble, and Louis Vuitton or Goyard trunks were immediate markers of socio-economic status [186]. Steamer travel and luxury branding evolved on a parallel course, and new spaces for display facilitated the creation of easily identifiable and distinctive fashion logos, such as the Louis Vuitton 'LV' monogram (introduced in 1896 and still a powerful marker of status today).[14] Founded in 1854 as a trunk-making and packing company, Vuitton became known for its speciality trunks for specific forms of attire (hats, dresses, shoes and lingerie) with flat, rather than domed, tops, which allowed them to be stacked. A photograph of Marlene Dietrich from around 1936 shows the star surrounded by innumerable trunks, stacks of luggage and hatboxes, and illustrates how an overabundance of varied trunks became standard props that identified the owner as a seasoned and stylish traveller.

What did the passenger actually pack in their trunks? While advice in articles and travel manuals abounds, the compensation claims made against the White Star Line after the sinking of *Titanic* (1912) offer tangible evidence of the luggage contents of

GRANDE · DESCENTE · DU
PAQUEBOT ☰ PARIS
HALL · D'ENTRÉE · AU · CENTRE · DU · NAVIRE

181 OPPOSITE LEFT

Elizabeth Taylor and Richard Burton disembarking
from *Queen Elizabeth* in Cherbourg, France, October
1964. Taylor is wearing the 'Night of the Iguana'
brooch.

182 OPPOSITE RIGHT

'Night of the Iguana' brooch, designed by
Jean Schlumberger, Tiffany & Co.
New York, United States, *c*.1964
Diamonds, gold, cabochon sapphires,
emeralds and platinum
PRIVATE COLLECTION

183 ABOVE

View of the grand staircase and main hall on *Paris*,
by Richard Bouwens van der Boijen
1921
Ink and watercolour on sepia print
ACADÉMIE D'ARCHITECTURE/CITÉ DE
L'ARCHITECTURE ET DU PATRIMOINE/ARCHIVES
D'ARCHITECTURE DU XXE SIÈCLE: RBB-DES 2/1.1

184 ABOVE LEFT

Day suit worn by Marlene Dietrich, by Christian Dior

*c.*1949

Wool

GIFT OF THE DEPARTMENT OF RECREATION

& PARKS, CITY OF LOS ANGELES

COURTESY OF THE FIDM, MUSEUM AT

THE FASHION INSTITUTE OF DESIGN &

MERCHANDISING, LOS ANGELES, CA: L88.1.250AB

185 ABOVE RIGHT

Marlene Dietrich wearing the day suit by Christian

Dior on *Queen Elizabeth* arriving in New York,

21 December 1950

186 OPPOSITE

Special secretary trunk for linen in monogram

canvas, by Louis Vuitton

France, 1922

Coated canvas, wood, lozine, brass, leather,

metal and textile

COLLECTION LOUIS VUITTON

a wide variety of passengers. The high value assigned to fashion and accessories is apparent in the meticulous accounting of the wardrobe of first-class traveller Charlotte Cardeza (1854–1939). Cardeza's claim reveals she travelled with a total of 12 trunks, including Vuitton wardrobe trunks, hat trunks, shoe trunks, tray trunks and a dress trunk. Most of the ensembles were valued between $200 and $500 each (around $5,000 to $12,000 in today's terms) and included designs by Redfern and Rouff in Paris, S. Ungar in Vienna and from American department stores such as Lord & Taylor.[15] While very little clothing survives, passenger Edith Russell's (1879–1975) fashionable French silk, flower-adorned evening slippers are an exception. In contrast, Mrs Allen Becker (1873–1961), who was travelling in second class with her children, claimed for clothing of much lower value and no specific designers were singled out.

Women were often advised to leave their valuables at home, but surviving photographs and jewellery reveal that this was challenging for many. *Titanic* first-class passenger Mrs Margaret Brown (1867–1932) claimed she lost a necklace worth $20,000 (over $480,000 in today's terms), while Lady Marguerite Allan (1873–1957) managed to escape the sinking *Lusitania* in 1915 with her diamond and natural pearl Cartier tiara [187]. Celebrities such as Elizabeth Taylor, a renowned jewellery enthusiast, could not part with her fabulous jewels onboard ship, and probably had an interest in maintaining her public persona as a style icon [181 & 182].

In every class of travel, the 'acid test of true chic' applied equally to the practicality of garments as well as one's personal sense of style. A 1907 traveller's handbook recommended 'the most sensible clothing possible for her sex': a plain tailored suit, silk or woollen tights, thick stockings, shirtwaists, a woollen knitted sweater, woollen wrapper for going to bathe, woollen slippers, shoes with rubber soles and, instead of an evening gown, a pretty, dressy bodice for dinner. Men could pack even more sparingly: a black coat for dinner and appropriate shirts were the only luxury items needed. Anything more decorative, such as coats with loud checks, 'which belong to the race-course', or 'fancy shirts are entirely out of place'.[16] The rules had changed by 1934, when *Vogue*'s illustrated article 'Packing for Pleasure' recommended at least 16 ensembles including beach pyjamas, bathing suit, three evening dresses, cocktail dress, day suit, evening wraps and at least seven pairs of shoes, by couture designers such as Chanel, Lanvin, Patou and Alix. By this time, *Vogue* was a magazine consumed by the masses and, even if its readers were not travelling first class, these were the standards promoted to all.[17]

The advent and increased accessibility of liner travel had an undeniable impact on the evolution of sports and casual wear.

Coco Chanel (1883–1971) opened up her resort boutiques in fashionable Deauville in 1913, with Jean Patou (1887–1936) following suit in 1924.[18] Both designers also started offering a *demi-saison* to present resort or 'cruise' wear for those who were wintering in warmer climes or planning to engage in sporting activities during their transatlantic travel. As key figures in the evolution of sports-oriented fashion for women and the use of the ever-practical jersey knit for daytime attire, their designs appealed to a younger set that enjoyed golfing, tennis and swimming. One article noted that the sun deck and outdoor swimming pools of the new ships 'have revolutionized life on the ocean wave and banished traveling clothes forever from the fashion dictionary'.[19] This new category of clothing included bathing suits with matching cover-ups, cardigan jackets, jersey skirts and pyjama-style pants [188].

By this time, 'Cruise Clothes' had evolved into a specific genre, with magazines such as *Harper's Bazaar* including the category as a regular section. The 'Cruise' collection on the couture calendar today is a noteworthy holdover from the age of ocean liners,

and many runway shows for the *demi-saison* are shown in cruise destinations such as Rio de Janeiro and Havana.[20]

The ocean environment influenced the type of fabrics best suited for cruise clothes, favouring those that would perform better in the humid air. Helen Eva Yates, author of *The World is Your Oyster: The Art of Traveling Smartly* (1939), devoted an entire chapter to wardrobe, recommending gingham, non-crushable linens, piqué, seersucker and cottons for sports attire. For evening clothes, passengers travelling on large liners should pack their best gowns, but they should avoid ostrich feathers, velvet, tulle or ruffles. Lace and printed chiffon were deemed practical, but there is a particular word of warning to '[s]idestep the metallic evening gown for an ocean trip – it is too dressy and it turns "green" at sea'.[21]

Transatlantic travellers who did not have the appropriate raiment however, were, of course, heading towards the shopping capitals of London, Paris and New York, and steamship companies promoted the ocean voyage as an opportunity to seek out luxury goods. The deluxe *Album de la Compagnie Transatlantique* of 1877, created for the first-class lounge, presented 30 advertisements for Parisian purveyors of '*Modes, Toilettes, Bijoux, Parfums*' as well as corsets and riding outfits, from smaller boutiques to the '*grands magasins* [department stores] *de la Paix*' [189]. Specifically targeting women travellers became even more common in the 1920s, and the International Mercantile Marine Company's publication *The Ocean Ferry* encouraged advertisers to stress the 'joys of shopping abroad, the extreme luxury and niceties of service' for readers of *Vogue* and *Harper's Bazaar*.[22]

For many Americans, shopping at Parisian couture houses and London tailors was an essential part of the 'Grand Tour'. Mary Elizabeth Staples, who travelled to Paris a number of times, arrived in New York in 1927 on board *Majestic* (1922), carrying with her at least three beaded evening dresses from the Paris couture house

---

187 ABOVE
Tiara, by Cartier Paris
France, 1909
Platinum, one old-cut cushion-shaped diamond,
old-cut diamonds, natural pearls, millegrain setting
Formerly the property of Lady Marguerite Allan
(1873–1957)
CARTIER COLLECTION

188 OPPOSITE FROM LEFT TO RIGHT
Bathing suit, by Viking
United Kingdom, 1925–9
Knitted wool
GIVEN BY AMY DE LA HAYE
V&A: T.93–1994

Man's bathing suit, by Meridian
United Kingdom, c.1925
Wool jersey knit
GIVEN BY CAPT. G.P. WILLIAMS
V&A: T.299–1982

Two piece bathing suit, retailed by Finnigans Ltd
London, 1937–9
Wool jersey
V&A: T.294&A–1971

Jenny.[23] Jenny Sacerdote (1868–1962) was then at the height of her fame and success, and all three dresses are beautiful examples of haute-couture craftsmanship [191]. In addition to their steep purchase price, the buyer had to pay customs tax on arrival at home.[24] Staples reputedly wore multiple dresses under her fur coat to avoid paying duty on her Paris purchases and two of the dresses, while undoubtedly by Jenny and documented on the receipts, have had their labels taken out. Emilie Grigsby (1876?–1964), an American who eventually settled in London, travelled on ocean liners throughout her life and her wardrobe contains pieces by many avant-garde designers of the early twentieth century, including Paul Poiret and Natalia Goncharova (1881–1962). Certain clothes that she probably transported from Paris, such as a 1925 Jeanne Lanvin dress, have the labels cut out; while others, including an Art Nouveau dress by London maker Anne Talbot, do not [190]. Fear of the customs officer was the subject of much satire in the popular press and one 1909 account of ocean-liner travel notes the standard practice of replacing a Parisian Doucet label with one from Siegel-Cooper, New York. The author comically proceeds to

describe the encounter with the customs officer as 'some of the very best acting done outside of a theatre ... on any dock after the arrival of a crowded steamer'.[25]

The same observer also tells of a 'shopping woman' who suffers at sea for seven days, anxiously searching for something, *anything*, to buy. The author wonders if better shopping would alleviate the 'dull and eventless' monotony of a transatlantic journey for such passionate consumers.[26] *L'Atlantique* was among the first liners to carry a fully-fledged shopping mall, or rue, on board [88]. The ship boasted a satellite boutique of the French department store Au Printemps, a florist, candy store and hair salons. A cinematic depiction of shipboard shopping appeared around the same time in *What a Widow!* (1930) starring Gloria Swanson (1899–1983). The film is lost, but promotional stills reveal that shopping was a vital part of the protagonist's liner experience. The ultra-modern Art Deco sets show Swanson surrounded by piles of shoes, trying on diamond jewellery, being shown hats and being fitted for a custom-made dress. By 1934, it seemed that 'all of the boats have shops on a par with Burlington Arcades' selling a range of goods: perfumes,

ROBES ET MANTEAUX

Mme HERMANTINE DU RIEZ

8, rue Halévy, place du Nouvel-Opéra
PARIS

clothing and cocktail shakers could readily be had on board *Europa* (1930), *Santa Rosa* (1932), *Santa Paula* (1933) and *Kungsholm* (1928). *Aquitania* (1914) carried an Austin Reed boutique and *Lafayette* (1930) had an outpost of the famous Parisian department store Au Bon Marché.[27]

DESIGNER: MODE SUR MER

For the fashion designer, the liner was a modern mode of transportation that opened up new vistas for overseas exposure and expansion. The world of haute couture became increasingly international and the golden age of liner travel brought direct access to a global clientele. In addition to designers, department-store buyers, retailers, dressmakers and copyists for the ready-to-wear market all began travelling overseas. Business travellers, including fashion-industry professionals, made up a substantial portion of the liner population, and their increased transatlantic travel was directly responsible for the growth of second-class accommodations.[28] From the early twentieth century, when it was a novelty for designers to make well-publicized trips with their models, to the routine twice-yearly trips of London Savile Row tailors to fit their American clientele in the 1960s, ocean liners played an essential role in how fashion information was transmitted and transported.

Paul Poiret, whose press and marketing savvy helped to position him as one of the most recognizable designers in the fashion world, was the first to embark on a much-heralded tour of the United States, arriving in New York City on *La Provence* (1906) in 1913.[29] Poiret and many other designers were actively fighting the copyists who were stealing their designs, and this was an attempt to control access to his latest work. From the perspective of the couture industry, the rampant piracy was one of the downsides of the increased access to Parisian designs. Jeanne Paquin (1869–1936) had a similar mission when she personally accompanied her latest designs to the United States in 1914, also on board *La Provence*, with 100 garments in 100 trunks, and an entourage that included models, a press agent and a builder to erect the elaborate set in

189 ABOVE
Page from *Album de la Compagnie Transatlantique: aquarelles pour les modes, toilettes, bijoux, parfums, etc.*, by Léon Sault
Paris, France, 1877
Hand-embellished chromolithograph
PHILLIPS LIBRARY, PEABODY ESSEX MUSEUM

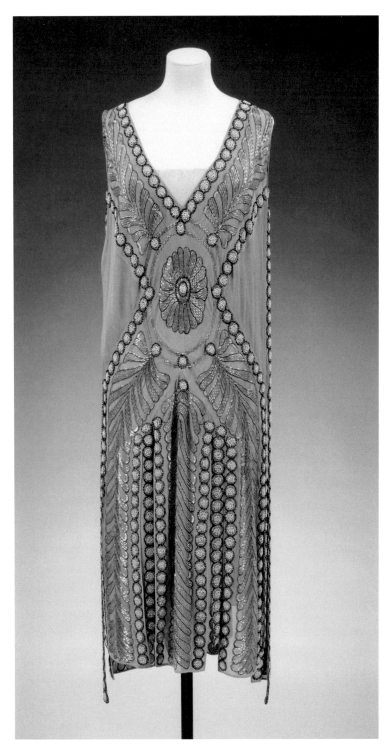

190 ABOVE

'Salambo' dress, by Jeanne Lanvin,

belonging to Miss Emilie Grigsby

France, 1925

Silk georgette and glass beads, lined with chiffon

191 ABOVE

Dress, by Jenny

Paris, France, 1926

Silk, gold lamé and glass beading

I am returning on
S. S. Majestic with many
clever creations for our
early Spring showing from
the best known couturiers
of Paris.

The originals and our copies
will be on display in our
showroom on December 7th.

Your early inspection is
invited.

Respectfully yours

l. a. Chaikin

PICKWICK DRESS C° INC.

62, Rue Beaubourg
PARIS

230 West 38th Street
NEW YORK

which the creations would be shown. Paquin was showcasing her 'tango' gowns that allowed more movement for the then wildly popular dance. The runway show, which was as complex as a Broadway production, was to premiere in New York and then travel to various American cities.[30] Upon her arrival, the dresses were held in customs but as Paquin claimed she was showing them for exhibition purposes only, they were admitted free under bond.[31] This caused great resentment on the part of the American buyers, who always had to pay customs, fees and viewed Paquin as competing with the New York fashion industry.[32] Jean Patou also conducted a heavily publicized voyage that would help him better fit

his garments to the American physique. In 1924 he travelled back on board *France* (1912) after recruiting and importing American models who were 'smart, slender ... with well-shaped feet and ankles'.[33]

In her book *Fashion is Spinach*, American designer Elizabeth Hawes (1903–71), who started her career as a copyist for a ready-to-wear manufacturer, wrote that at the beginning of every Paris season, the city was 'flooded with dress buyers from all over the world', including America, Germany, the Netherlands and South America. The high-end department store Bergdorf Goodman and luxury retailer Hattie Carnegie were among many businesses

---

192 & 193 ABOVE LEFT AND RIGHT

Invitation for Pickwick Dress Co., illustrated by
Robert Polack, printed by Georges Gotscho
*c.*1926
Planographic print with pochoir (colour stencil)
GIFT OF SUSAN B. KAPLAN
MUSEUM OF FINE ARTS, BOSTON, MA: 2016.142

194 & 195 OPPOSITE ABOVE AND BELOW

Fashion show on *Normandie*, photographs
by Roger Schall, 1 July 1935

frequently travelling back and forth, and it was common for even small fashion suppliers to make the pilgrimage to Paris twice yearly.[34] The ready-to-wear manufacturer Pickwick Dress Company had offices in both New York and Paris, and on return from Paris on board *Majestic* in 1926, an agent sent out invitations to its clients (probably department-store buyers) offering them a look at both the originals and their ready-made copies [192 & 193].

The maiden voyage of *Normandie* in 1935 was perhaps the most directed effort to position an ocean liner as integrally entwined with the business of fashion. The trip boasted '100 fashion experts' among the 519 first-class passengers, held an on-board fashion show mid-passage, and the ship's modern design inspired fashion accessories and perfume.[35] Representatives from the couture houses of Callot Soeurs, Jenny, Maggy Rouff, Jeanne Lanvin, Lucien Lelong, Vionnet, Worth and Lucile Paray, Max and Weil furriers, and milliners Caroline Reboux, Rose Valois, Le Monnier, Maria Guy and Agnes were all on board to participate in a fully-fledged *défilé*, in which each house showed a garden-party dress, a *tailleur de minuit* (a tailored ensemble) and three evening gowns. Organized by Jean Labusquière (1895–1941), a kingpin of the Parisian couture industry, the event promised *Normandie*'s passengers the first viewing of the very latest fashions.[36]

Magazine and newspaper coverage was rampant, with countless articles in *Vogue* related to the trip; photographs by Roger Schall (1904–95) offer rare glimpses into the behind-the-scenes preparations for the grand show [194 & 195]. The *défilé* took place in the dramatically lit grand salon – the most spectacular space on the ship – and the formal dress of the passengers illustrates that the viewers' ensembles were as important as the designs featured on the models. Couturier Lucien Lelong (1889–1958), a great proponent of applying modern concepts of movement to dress, included two evening dresses that show how the lissom, lean cut of the 1930s reflected the streamlined modern design of the ship itself. With Lelong, the line between wearer, spectator and designer coalesced on many levels, and passengers were also wearing his designs, including Bernadette Arnal (1898–1986), the wife of a partner of the important shipping company Worms & Cie. As a regular client of Lucien Lelong, she had three evening dresses in France's national colours of blue, white and red made for *Normandie*'s maiden voyage [196]. Perhaps the most telling illustration of the deep associations between fashion, *moderne* style and the ocean liner, however, was Jean Patou's commission to create a special perfume bottle in the shape of *Normandie*. Patou had capitalized on the international access to clients that ocean-liner travel brought throughout his career, and it is fitting that he created

a unique scent in a limited edition that was presented to all the female first-class passengers on the maiden voyage [197].

The ocean liner continued to hold great appeal as a modern stage for premiering new fashion and countless fashion shows occurred on ships both at dock and at sea throughout the 1960s. The rise to prominence of the Italian couture industry after the Second World War, no doubt aided by ocean liner crossings, benefited womenswear designers such as Emilio Pucci (1914–92). He began his career with resort wear in Capri, and liners visiting nearby Naples brought waves of customers who obediently spread his gospel of vibrantly patterned and richly hued cruise clothes far and wide. The Roman menswear firm Brioni successfully introduced the more relaxed Continental cut through transatlantic travel, allowing the firm to compete with the Savile Row tailors who were continuing their twice-yearly journeys to fit overseas clients.[37] Much like *Normandie*'s tight relationship with the French couture industry in the 1930s, *Queen Elizabeth* became a frequent site for filmed and live fashion shows, including the heavily publicized *British Fashions – U.S.A. '66*. This show of 17 British ready-to-wear designers travelled to America to promote the mod creations of John Bates (b.1938) for Jean Varon and Wallis of London among others. Cunard went as far as to build runways and install lighting for four fashion shows while the liner was berthed in New York.[38]

For the wearer, the formality and appropriateness of dress for specific spaces on board continued to hold sway, even in the midst of the swinging '60s. One passenger sailing from New York to Southampton on board *Queen Elizabeth 2* in 1969 misinterpreted the mandates of shipboard style and wore a vibrantly patterned evening suit designed by Tom Gilbey (b.1939) for dinner at the Captain's table [198]. Gilbey's design, while fairly straightforward

in cut, was made from a striking blue fabric with a zigzag pattern, and worn with a cravat with floral sprays and paisley motifs. The wearer was the sole diner without a more conservative dinner jacket and the occasion was evidently memorable, recorded in perpetuity in the records of the Museum of London. The consistent refrain throughout all of these stories, accounts and histories, is that, for many travellers, fashion was of utmost importance to the ocean liner experience. As Henriot noted in his 1926 *Vogue* article, both fashion and 'the ships ... act as shuttles between our desires and our dreams'.[39]

196 OPPOSITE LEFT
Dress worn by Bernadette Arnal on the maiden voyage of *Normandie*, by Lucien Lelong
France, 1934–9
Silk crêpe
MUSÉE DES ARTS DÉCORATIFS, PARIS,
DÉPARTEMENT DE LA MODE ET DU TEXTILE:
998.178.5

197 OPPOSITE
Jean Patou perfume bottle in the shape of *Normandie*, presented to female first-class passengers on the ship's maiden voyage, designed by Louis Süe
France, c.1935
Glass, steel and paper
COLLECTION OF MARIO J. PULICE

198 RIGHT
Suit worn by Geoffrey Osmint at the Captain's table on *QE2*, by Tom Gilbey
United Kingdom, 1969
Mixed fibres, cotton and metal
GIFT FROM GEOFFREY OSMINT IN MEMORY OF
KEITH WEBBER, AUGUST 2001
MUSEUM OF LONDON: 2001.74/5

CHAPTER 8

MODERNIST ARCHITECTURE AND THE LINER

le navire

le palais

le paquebot

SDN

le gratte ciel

la colline artificielle

MODERNIST ARCHITECTURE AND THE LINER

TIM BENTON

FOR THE MORE RIGOROUS THEORISTS of modern architecture and design, the ocean liner was a symbolic rather than an iconic reference, a motive rather than a motif. Le Corbusier (Charles-Édouard Jeanneret, 1887–1965), a pioneer of Modernist architecture, made ocean liners the subject of the first of his three essays comprising the text 'Des yeux qui ne voient pas' (1921, 'Eyes That Do Not See') [200].[1] Together these essays argued that modern engineering had made the old ways of thinking redundant, and – using the examples of liners, aeroplanes and automobiles – urged architects to change radically their approach to design.

If we forget for a moment that a liner is a transport tool and look at it with new eyes, we will sense that we stand before an important manifestation of temerity, discipline and harmony, a beauty that is calm, vigorous and strong. A serious architect who looks as an architect (a creator of organisms) will find in the liner a liberation from cursed enslavement to the past. … The liner is the first stage in the realization of a world organized in accordance with the new spirit.[2]

This was an argument widely shared in Modernist circles and even among defenders and practitioners of Art Deco. For example, in a long article written to introduce the 1925 *Exposition des Arts Décoratifs et Industriels Modernes* to the readers of the journal *Art et Décoration*, an authoritative member of the arts establishment,

Guillaume Janneau (1887–1968), referred positively to 'revolution' and 'rupture' in the decorative arts.[3] Instead of replacing one style of decorative art with another, what was needed was a fundamental revision of principles:

Contemporary society, which is conditioned by machinery, the primary cause of the transformation of the economic and social system, and by scientific discoveries requires a new architecture – one that reflects the new realities – and logical solutions that have broken away from the traditional canons.[4]

Even if the designers and decorators who dominated the 1925 exhibition worked in what we would now call the Art Deco style, they accepted the principle that they should follow the example of modern engineering in simplifying and rationalizing design. Many Art Deco designers hoped to standardize their work for a wider market. For example, André Ruhlmann, apparently no relation to Jacques-Émile Ruhlmann (1879–1933), specialised in sheet metal furniture and was responsible for one of the third class cabin designs on *Normandie* [201].

The differences between Art Deco and Modernist designers should not be exaggerated, but the polemics of the time did emphasize the differences rather than the similarities. For example, by 1929 it was common among Modernist designers to derisively describe Art Deco as '*le style paquebot*' because the style that took

199 PREVIOUS

Sketch made for a conference given in South America, by Le Corbusier
Buenos Aires, Argentina, 1929
Charcoal on Canson paper
FONDATION LE CORBUSIER, PARIS: 33526A

200 OPPOSITE

'Des yeux qui ne voient pas... Les Paquebots',
by Le Corbusier-Saugnier, in *L'Esprit Nouveau*,
(8 May 1921)

Paquebot « FLANDRE », Cie Transatlantique, construit par les Chantiers et Ateliers de St-Nazaire.

DES YEUX
QUI NE VOIENT PAS...

★

Les Paquebots

PAR

LE CORBUSIER-SAUGNIER

« Il y a un esprit nouveau : c'est un esprit de construction et de synthèse guidé par une conception claire.

Quoi qu'on en pense, il anime aujourd'hui la plus grande partie de l'activité humaine.

UNE GRANDE ÉPOQUE VIENT DE COMMENCER
Programme de l' « Esprit Nouveau », N° 1, Octobre 1920

« Nul ne nie aujourd'hui l'esthétique qui se dégage des créations de l'industrie moderne. De plus en plus, les constructions, les machines s'établissent avec des proportions, des jeux de volumes et de matières tels que beaucoup d'entre elles sont de véritables œuvres d'art, car elles comportent le nombre, c'est à dire l'ordre. Or les individus d'élite qui composent le monde de l'industrie et des affaires et qui vivent, par conséquent, dans cette atmosphère virile où se créent des œuvres indéniablement belles, se figurent être fort éloignés de toute activité esthétique. Ils ont tort, *car ils sont parmi les plus actifs créateurs de l'esthétique contemporaine.* Ni les artistes, ni les industriels ne s'en rendent compte. C'est dans la production générale que se trouve le style d'une époque et non pas, comme on le croit trop, dans quelques productions à fins ornementales, simples superfétations sur une structure qui, à elle seule, a

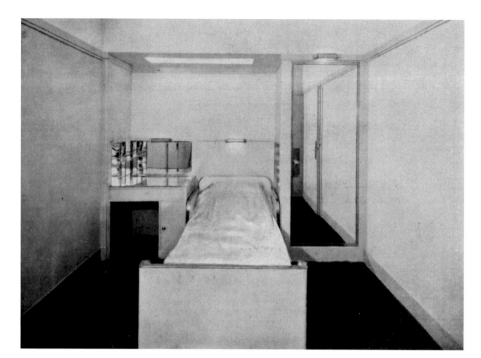

201 LEFT

Third-class cabin on *Normandie*, made entirely
in steel, by A. Ruhlmann, from *L'Illustration*,
special issue on *Normandie* (1935)

over from historicism in the great ocean liners was not Modernism
but Art Deco. It was the Art Deco designers who best knew how to
combine the realities of ship design with the comforts of modern
life, imbuing the results with symbols of luxury and escapism.
None of the great inter-war ocean liners was designed by leading
Modernist architects or designers. Although ships such as *Bremen*
(1929) or *Orion* (1935) came close, in their use of modern materials
and little ornamentation, purists still regarded them as Art Deco.

Fritz August Breuhaus de Groot (1883–1960), who also
designed the interiors of the Hindenburg airship, designed the
interiors of *Bremen* [202]. Franz Kollmann criticized his efforts in
the pages of the journal *Das neue Frankfurt*, in the typical terms
of the Modernist/Art Deco polemics: 'As with the Zeppelin, the
beautiful and clear simplicity of the technical form stands in
contrast to the frantically emphasized luxury of the social spaces
of the interiors.'[5] This was the caption to a detail of the exterior
of the ship, to which were compared three views of the interior.
Kollmann's comment is perhaps unfair, but reflects the
general feeling among left-wing, Modernist critics that the
ocean liner was a lost cause for modern design.

For Le Corbusier, however, as we have seen, the ocean liner
was a metaphor. If architects designed houses like the engineers
designed the functional parts of a ship, they would create a new
architecture. He illustrated a promenade deck from *Aquitania*
(1914) in his book *Vers une architecture* (1923, which contained
and expanded upon the 'Des yeux qui ne voient pas' essays).
Here he appears to be ready to copy features of the ocean

liner in his own architecture. The caption accompanying the
photograph explained:

> For architects: a wall that's all windows, a room flooded with
> light. What a contrast with the windows of our houses, which
> pierce the wall and create patches of shadow on either side,
> rendering the room drab and making the light so bright that
> curtains are indispensable to filter and soften it.[6]

But his real point was not that the steel openings in a promenade
deck should be converted into long windows in a reinforced
concrete frame. Instead, he wanted to associate his architecture
with the structure of the ship rather than its decoration. He featured
another photograph of a promenade deck on the cover of the book
and captioned it as follows: 'A pure architecture, precise, clear,
clean, healthy. Contrast this with the carpets, the cushions, the
baldachins, the damask wallpapers, gilded and sculpted furniture,
dowager duchess colours or *ballets russes* hues; the mournful
sadness of this Western bazaar.'[7]

This contrast between the engineering of the ocean liner and
its decorated interiors was spelled out in his lectures and again in
his book *L'Art décoratif d'aujourd'hui* (1925, The Decorative Art of
Today).[8] Here the contrast is made between the structure of the
liner *Paris* (1921) and her Art Deco and Art Nouveau interior, with
its staircase by Edgar Brandt (1880–1960). Le Corbusier used the
example to test the taste and judgement of his audience. At a lecture
at the Salle Rapp in Paris in October 1924 he announced:

202 ABOVE

Shopping street on *Bremen*, designed by Fritz
August Breuhaus de Groot, 1928–9, from
Der Ozean-Express 'Bremen' (Munich, 1930)

only 56 m² for 5 to 7 persons. This means that they provide only 11 m² or 8 m² per person. The ocean liner can only continue to function within these astonishing physical limitations because its communal services are rigorously organized, because the living quarters are stripped of all parasitical elements, and because life aboard ... is governed by an intelligent use of innovations that *permit a solution of the space problem*, on the one hand, and that REJECT ALL WASTE, on the other.[12]

He would go on to use these figures to propose a system of bedroom units for his unrealized Ville Radieuse apartments (1935), based on 14 m² per person, in different combinations.

THE DANGERS OF IMITATION

The German architect Bruno Taut (1890–1938) begins his book *Die neue Baukunst in Europa und Amerika* (1929, published in English as *Modern Architecture*) with the Zeitgeist arguments: 'we have railway engines, ocean liners and automobiles, why do we build as if we were in the age of the horse-drawn carriage'.[13] Yet, in a barely disguised criticism of Le Corbusier's *Five Points Towards a New Architecture* (1926), Taut goes on to criticize the unthinking use of flat roofs, large strip windows, pilotis and so on. He goes on to warn against a fashionable imitation of modern engineering:

> You can imitate the forms of transportation – railway wagons, buses, automobiles, even airplanes, boats and ocean liners – and concoct a free-standing house made up of such elements, as if it was going to move about on wheels or sail off over the ocean. The word 'dynamic' became a slogan for a long time, whereas any buildings must remain static. ... You can identify motifs derived from this romantic attachment to machines and vehicles of transportation in several good architects today. Again and again we find balconies detailed with two or three horizontal tubes, as if to allow the seawater to evacuate easily in a storm, and the forms of a ship's bridge or promenade deck easily identifiable in modern house designs ...[14]

Taut went on to suggest that all you needed was a photograph of a ship, with identifiable parts such as the masts and funnels covered over with white paper, and a landscape drawn in the style of Le Corbusier to design a modern villa. He illustrated this with a sketch based on a photograph of *Australia*. The attractive dynamic curves natural to an ocean liner made no sense, according to Taut, in works of static architecture [203].

Just now I showed you the ocean liner *Paris*, which you regarded as a remarkable thing, superb. Then, from the same ship, I showed you the salon, which certainly left you feeling depressed; it seems in fact astonishing to find at the heart of such a perfectly ordered construction, such a contrast, such a contradiction, such a lack of coherence between the great lines of the ship and its interior decoration.[9]

So what did Le Corbusier find admirable in the ocean liner? One argument he made was that of physical scale. He illustrated *Aquitania* as a backdrop to Notre-Dame cathedral, the Tour Saint-Jacques, the Arc de Triomphe and the Hôtel de Crillon, arguing that urban building regulations made such ambition impossible.[10] A critic of one of his lectures, however, misunderstood this argument and claimed that Le Corbusier identified sheer scale as an aesthetic value in itself, a fallacy that the critic attributed to Romanticism.[11] Another virtue of the ocean liner, for Le Corbusier at least, was the distribution of space. Wealthy clients accepted a severely restricted scale for their sleeping quarters, compensated by vast and lavish dining rooms, ballrooms, promenade decks and other reception areas. This was a model for a different kind of living, comparable to the American apartment hotel, where cooking, recreation and leisure facilities were provided outside the individual apartment. It was also a model that fascinated Socialist and Communist designers of the period, who imagined a collective sharing of food production, child-rearing and social interaction.

In the April 1931 issue of *Plans* magazine, Le Corbusier analysed the space distribution on board *Bremen*:

> I must point out that the *luxury suites*, which are intended only for the most exceptionally wealthy passengers, measure

Le Corbusier would have agreed that imitating the forms of transportation in architecture was a mistake. This seems to have been one of his criticisms of Eileen Gray's (1878–1976) design for E-1027 (1929), her Modernist villa in Roquebrune-Cap-Martin, south-eastern France. Gray had taken pleasure to evoke not only the presence of the sea (in her rugs and the marine chart in the living room) but also explicitly to cite ocean liners, in the villa's railings, canvas awnings and a life-saver on the balcony. Her Transat chair, based on ocean-going deckchairs, was a delightful conceit, taking a functional object and turning it into an Art Deco masterpiece,

with its black lacquered or sycamore wooden laths immaculately finished and jointed with nickelled connectors [204]. Le Corbusier even referred to Gray's beautiful villa Tempe a Pailla at Castellar, near Menton, as 'that submarine of Modernism', although the naval references are hard to discern.

THE MODERNIST AT SEA

Le Corbusier himself seems to have enjoyed travel by sea. Offered a place on the Hindenburg Zeppelin for his trip to Brazil in 1936, he said:

---

203 OPPOSITE

Sketch of a modern villa based on *Australia* by Bruno Taut, *c.*1929, from *Die neue Baukunst in Europa und Amerika* (Stuttgart, 1929)

204 ABOVE

Fauteuil Transatlantique (Transat chair), designed by Eileen Gray
Paris, France, 1925–30
Sycamore, chromium-plated metal and faux leather made from a kaolin-filled polyacrylate resin (1960s)
GIVEN BY THE DESIGNER
V&A: CIRC.578–1971

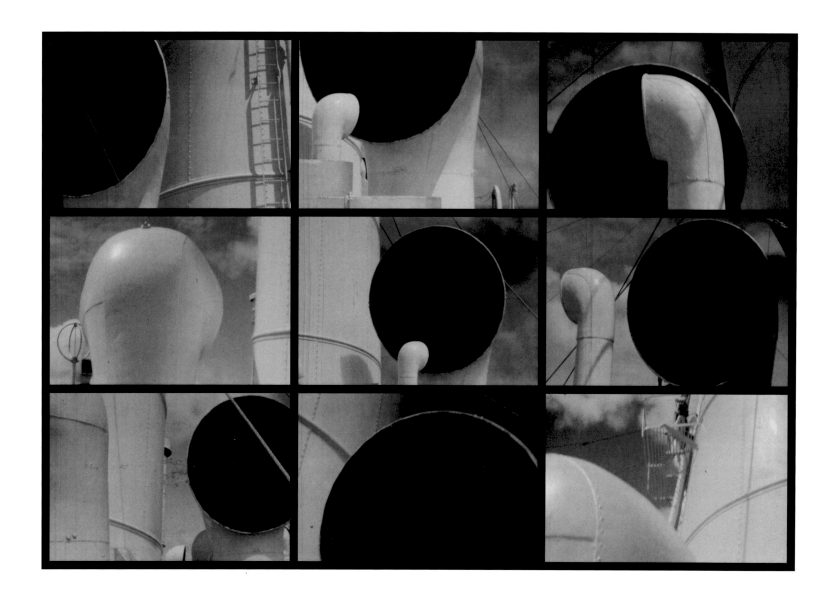

205 ABOVE

Photographs taken on *Conte Biancamano*,

by Le Corbusier

1936

Photographs taken with a 16-mm film camera

FONDATION LE CORBUSIER, PARIS

I have no desire to go by Zeppelin. I would much rather take the boat – in true bourgeois fashion – and spend 11 days of rest and meditation. The Zeppelin, on the other hand, like an aeroplane, is a tool in which you become very bored. I consider sea voyages as a haven of tranquillity in my busy life ...[15]

In the event, he did travel by airship (not on the Hindenburg but on board the Graf Zeppelin, because of a change of schedule). He had crossed the Atlantic once, in 1929, en route to Buenos Aires on the *Massilia* (1920) – 'a trip like this is enormously comforting'[16] – returning two months later on board the *Lutetia* (1915) from Rio de Janeiro to Bordeaux in the company of Josephine Baker (1906–75). He noted, however, in a letter to his mother that he chose to avoid the social temptations of the ocean liner.

I live a very solitary life on board, by choice. There are countless opportunities to amuse oneself. Every evening there's a party. I don't go to them. I am anti-social. In 'bourgeois' circles these people give me a sinking feeling. They have no thoughts in their heads except those derived from others.[17]

By contrast, he loved the Punch and Judy shows in the afternoon: 'I amuse myself royally. I would like to compose puppet plays. It's a magnificent medium for communicating to one's peers.'[18] Le Corbusier also admitted that his best friend on the trip was the PT instructor who gave him a workout at 7 am every morning – 'a terrific chap, a real free spirit'. This man had written his life story and Le Corbusier read all 300 pages. He thought he might have discovered a 'Bauchant of literature', a reference to the primitive painter André Bauchant (1873–1958) whom Le Corbusier had befriended in the 1920s.

Le Corbusier also made some influential friends while travelling at sea. In October 1935, on board *Normandie,* he became friends with the industrialist André Jaoul, who would later commission two houses from him in the suburb of Neuilly-sur-Seine in Paris and who helped him meet people in New York. And yet, although he described the trip as 'a dream', there is not a word in Le Corbusier's letters or diaries about the decor of *Normandie*.[19]

Next year, Le Corbusier returned from Brazil on *Conte Biancamano* (1925). The Florentine Coppedè brothers decorated the ship in the Italian Renaissance style with exotic Art Nouveau furniture by Carlo Bugatti (1856–1940). Le Corbusier noted that, on crossing the equator, the stewards had 'lit' a fire in the enormous Renaissance fireplace in the smoking room. 'Don't worry!' he added, 'it is only tinted mica lit by electricity. We made them switch it off; it was physically insufferable.'[20] Every evening, Le Corbusier dined with Bertie Landsberg, a Brazilian count who owned Palladio's Villa Foscari, where Le Corbusier had stayed the year before.[21] Le Corbusier had a 16-mm cine camera with him, which was capable of taking still pictures. He took over 700 pictures on this trip but, consistent with his aesthetic, there are none of the historicist interiors and only one of his fellow first-class passengers. Instead, there are some astonishing views of functional parts of the ship – funnels, air intake cowls, pulleys, lifeboats, winches and coils of rope – as well as a number of photos of the third-class passengers let out onto the bow of the ship for a breath of fresh air [205].[22]

A MODERNIST CABIN

This double standard, taking pleasure in the luxury of first-class travel while celebrating only the mechanical aspects of the ship, is characteristic of Modernist views towards ocean liners. For the ocean liner to be a true 'problem' for the modern designer, it would have to be cast in functional and material terms consistent with the engineering of the vessel. This is exactly what happened in 1933, when the French Office technique pour l'utilisation de l'acier (OTUA, the Technical Office for the Use of Steel) commissioned a number of architects, designers and construction companies to design an all-steel ship's cabin. The OTUA was an industrial lobby group dedicated to improving an understanding of the potential of steel products in architecture and design, which was doubly motivated by the crash of 1929 to keep the French steel industry afloat. The key problem, as presented by the members of the commission, was fire. Of the ships discussed so far, *Paris* suffered a serious fire in 1929 before burning and sinking in Le Havre harbour in 1939. *Bremen* was set alight by an arsonist in March 1941. *Normandie* burned in New York during refitting in 1942. As the architect and designer Robert Mallet-Stevens (1886–1945) noted in the OTUA's journal, 77 ships were completely burnt out between 1930 and 1934, while a further 1,523 ships were seriously damaged by fire.[23] The solution was not to blame whatever caused each fire but to make fire on board ships impossible, or at least less likely. The trouble was that the luxury liner had reduced the fire resistance of the more functional immigration ships, with the introduction of more and more exotic materials. Some experiments in creating all-steel cabins had already been made by G.A. Harvey and Co. of London, Roneo of Romford and Art Steel. M. Séguenot, OTUA's chief engineer, had worked up a detailed specification for a steel partition with sound insulation and excellent fire resistance. It was

based on this specification that the selected architects, associated
with different manufacturers, were asked to design passenger
cabins for first-, second- or third-class passengers.[24]

René Herbst (1891–1982), the leading figure of the Union des
Artistes Modernes (UAM), co-ordinated the competition and also
submitted a design [208]. The UAM was formed by a breakaway
group of Art Deco designers who wanted to move towards a more
modern position. Charlotte Perriand (1903–99) was one of the
early members, and Le Corbusier and Pierre Jeanneret (1896–1967)
later joined the group. Pierre Chareau (1883–1950), Robert Mallet-
Stevens, Pierre Barbe (1900–2004) and Georges-Henri Pingusson
(1894–1978) all inhabited the border between Art Deco and
Modernism, designing tubular steel furniture and modern

207 ABOVE

Third-class cabin for the OTUA competition for all-
steel cabins, by Robert Mallet-Stevens with Flambo,
from *Acier* (1935/8)

PHILLIPS LIBRARY, PEABODY ESSEX MUSEUM

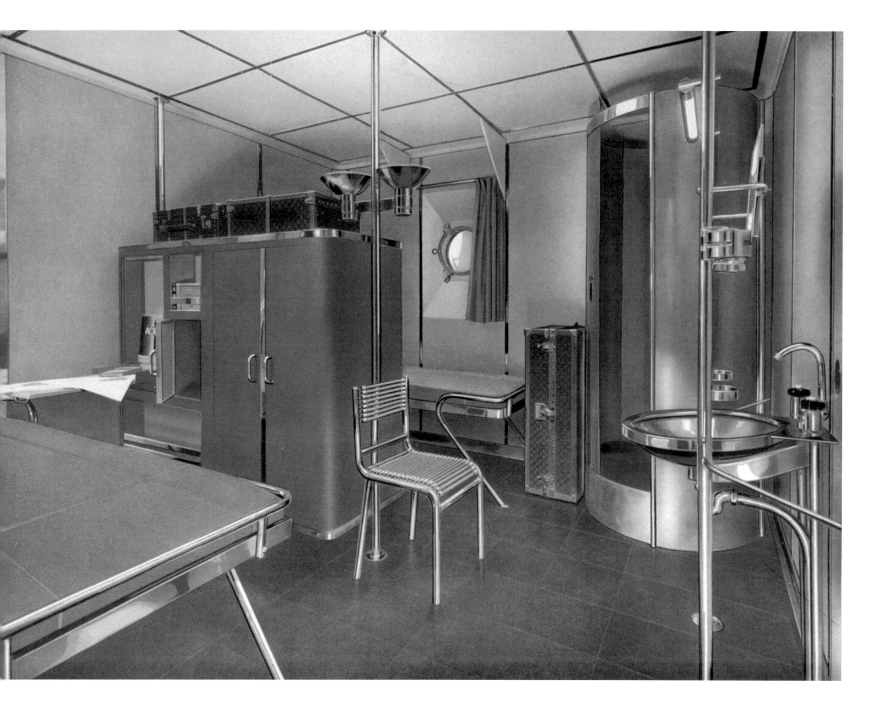

buildings that usually retained enough of a decorative element
to draw condemnation from Modernist purists. Nevertheless this
competition, with its strict functional regulations, met all the
requirements of Modernist exigencies. Each team had to
demonstrate the fire resistance and weight of their design and give
details of the partition sections. The competition was exhibited at
the Salon d'Automne in 1934 and the Salon Nautique International
in 1935, and made a big impression.

The question faced by all the designers and architects was how
to make all-steel, fireproof cabins appeal to passengers who were
used to wood veneer, lacquer and textile surfaces? As Léandre
Vaillat (1878–1952), normally a critic of Modernism, very reasonably
explained:

Whereas the apartments in which we live on terra firma often parody the style of the ocean liners, the cabins and salons of the latter try to copy, with an ignorance that might be comic if it did not so often turn into tragedy, the decor of houses and apartments on dry land. In both cases, no truth, no honesty but a decorative mask which is insufficient to protect against asphyxia from smoke and fumes.[25]

Further problems presented themselves during the project however. Designers discovered, for example, that they had to find ways of making the sheet steel sections rigid, reducing the squeaking effect produced by the ship's movements and distributing electricity and lighting in a way that was both safe and accessible. Chareau introduced rigidity by bowing the wall sections, as he had with the cupboards in the famous Maison de Verre in Paris that he had recently designed with Bernard Bijvoet (1889–1979). He also proposed the same system of electric light switches in chrome-plated steel boxes attached to the electric conduit tubes.

Some of the construction companies associated with this venture already had experience of building in steel. Constructions Métalliques Fillod, for example, had exhibited steel houses in 1929 and Le Corbusier had used their hollow-wall steel panels as an inspiration for the house he designed for Hélène de Mandrot (1867–1948) in 1929–30.[26] Jean Prouvé (1901–84), who was just starting out as an industrial producer of sheet-steel products, created one of the most radical designs for a third-class cabin with the architect Marcel Gascoin (1907–86). Prouvé explained that the steel panels had no horizontal joints and could therefore be cleaned by pressure hose [206].

The principle of 'building-in' all the furniture, making cleaning easier and reducing clutter, was a key feature of Modernist thinking in interior design. Le Corbusier's slogan, that furniture should be replaced by equipment, is here perfectly exemplified, and it is

209 ABOVE
'Chaise Mi-Longue', by René Herbst
Paris, France, 1931
Nickel-plated tubes with metal strappings (sandows)
VILLE DE BOULOGNE-BILLANCOURT, MA-30/
MUSÉE DES ANNÉES TRENTE: 2016.0.36

210 OPPOSITE
Model for 5 rue Denfert-Rochereau, Boulogne-Billancourt (1932–8), designed by Georges-Henri Pingusson, and built on top of Maison Ternisien (1924–6), designed by Le Corbusier. Model by Philippe Velu
Paris, France, 1998
Cardboard, wood and resin
VILLE DE BOULOGNE-BILLANCOURT, MA-30/
MUSÉE DES ANNÉES TRENTE: 2013.0.94

evident that the architect admired Prouvé and sought opportunities to work with him. He adopted the stainless-steel washbasin in his own work (for example in the *cabanon* he designed in 1952 at Roquebrune-Cap-Martin).

Mallet-Stevens, first president of the UAM, designed one of the most elegant of the third-class cabins, using Flambo, his preferred firm of carpenters, to assemble the elements [207]. He used built-in cupboards and the space under the bunk beds to accommodate luggage and clothing. All the elements in his cabin, including four bunk beds and four washbasins, are made from stainless steel. His interior is characteristic of the functional but elegant UAM look.

In many ways, it was easier to design third-class cabins, with their built-in economies, rather than trying to meet the needs of the first-class passengers. Herbst exhibited a first-class cabin in which his origins as a designer of tubular steel furniture and Art Deco shop fronts are apparent. The requirements of a first-class cabin are met with a shower, a writing desk and an additional bed for a child without the ingenious economy of the Prouvé design. The architect Georges-Henri Pingusson – who had a taste for the *paquebot* style, as seen in the hotel Latitude 43 near Saint-Tropez – also had a go at a first-class cabin. The horizontal pleating introduced into the sheet steel to ensure rigidity created a decorative effect and the well-upholstered furniture provided a little more warmth compared to Herbst's design, although with an added fire risk.

These designs, and the discussion they caused in the press were the closest designers came to tackling the mixture of aesthetic and technical problems of the ocean liner from the perspective of the Modernists.

A final ironical note: between 1932 and 1938, Pingusson built a small block of flats, in a marine style, on top of a villa Le Corbusier had designed for the musician Paul Ternisien (1924–6), of which only the triangular projection survived [210]. It seems that the *paquebot* style won, after all.

STREAMLINING

GHISLAINE WOOD

IN 'SPEED. TOMORROW' A CHAPTER in his book *Horizons* (1932), the American industrial designer Norman Bel Geddes (1893–1958) signalled the importance of ship design for contemporary architects, artists and designers, writing: 'For years when aboard ship, if you are observing, you have seen better modern architecture than you have ashore.'[1] As the most complex industrial objects of the age, liners acquired a key role in Modernist culture that was at once typological and metaphorical. The liner presented models for new ways of structuring modern living while also providing – in the form of 'streamlining' – a new iconography, symbolic of progress and technological advancement. Streamlining emerged as a style in the United States in the late 1920s, and was in large part inspired by the design of liners. In turn it affected the design of everything from cars and buildings, to pencil sharpeners and beauty compacts. Bel Geddes's *Horizons* did much to promote streamlining and,

211 ABOVE
'Normandie' pitcher, designed by Peter Müller-Munk, made by Revere Copper and Brass Inc.
New York, United States, 1935
Chrome-plated brass
MIOTTEL MUSEUM, BERKELEY, CA

212 RIGHT
Starboard view of the Coca-Cola Bottling Plant,
Los Angeles, designed by Robert V. Derrah, 1936–7

213 OPPOSITE ABOVE
Model for a streamlined ocean liner, by Norman Bel Geddes
1932
Wood and paint
GIFT OF NORMAN BEL GEDDES, 1941
MUSEUM OF THE CITY OF NEW YORK: M41.29A-B

although never realized, his own design for an ocean liner was one of the most ambitious streamlined designs of the age. The project stood no chance of coming to fruition in a notoriously conservative industry that favoured incremental improvement over radical departures in design, but it did away with the notion of a floating hotel and created a ship that was entirely new and powerfully evocative of modernity. Its accentuated teardrop form, theoretically capable of extreme speed, presented a vision for the future [213].

Many modern architects and designers emulated the technological forms of ships to suggest progress, and designs were often mimetic, such as Georges-Henri Pingusson's (1894–1978) Parisian apartment block in the form of a ship's prow (1932–8) [210] or Robert V. Derrah's (1895–1946) iconic Coca-Cola Bottling Plant (1936–7) in Los Angeles with its portholes, walkways and

simulated rivets [212]. The idea of the liner as symbolic of modernity also entered the home in designed objects around the world, from the American designer Ruth Reeves's (1892–1966) *Manhattan* hanging with its fragmented, Cubist-inspired liner, to the Japanese kimono and haori printed with scenes of liners and modern cityscapes. Innumerable mass-produced objects were also enclosed in moulded, contoured shells, the forms of which were derived from machines such as liners, zeppelins, trains and planes, giving the illusion of speed. Some pieces, such as Peter Müller-Munk's (1904–67) 'Normandie' pitcher [211] or Steubenville's ceramic service of the same name, directly evoked the design of ships. However, the fashion for streamlining was relatively short-lived and the Second World War marked the end of the style.

CHAPTER 9

THE LINER AS MACHINE

THE LINER AS MACHINE

ANNA FERRARI

Here was something unusual, certainly, by one of those Americans who love to smash tradition by doing unusual things. ... It was a flaming, vivid affair. Unmistakeably it was the picture of a great ship, and more unmistakeably the great ship had three immense smokestacks that struck one, so to speak, and made no apologies for it.[1]

WHEN GERALD MURPHY (1888–1964) exhibited his painting *Boatdeck* at the Paris Salon des Indépendants in February 1924, it caused an outcry worthy of a revolutionary work of art [215].[2] Paul Signac, president of the Society of Independent Artists, and several members of the committee resigned, albeit briefly, when Murphy refused to move his work from the American section to a less prominent space. A New Yorker and the son of a wealthy leather goods store-owner, Murphy had come to Paris in 1921 with his wife Sara and discovered the work of Pablo Picasso, Georges Braque, Juan Gris and Henri Matisse. Murphy at once decided to become a painter. He took lessons from Russian artist Natalia Goncharova and soon gained recognition from Picasso and Fernand Léger, who praised him as 'the only *American* painter in Paris'.[3]

Although *Boatdeck* was gigantic (at over 5 m tall it dwarfed the other works on display) it was the subject itself that the reporters suggested was iconoclastic.[4] A photograph of the painting at the Salon reveals its gleaming funnels and sharply delineated ventilation cowls boldly standing out against other works representing traditional subjects painted in a Cubist style. Murphy explained that he had based his painting on his photographs of *Olympic* (1911) and *Paris* (1921) on which he had recently travelled [216].[5] Towards the end of his life, the artist remembered how he had been 'struck by the look (especially with the floodlights at night) of the huge almost vertical red-lead-colored smoke-stacks against the sky ... dead-white mushrooming ventilators with black, gaping pure-circle mouths cut across with white rods spaced into six geometrical segments. Gray, white, black & red-lead: the whole.'[6]

In the first decades of the twentieth century, many Modernists recognized that liners, among other new modes of transport such as the aeroplane or the car, were a worthy subject matter reflecting the radical changes occurring in modern life. In Europe before the First World War, the Futurists glorified the machine as a symbol of modern times and the antithesis of the past that they denigrated. In the Futurist manifesto of 1909, the movement's leader Filippo Tommaso Marinetti (1876–1944) praised the 'beauty of speed', and evoked 'daring steamers' as well as 'full-breasted locomotives ... the gliding flight of the aeroplanes ... [and] the racing automobile with its explosive breath', all of which he provocatively claimed were 'more beautiful than the Victory of Samothrace'.[7] After the First World War's unprecedented casualties resulting from the mechanization of warfare, the Futurists' violent rhetoric associated with the machine became unacceptable. The machine nonetheless continued to inspire awe and signify the dawn of a new epoch for many. In 1923, Léger defended a machine aesthetic, confidently affirming that: 'Geometric relations, volumes, lines and coloured surfaces (aeroplanes, automobiles, agricultural machinery, all commercial objects, etc.) can be beautiful, it is *absolutely indisputable*.'[8] This was the premise of two pivotal exhibitions in New York that asserted the relation between art and machines, machine parts or industrial complexes. The 1927 *Machine-Age Exposition*, organized by the Little Review Gallery, juxtaposed machines, photographs and drawings of machines with painting, sculpture and architecture by international modern artists to show the interrelation and influence between art and industry. The Museum of Modern Art went on to cement the aesthetic status of industrial objects when it opened its *Machine Art* exhibition in 1934, where the curator, Philip Johnson, and the Museum Director, Alfred H. Barr Jr, presented objects such as ball bearings, springs and an outboard propeller as though they were works of art.

Against this backdrop, the ocean liner became a key iconographic motif of the inter-war period. The liner that Modernist

214 PREVIOUS

Paquebot 'Paris', by Charles Demuth

United States, 1921–2

Oil on canvas

GIFT OF FERDINAND HOWALD

COLUMBUS MUSEUM OF ART, OH: 1931.139

215 ABOVE

Boatdeck by Gerald Murphy on display at the Paris Salon des Indépendants, 1924 (*Boston Evening Transcript*, 15 March 1924)

artists represented was not exactly that advertised by the shipping lines, which promised fast crossings in luxurious and grand interiors laden with nationalist overtones. For these painters and photographers, the appeal of the liner lay in the ship as machine – whether for its speed, its ability to convey a modern sensation and transform the perception of time and space, or its formal beauty and its metaphoric association with New York and other metropolises as symbols of modernity.

'A MODERN SENSATION': EUROPEAN AVANT-GARDES AND THE LINER IN THE 1910S

In early 1913, the Frenchman Félix Del Marle (1889–1952) met the Italian Gino Severini (1883–1966) who introduced him to Futurism. Soon after, Del Marle declared his allegiance to Futurism and his pursuit of a new type of painting that took 'a modern sensation' as its starting point.[9] In a text indebted to the then-popular philosopher Henri Bergson (1859–1941), Del Marle explained he wished to paint the 'sensation of dynamism', or movement, itself rather than a fixed moment in a series of successive moments.[10] At the same time, Del Marle began work on a painting representing liners in port.[11] Le Port represented liners and the numerous sensations experienced when travelling; feelings with which Del Marle would have been well acquainted, having worked in the engine rooms of Compagnie des Chargeurs Réunis liners between 1907 and 1909.[12] In a surviving study, Del Marle fragmented the picture plane, representing two hulls in the centre with, in the distance, smoke billowing from funnels, framed by an industrial iron bridge [217]. The upper half of the painting is bathed in light, yet the lower half is a night view. 'Simultaneity' as an expression of modern life was a central idea of Futurism. Del Marle conveys the impression of a multitude of events occurring at the same time, suggesting the then-novel experience of travelling vast distances at speed. As he explained to Marinetti:

> representing a liner, in a port, while expressing the profiles characteristic of the ship, its essential properties and noises,

will evoke for example the arrival at the port of destination, or life on board, during the crossing or even the liner plunging into the night, all lights ablaze.[13]

The painted lettering also contributes to the sense of simultaneity, bringing to mind different places. In the lower left, a leaflet or poster reads 'New York', which echoes the American flag above, while the red and white abbreviation 'CGT' stands for the French shipping line, Compagnie Générale Transatlantique. Both references suggest the transatlantic route, but 'Niagara', inscribed on one of the hulls, identifies a new liner completed in 1913 for the Union Steam Ship Company of New Zealand, which was intended for the trans-Pacific route. Le Port therefore synthesizes the whirling speed of modern life and the global routes criss-crossed by liners.

As modern symbols of engineering and speed, liners were a priviledged subject for Futurists. About the same time, Christopher Richard Wynne Nevinson (1889–1946) painted The Arrival, which depicts a liner in port [218]. Nevinson was struck by the Futurist Exhibition, held at the Sackville Gallery London in March 1912, which featured works by Severini, Umberto Boccioni, Carlo Carrà and Luigi Russolo. Nevinson met Severini and returned with him to Paris. He cemented his affiliation with Futurism when he co-authored the 'Vital English Art: Futurist Manifesto' with Marinetti in 1914. The Arrival focuses on the fragmented prow of a transatlantic ship sailing into port amid iron bridges, maritime signal flags and the smoke of tugboats. While the theme and pictorial devices are similar to Del Marle's work, Nevinson's strong diagonals of ropes and iron bridges create a more ordered structure.

For Francis Picabia (1879–1953), the experience on board La Lorraine (1900), which took him to New York in 1913, proved decisive. Where for Del Marle the liner stood for simultaneity, for Picabia it was inextricably linked to his experience of New York. In January 1913, Picabia and his wife Gabrielle Buffet-Picabia (1881–1985) sailed to America to attend the opening of the landmark Armory Show, which was the largest exhibition of contemporary art ever organized in America and introduced avant-garde art to the country. Picabia exhibited several works that drew the attention of the press and earned him the reputation of art 'rebel'.[14]

While in New York, Picabia painted a highly abstract watercolour recalling his encounter on board La Lorraine with the dancer and actress Stacia Napierkowska, who was on her way to perform in New York. Her dance rehearsals during the crossing bewitched Picabia and other passengers.[15] Danseuse étoile sur un transatlantique (Star Dancer on an Ocean Liner) refers to this encounter in a highly abstracted watercolour of black forms, grey

shapes fading into white and red funnel-like rectangles [219]. The dancer Picabia refers to in the title remains teasingly elusive.

Danseuse étoile sur un transatlantique is as much about this meeting as Picabia's stimulating and invigorating experience of the modern city he discovered on his arrival. It was one of 16 watercolours painted in New York that he presented at a one-man show at Alfred Stieglitz's '291' gallery in the spring of 1913. Picabia himself explained to the press 'the studies which I have made since my arrival ... express the spirit of New York as I feel it, and the crowded streets of your city as I feel them, their surging, their unrest, their commercialism, and their atmospheric charm.'[16] In exhibiting these watercolours together at 291, Picabia suggested he fused Napierkowska's seductive dance on board the liner with the dynamic life of the city.

During the First World War, Picabia returned to New York where fellow French artists Marcel Duchamp (1887–1968) and Albert Gleizes (1881–1953) joined him. Gleizes had exhibited at the Parisian salons that turned Cubism into a recognized (albeit mocked) movement between 1911 and 1912, and had co-authored the hugely influential theoretical account *Du Cubisme* (On Cubism, 1912) with Jean Metzinger (1883–1956). He was revolted by the war and as soon as he was demobilized in 1915, he married Juliette Roche (1884–1980) and they sailed to New York.

Gleizes's *In Port* (1917) depicts another busy port scene with jostling prows, sterns, funnels and skyscrapers that appear stacked on top of one another [220]. The superimposed, brightly coloured planes merge these multiple viewpoints while pivoting the scene, provoking a sense of disorientation and movement. Gleizes combined motifs sketched in New York and Barcelona, where he and Roche lived between May and December 1916.[17] *In Port* echoes the subject of Del Marle's earlier painting and Picabia's fusion of liner and city but, painted during the war, the interweaving of motifs from Barcelona and New York betrays the artist's sense of uprootedness.

Gleizes recognized the significance of modern travel, and in particular ocean liners, in altering his conception of space and time.[18] As he explained to a friend, the poet Henri-Martin Barzun in 1916, in a passage that could easily relate to *In Port*:

219 ABOVE

Danseuse étoile sur un transatlantique (Star Dancer
on an Ocean Liner), by Francis Picabia

New York, United States, 1913

Watercolour on paper

220 OPPOSITE

In Port, by Albert Gleizes

New York, United States, 1917

Oil and sand on cardboard

The knowledge of vast horizons that trains and ocean liners have opened to me has drawn me away forever from metaphysical spaces. ... Our space has not been used as it should, far from being exhausted, it flourishes more multiple than ever ... And we are in the age of syntheses. One hour in the life of a man of today raises more levels, insights, actions, than one year in the life of a man in the other century – it is what I am trying to say in my art. ... Painting today must crystallize a thousand sensations in an authentic order...[19]

'THE PICTURE OF A GREAT SHIP':
THE AMERICAN AVANT-GARDE AND THE LINER

After the war, the liner emerged in American avant-garde painting with *Paquebot 'Paris'* (1921–2) by Charles Demuth (1883–1935), *Boatdeck* (before early 1924) by Murphy and *Upper Deck* (1929) by Charles Sheeler (1883–1965) [214, 215 & 222]. These works are similar in their metonymic focus on liner machinery above deck and the conspicuous absence of people. Demuth and Sheeler, who were later identified as part of the loosely defined American avant-garde Precisionists, were indebted to European artists, some of whom they met at the New York home of avant-garde art collectors Walter and Louise Arensberg. In particular, the Cubists' flattening of space and Picabia's and Duchamp's embrace of the machine proved important.

In November 1921, after several months spent in the French capital, Demuth sailed back to America on board *Paris*. During the journey he produced a series of sketches that served as the basis for *Paquebot 'Paris'*. Demuth's imagery was strikingly new, focusing on white ventilators and two red and black funnels framed so close that the top of the first is cropped out.[20] Between 1916 and 1920, Demuth evolved a new style influenced by Paul Cézanne and Cubism, flattening space and abstracting forms. This development was accompanied by a shift in subject matter as Demuth, who had painted watercolours of flowers, also began to depict the modern industrial landscape of factories, smokestacks and water towers near his native Lancaster in Pennsylvania.[21] Such scenes and subjects seemed to capture America's new identity as the undisputed world leader of industrial production after the First World War, at a time when intellectuals such as Demuth's friend, the poet William Carlos Williams, advocated indigenous American subjects and styles. Demuth's new imagery in *Paquebot 'Paris'*, focusing on the machinery of the liner, can thus be understood as a celebration of the machine and, metaphorically, of America.

The title, referencing the city where Demuth had spent several months, may also suggest a symbolic acknowledgement of his encounters there. In a letter written to Stieglitz from Paris, Demuth mentioned two art journals of particular interest: *L'Amour de l'Art* and *L'Esprit Nouveau*.[22] The latter was published by Charles-Edouard Jeanneret (who would soon establish himself as Le Corbusier) and Amédée Ozenfant, who together had penned the Purist manifesto, *Après le Cubisme* (After Cubism, 1918), in which they argued for a clarified aesthetic and celebrated the manufactured object. Demuth was familiar with this text and is likely to have been aware as well of Jeanneret and Ozenfant's article 'Purisme' published in *L'Esprit Nouveau* in 1920.[23] They praised subjects such as mass-produced objects that resulted from a 'purifying' mechanical selection. Examples included modes of transport like 'boats and cars'.[24]

The 1927 *Machine-Age Exposition* held in New York signalled international artists' embrace of the machine. It sought to draw a parallel between the artist and the engineer and presented art together with objects such as propellers, a model of a plane or a gyroscope stabilizer. Sheeler was part of the artists' committee and, although he did not exhibit, his involvement indicates his interest in machinery at the time. Late in 1927, he accepted a commission

221 OPPOSITE

Upper Deck, by Charles Sheeler

*c.*1928

Gelatin silver print

222 ABOVE

Upper Deck, by Charles Sheeler

United States, 1929

Oil on canvas

Looking as though it had been built with
an Erector set, this boat-and-davit on
the "Liberté" port side is on top but a very
robust, electrically powered mechanism.

Gallery

Ship shapes and shadows

Just as time puts a soft patina on land-based buildings—and often improves
their appearance—so it adds a softening touch to the lines and forms of naval
architecture. The caky, almost edible quality that shipboard structures take
on after years of use and exposure is noted in the pictures on these pages.
Several corners of the R.M.S. "Queen Mary" and the S.S. "Liberté" were
chosen in illustration of how patina is acquired at sea. It comes down, in
effect, to paint on paint over paint. The result might rather be called impasto.
   The "Queen Mary" is 24 years old now. But truly venerable, as primary
Atlantic liners go, is the "Liberté". She is 30. Yet her lines and forms are
still handsome and, indeed, stylish.

122

from the Ford Motor Company to photograph the new River Rouge
plant in Michigan. The resulting series of photographs focusing on
parts of machinery designed to increase efficiency and productivity
attests to this fascination. Sheeler later expressed the fundamental
Modernist appreciation of the functional when he recalled the Ford
plant in his autobiography: 'There I was to find forms which looked
right because they had been designed with their eventual utility
in view and in the successful fulfilment of their purpose it was
inevitable that beauty could be attained.'[25]

   Such ideas probably informed his shots of a liner taken around
1928, when he was commissioned to photograph a vessel named
Majestic for a brochure [221].[26] In 1929, Sheeler painted *Upper
Deck*, a crisply delineated close-up view of white-grey fan units with
electric generators that served to ventilate the lower decks of the
ship.[27] The painting is closely based on his photograph although he
reduced contrast and abstracted details, eliminating rivets.

   Sheeler had previously employed the symbolism of ocean liners
in *Manhatta*, a documentary film made in 1920 or 1921 with the
photographer Paul Strand (1890–1976). The film traces a day in
the vibrant city through disconnected sequences presenting New
York as an urban metropolis of skyscrapers and thronging streets,
and features *Aquitania* (1914) docked in New York. In the film the
liner stands as a metaphor for modernity and the city, whereas
Upper Deck appears to be a statement about Sheeler's technique and
his preoccupation with form and structure as well as a testament
to the authenticity of a functional machine. For Sheeler, this work
proved to be a pivotal moment in his career and from this point on
his photography played a determining role in his painting, often
serving as the basis for his compositions.

   When Walker Evans (1903–75) took up photography in
1927 following his return from Paris to New York, he initially
focused on the city's architecture, shot in a style comparable to
Sheeler's.[28] Evans's photographs of *Liberté* (completed in 1930 as
Norddeutscher Lloyd's *Europa* and in 1950 as the CGT's *Liberté*)
and *Queen Mary* (1936) taken over 30 years later in 1958, however,
convey an altogether different idea of the liner than Sheeler's
pristine machinery [223]. Evans photographed mechanisms
such as the winch system of a lifeboat, a valve wheel and a

ventilation cowl, relishing their worn aspect, or the 'softening touch' of patina, revealing the years of service of both ageing liners.[29] In the evocative text he wrote to accompany his portfolio of photographs in *Architectural Forum*, Evans described the 'caky, almost edible quality that shipboard structures take on after years of use and exposure' and how 'paint on paint over paint' produced 'impasto'.[30] Evans's reaction to the liner not only reflected his interest in vernacular architecture and structures, but also revealed the changing status of the liner in the decades after the Second World War, when commercial aviation superseded sea travel.

The liner no longer stood for speed, progress and the most advanced engineering, and instead Evans noted the age of each ship, remarking that *Liberté*, at 30 years old, was 'truly venerable'. Still, even after the liner's heyday, it continued to be identified with the metropolis. In 1964, Hungarian émigré André Kertész (1894–1985) played on these associations in his photograph *New York*, conflating the city's architecture seen in a reflection, the model of a liner and a couple leaning against railings in a visual synthesis of the city [224].

---

223 OPPOSITE

'Ship Shapes and Shadows', by Walker Evans, in *Architectural Forum* (October 1958)

224 ABOVE

New York (Model Ship and Reflection, New York), by André Kertész
1964
Gelatin silver print
MUSÉE NATIONAL D'ART MODERNE, PARIS:
AM 1978-198

CHAPTER 10

THE AFTERLIFE OF SHIPS

BRITISH AIRWAYS

THE AFTERLIFE OF SHIPS

DANIEL FINAMORE AND GHISLAINE WOOD

THE SECOND WORLD WAR marked the beginning of the end for the ocean liner as the primary means of transoceanic travel. Although commercial aviation started before the war, the need for reliable, long-range aircraft, particularly bombers and troop carriers, spurred its growth. Furthermore, the development of the jet engine and tremendous investment made in the infrastructure of airports and radio-navigation technology laid the foundations for a flourishing post-war industry. The De Havilland Comet (1952) and the Boeing 707 (1958) marked the rise of a new generation of long-haul aeroplanes with the capacity to carry a large number of passengers. By the 1970s, the success of commercial air travel coupled with the steep rise in oil prices had resulted in most liners being taken out of service [225].

Liners were usually constructed with anticipated lifespans of approximately 20 years (paying off their construction costs only after many seasons of operation) and most of the world's historic liners have now been lost. A small number remain, however, and their survival has not been accidental, but rather the result of owners whose interests in preserving and promoting them has outweighed practical financial decisions.

In an ambitious conservation project in 1970, Brunel's *Great Britain* (1845) was towed back to Bristol from the Falkland Islands (where the vessel had served for many years as a coal bunker before being scuttled) and was restored as a historic ship and visitor attraction. The Nippon Yusen Kaisha Line's *Hikawa Maru* (1930) sailed in one capacity or another for 30 years until being tied up in Yokohama harbour to serve as a maritime museum, hostel and restaurant. The modest liner carried fewer than 350 passengers on the trans-Pacific route, until much of her interior was gutted during conversion to a Second World War hospital ship. Now partially restored, the metalwork and other interior elements display a European *moderne* aesthetic infused with Japanese decorative elements. Other liners such as *Rotterdam* (1959) and *Queen Mary* (1936) have become floating hotels. Since 1967, *Queen Mary*, an exemplar of surviving British Art Deco design, has sat dockside in Long Beach, California, as a self-contained hotel, convention centre and entertainment destination [226]. Many cabins and public spaces on 'the ship of beautiful woods' retain their original panelling and artwork, most notably in the Grand Salon. The diverse on-board entertainments (such as popular period-dress events) offer what is perhaps the most effective simulation of the ocean-liner experience available today.

SS *United States* (1952) has been less fortunate since coming out of service in 1969. The liner has been the subject of multiple studies for repurposing as a cruise ship, hotel, casino and centrepiece of shore-side revitalization projects. Furniture and fittings were sold at auction in 1984, and in 1993 the ship was towed to Sevastopol, Ukraine, for an extensive and a highly

225 PREVIOUS

Poster showing *QE2* and a British Airways Concorde

flying in formation with the Royal Air Force Red

Arrows over the Solent, photograph by Arthur

Gibson

1985

Colour offset lithograph

BRITISH AIRWAYS HERITAGE COLLECTION

THE AFTERLIFE OF SHIPS

controversial asbestos abatement before returning to Philadelphia. Despite dedicated efforts by the current owners, a non-profit group committed to preserving and restoring the ship, it remains at the time of writing a stripped-out hull in financial limbo on the Delaware River. The most recent analysis by an ambitious cruise line concluded that the costs for restoration would far exceed a new build, and the nostalgic appeal of a 1950s design with powerful nationalist symbolism was not an adequate incentive.

QE2 (1969) meanwhile ended her cruising career in 2008 in Dubai where she remains today having been sold to an investment arm of the Dubai Government for $100 million. With original furniture and decorations still on board, she is a time capsule of British design at the 'dawn of the age of postmodernity' and represents 'the pop palette and novel materials of Swinging London'.[1] The once iconic British Liner sits frozen in time, her future incarnation as yet unknown.

For many years, the rusting, partial hull of SS *America* sat off the coast of Fuerteventura in the Canary Islands, where it came to rest having broken free from its tow across the Atlantic in bad weather. The poignant sight of the giant decaying structure slowly dissolving into the sea formed part of the tourist economy of the island until it finally disappeared. The power of the ocean liner to inspire awe and wonder even in its afterlife remains undiminished.

Another remarkable survival is a panel from a luxury suite of the *Andrea Doria* (1953), which was struck by the *Stockholm* in fog and sank in 1956. The panel washed ashore on a Nantucket Island beach, chipped and scraped with salt-water stains. The panel bore a blue-green zodiac pattern created by Piero Fornasetti (1913–88), a leading Italian artist of the day. Today it appears as a palimpsest of stories relating to the life and death of a liner [227].

When Cunard launched *Queen Mary 2* in 2003 – the only passenger vessel currently providing a service across the Atlantic – she was the first liner to have been built in over 30 years [229]. Like her predecessor the *QE2*, she was designed to withstand a transatlantic crossing, but also had the amenities to operate primarily as a cruise ship. The origins of cruising date back farther

---

227 ABOVE

Panel from a luxury suite on *Andrea Doria*, by Piero Fornasetti

1951

Ink and paint on Masonite mounted to plywood

COLLECTION OF THE NANTUCKET HISTORICAL

ASSOCIATION: 1970.0009.001

228 OPPOSITE ABOVE

Britannia Restaurant on *Queen Mary 2*, following refurbishment in 2016

229 OPPOSITE BELOW

Queen Mary 2, c.2003

than the modern industry, tied to the great age of ocean travel. From the mid-nineteenth century, P&O offered the possibility of pleasure tours round the Mediterranean, using the line's scheduled services. Similarly, as Albert Ballin (1857–1918) was managing the design of Germany's grandest liners, he also directed construction of the first purpose-built cruise ship, *Prinzessin Victoria Luise* (1901).

Many ocean liners engaged in purely recreational cruises during their working years, especially in winter months when there was less demand for North Atlantic passages. Cunard painted the hull of *Franconia* white for winter world cruises during the 1930s (on one of which Cole Porter wrote *Begin the Beguine*), and in the post-war years many shipping companies increasingly turned to cruising as the way forward in the face of competition from the aviation industry. Ships such as *Caronia* (1949) accommodated so many amenities that they dramatically impacted upon the vessel's speed and profitability as a liner.[2] At the outset, the hull design differed somewhat from liners, since accommodating for a cruise experience took precedence over withstanding harsh conditions while keeping to schedule. The industries advanced in parallel for a time, but as ocean liners gradually increased amenities and promoted the experience over the destination, the public demand for cruising expanded. A particular development in the industry saw the introduction of educational cruises operated by, among others around the world, the British India Steam Navigation Company, which took thousands of school children on educational trips around Europe. *Uganda*, for instance, was converted for use as a schools' ship in 1966–7 and operated from several cities including the port of Dundee in Scotland.

The largest cruise ships operating today are only 45 m longer than the largest ocean liners, but with dramatic differences. At 315 m, *France* (1962) carried approximately 3,300 passengers and crew, while *Harmony of the Seas* (2016), currently the world's largest cruise ship, is 362 m, but can carry more than 6,750 travellers [230]. As industry demands transitioned from the requirements of North Atlantic winter crossings to maximizing recreational amenities – such as increased cabin space, private balconies, entertainment venues and dining opportunities – designs evolved towards towering superstructures (with up to 16 passenger decks) that stay largely in protected waters. The largest modern cruise ships bear little exterior resemblance to traditional liners. By contrast, the external profile of *Queen Mary 2* emulates James Gardner's (1907–95) design for the *QE2*, but the interior offers the requirements of a modern cruise ship, including a spa, several auditoriums and a planetarium. The naval architect Stephen Payne aimed for the design of the ship to reference the grand traditions of

the Cunarders, while also providing state-of-the-art facilities. The consciously historicizing decoration includes a double-height dining room with stained-glass lantern and the use of such materials as tapestry and verre églomisé, a medium most famously used on *Normandie* (1935) [228].

A record 24 million people are expected to take cruises in 2016, approximately 10 million more than a decade previously and new markets such as China are expanding.[3] With this surge in numbers, the international cruise industry has witnessed a diversification in the types of cruises on offer and is attracting a wider demographic. Brand identity today is different from that of the liner's heyday since cruise lines are now global and no longer tied to a region. Neither are ships any longer associated with particular routes, ports or destinations. National identity, once so crucial to liner design, has also been blurred. Initially the prevalence of Scandinavian naval architects in the 1970s brought certain similarities in style to ships of different nations, but today the homogeneity is intentional, since most cruise ships are designed for the American market and many contain design elements reflecting a northern European interpretation of Caribbean influence – coral carpet, palm-frond motifs, sea-creature imagery and a colour palette of aquamarine, turquoise and beige.[4]

All the major companies including Disney, Royal Caribbean, Carnival, Viking Cruises and the Italian firm Costa have injected tremendous impetus into the design and building of modern cruise ships. In the past, the design of a new ship was top secret, as in the case of SS *United States*, today all future plans for entertainment are as closely guarded and are used by cruise lines to set themselves apart from one another. Cruising is now one of the most valuable leisure industries and, with increasingly extensive on-board entertainment facilities, the design of contemporary cruise ships moves ever closer to the reality of a self-sustaining city.

Furthermore, the role cruising plays in the modern consciousness sustains the ship as a lasting icon in everyday life, an imagery and symbolism that was begun by the liner. It is therefore no surprise that the ocean liner has proved a particularly enduring subject in popular culture, and especially in film. In the early years of the medium, film-makers documented liners and their passengers, and extolled their technological marvels, disseminating a visual appreciation of them to global audiences. For those who lived far from a port city or the coast, such films were their first – and perhaps only – experience of these archetypal embodiments of Modernist values and accomplishments.

In the ensuing decades, the ocean liner became a privileged setting in Hollywood film, providing an environment replete with

230 ABOVE
Royal Caribbean cruise ship *Harmony of the Seas*
sailing to the Port of Palma de Mallorca, Balearic
Islands, Spain, 2016

THE AFTERLIFE OF SHIPS

potential for transformative events. Some movie plots hinge on the impossibility of maintaining the purity of mid-ocean romance, whether due to the onslaught of urban life or nature itself. In *Love Affair* (1939, and its remake *An Affair to Remember*, 1957 [231]) a woman steps into traffic while distracted by thoughts of the man she met on a voyage, while in *Titanic* (1997) love's young dream is shattered by an iceberg [232].

Such commentaries on modern life – and its discontents – were also delivered as comedy. The plot of *The Big Broadcast of 1938* (1938), for example, revolves around the race between two liners. Bob Hope laments his poverty (and its implicit impact on his social

position and aspirations) while drinking cocktails in a shipboard bar. His future is irrevocably affixed to the success of the ultra-modern liner *Gigantic*. The ship, which seems strikingly similar to Norman Bel Geddes's conceptual proposal for a streamlined liner, is pitted against a more conventional-looking contender, *Colossal*, in a transatlantic race. Overcoming technical challenges and human shortcomings, the futuristic ship prevails.

On the other hand, the Marx Brothers perceptively critiqued the optimistic declarations of Le Corbusier and others regarding ideals of modern living, such as efficiency of space and servicing the megastructure, in *A Night at the Opera* (1935). Service staff and elegantly dressed visitors bring all the perceived amenities of luxury travel into a first-class cabin, but, arriving all at once, they render it increasingly crowded and ultimately uninhabitable.

The liner voyage, with its exposure to cosmopolitan life, is also a rite of passage for the first-time passenger who emerges forever changed. In *Dodsworth* (1936), the introduction to the urbane and voguish world of the liner awakens a wife's desires for social advancement, distancing her from her seemingly unsophisticated husband and destroying their marriage. Conversely, for the

---

231 ABOVE

Deborah Kerr and Cary Grant in *An Affair To Remember*, directed by Leo McCarey for Twentieth Century Fox, 1957

emotionally repressed character played by Bette Davis in *Now, Voyager* (1942) the ocean voyage is an ablution that cleanses her from a youth of maternal domination. She emerges a self-assured and independent woman of the world.

Many films employ the plot line of the ill-fated liner as a vehicle for other narratives. While James Cameron's *Titanic* (1997) casts the disaster as the quintessential setting for tragic romance, the same disaster was employed by Nazi propagandists in 1943 to cast the tragedy as the result of a plan by greedy capitalists to profit by winning the Blue Riband. It features a fictitious German officer whose heroism stands out among the feckless British passengers and crew. *The Poseidon Adventure* (1972), meanwhile, presents the liner as the consummate dystopic vision of the failure of modern technology. At the stroke of the New Year, party horns turn to screams as a tidal wave capsizes the ship, trapping passengers in a hazardous maze of bent metal, flooded corridors and flaming machinery. The inverted vessel becomes a purgatory to be traversed and survived by only a few. Thoughts turn from frivolity to survival, while social classes are reversed, villains become heroes and vice versa.

Other forms of popular entertainment such as fun-fair attractions also appealed to audiences by creating the experience of being onboard a ship and have a long tradition. For instance, at the 1900 *Exposition Universelle* in Paris an exhibit called the 'Mareorama' by Hugo d'Alési (1849–1906) allowed visitors to experience liner travel by standing on a replica deck with a painted seascape rolling past.[5] Just two years after the *Titanic* disaster, a Coney Island amusement park attraction lured audiences to an enormous diorama of the North Atlantic Ocean and a moving model of the ship designed to 'sink daily and nightly'.[6] In a re-enactment of events *Titanic* travels across the ocean, strikes an

232 ABOVE
Kate Winslet and Leonardo DiCaprio in *Titanic*, directed by James Cameron for Twentieth Century Fox, 1997

iceberg and trembles while *Carpathia* approaches, arriving too late for many [233]. Today museums such as the Titanic Belfast Experience and the Escal'Atlantic in Saint-Nazaire are contemporary interpretations of this long-standing tradition, inviting visitors to experience the liner in a multisensory environment.

Great vessels also frequently find resonance among contemporary artists who today see them as potent allegories for global economic, social and environmental concerns. Canadian artist Edward Burtynsky's (b.1955) famous series of photographs entitled *Shipbreaking* (2000–1), which portrays enormous vessels driven up on the beaches of India and Bangladesh and broken up by distressingly rudimentary means, contrasts assumptions of progress with modern reality. In *Wine Dark Sea* (2016), Scottish-born artist of Guyanese ancestry Hew Locke (b.1959) employs the Christian votive tradition of suspending ship models in church naves to explore contemporary issues around globalization. His flotilla of 35 boats includes two cruise ships that are not only ornamented with gold chains and latticework, but also smeared with dirt and overgrown with tropical vegetation, alluding to the contrasting experiences of the ships by those on board and on shore. In *Sea of Tranquillity* (2010), video artist Hans Op de Beeck (b.1969) explores the blurring of reality and representation on a strikingly ambitious scale. The mystical film places the viewer on board a cavernous and strangely vacant cruise liner passing silently and eerily through darkness. In this setting he distils issues surrounding the creation of identity to mask the insignificance of the individual in postmodern existence into a quasi-narrative that is both ethereal and profoundly disturbing. These works remind us that great ships still loom large in our cultural imagination.

233 OPPOSITE

Advertisement for the *Titanic* Disaster attraction at Luna Park, Coney Island, printed by Eldredge Print Brooklyn, New York, 1914

Colour lithograph

GIFT OF THE ESTATE OF FRANCIS B.C. BRADLEE, 1928

PEABODY ESSEX MUSEUM: M11210

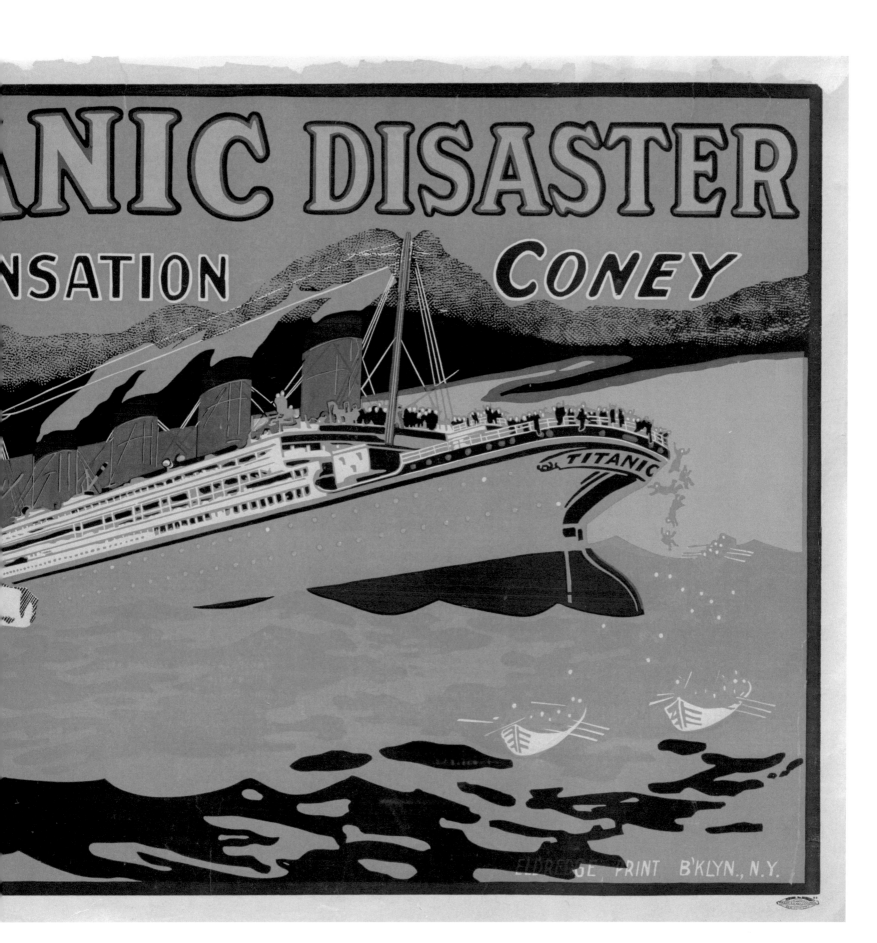

NOTES

INTRODUCTION

1. Dates given after ship names refer to their maiden voyage, once the fitting out was complete. The launch, when the ship slid into the water for the first time, usually took place about a year before. Gross ton (GT) is a unit of measurement for the internal volume of a ship.
2. Verne (1876), pp.5–6
3. 'a vast plain region'
4. Thackeray (1860), p.97
5. On 29 July 1840, following their arrival in Boston, Samuel Cunard, his son William, *Britannia*'s captain Henry Woodruff and Charles Clarke of Halifax visited the Salem East India Marine Society Museum, the founding institution of what is now the Peabody Essex Museum. Schwartz (2015), p.594
6. Twain (1883), chapter 20
7. Dickens (1883), p.598
8. Battcock (1980), pp.142–7
9. 'Foreign News', *Time Magazine* (8 June 1936), p.18
10. Walleans (2006), p.9
11. Charles A. Richter, unpublished manuscript notebook, 1928 (in possession of one of Richter's five grandchildren, Sally Festing)
12. W.A. Gibson-Martin, et al. (1932)
13. The large and safe Boeing 707 introduced in 1958 revolutionized travel, Dawson (2005), pp.145–6
14. F. Scott Fitzgerald (2003), p.205

ADVERTISING THE OCEAN LINER

1. See, for example, Ford Madox Brown, *The Last of England*, 1852–5; Richard Redgrave, *The Emigrant's Last Sight of Home*, 1858; Marshall Claxton, *An Emigrant's Thoughts of Home*, 1859 and John Watson Nicol, *Lochaber no more*, 1863.
2. *The Times* (12 June 1913), p.5
3. Apelt Schmidt (2011), p.218
4. Rieger (2005), p.43
5. *The Ocean Ferry* (September 1926), p.12
6. A.M. Cassandre quoted in Mouron (1985), p.47
7. Ibid., p.37
8. Artmonsky (2013), p.58
9. In 1972 Crosby/Fletcher/Forbes became the leading design consultancy Pentagram.

A CLOSE-UP PICTURE OF A MIGHTY PROJECT: PROMOTIONAL EXHIBITION MODELS

1. Bassett-Lowke Ltd (1929)
2. Lavery & Stephens (1995), pp.38, 102
3. Ibid., p.12; *A Guide to the Great Exhibition* (1851), p.189
4. 'The Centennial', *Harper's Weekly* (8 July 1876), pp.556–7
5. 'Vor dem Auskunftsbureau des "Norddeutschen Lloyd" in Berlin' (1893), p.487
6. 'Steamship Model Costs Run up to $25,000', *Daily Boston Globe* (24 November 1929)

7. Francis (1935)
8. Graves, 'Ship Models – Magnificent *Mauretania*', www.rmg.co.uk/discover/behind-the-scenes/blog/ship-models-magnificent-mauretania (accessed 15 March 2016)
9. Matthew, 'The *Kronprinzessin Cecilie* Project: Restoring Fleischmann's Forgotten Masterpiece', www.kronprinzessin-cecilie.com/index.html (accessed 17 February 2016)
10. 'Eine Zusammenstellung alter Kataloge der Firmen Gebr. Fleischmann, Leonhard Staudt, Ullmann & Engelmann', reproduced in C. Baecker et al. (1988) quoted by Matthew, ibid.
11. Object Files, Mariners' Museum and Park.
12. Fondazione Ansaldo Archives, Genoa, www.fondazioneansaldo.it/index.php?option=com_content&view=category&id=158&Itemid=284&lang=en (accessed 15 March 2016)
13. Callahan (1960), p.88
14. 'Marine Models at the Paris Exhibition', *Ships and Ship Models* (September 1937), vol. 6, pp.23–4
15. 'The French Quadruple-Screw Turbo-Electric North Atlantic Liner "Normandie"', souvenir edition of *Shipbuilder and Marine Engine-Builder* (June 1935), p.41
16. Fuller (1984), p.29
17. Ibid., p.55
18. British Pathé Newsreels, 'Queen Elizabeth Model 1949' (4 April 1949), www.britishpathe.com/video/queen-elizabeth-model/query/queen+elizabeth+cunard+model (accessed 17 February 2016)
19. Bassett-Lowke Ltd (1949), pp.10–12
20. 'Ship Model Exhibit Intrigues Visitors to Cunard Line Offices', *The Washington Post* (18 October 1936)
21. 'North German Lloyd Opens New Ticket Offices This Week', *Daily Boston Globe* (18 May 1931), p.7
22. 'Steamship Model Costs Run up to $25,000', *Daily Boston Globe* (24 November 1929)
23. 'How Long is the "Queen Mary"?', *Pittsburgh Post-Gazette* (18 May 1936)
24. 'Ocean Liner's Model', *Times-Picayune* (22 January 1911), reprinted from the *New York World*; 'Steamship Model Worth a Fortune', *Baltimore American* (7 April 1911)
25. Cerdan (1936)
26. '$40,000 Ship Model is at Travel Show: Reproduction of the *Berengaria* is Complete to Smallest Details', *The New York Times* (10 April 1923)

THE ARCHITECTURE OF PROMOTION

1. Figueiredo (2003), p.243
2. *The New Cunard Building*, Mewès & Davis Archive
3. Figueiredo (2003), p.249
4. 'The Cunard Building, New York', *Architecture and Building* (August 1921), pp.62–6
5. Anderson (1967), p.451

6. 'New Orient Line Building, Spring Street, Sydney', *Art in Australia* (23 May 1940), pp.75–80
7. Destrais (2002)
8. 'Two New Docks at Home and Abroad', *The Architects' Journal* (3 August 1933), p.129
9. 'Maritime Station, Le Havre, France', *The Architect & Building News* (30 August 1935), p.245
10. 'Introduction to English Architecture', *The Architects' Journal* (10 August 1950), p.130
11. Howarth & Howarth (1986), p.184
12. *P&O Building Leadenhall Street EC3* (1969)

SHIPBUILDING: SPEED, SAFETY AND COMFORT

1. William Denny and Brothers Ltd of Dumbarton, Scotland, constructed the first steel, ocean-going steamers in the late 1870s.
2. The method of making steel in quantity – the Bessemer process, introduced by Henry Bessemer (1813–98) in 1855 – did not produce metal of reliable consistency for shipbuilding, but the introduction of 'open-hearth' steel, made by the Siemens-Martin process (patented in the mid-1860s), yielded large quantities of homogenous steel and allowed ever-larger vessels to be built.
3. *Mauretania* factsheet (October 2013), Cunard Archive, Liverpool
4. *The Mild South Route to Europe* (1933)
5. '*California* is Herald of Electric Age in Sea Travel', *The Ocean Ferry* (February–March 1928), vol. 7, nos 5–6, p.12
6. 'First Radio at Sea was on the American Liner *Philadelphia*', *The Ocean Ferry* (November 1924), vol. 4, no. 2, p.13
7. Telegraph message (15 April 1912), Phillips Library, Peabody Essex Museum, Acc 2015.026f

FLOATING PALACES: VICTORIAN AND EDWARDIAN SHIPS

1. Dickens (1883), pp.585–7, 594, 601
2. Padfield (1981), p.57
3. Harcourt (2006); see also Howarth & Howarth (1994), pp.9–46
4. Kludas (1987), pp.147–8
5. Straub (2001), pp.32–41, 54–62
6. Rieger (2005), pp.227–36
7. *Parliamentary Debates* [Hansard], fourth series, vol. 127, col. 1104
8. *The Times* (9 September 1907), p.10
9. *Manchester Guardian* (12 October 1907), p.8
10. See Wealleans (2006), pp.59, 65; Miller (1984), pp.12, 63. The steerage number for Hamburg-American combines travellers categorized in 'steerage' and 'third class', a distinction for which no precedent existed.
11. *B.Z. am Mittag* (23 May 1912), p.1; *Berliner Tageblatt* (23 May 1912, evening edition), p.5
12. Osterhammel & Petersson (2005), pp.76–9
13. Bellmann (2015), p.57

14. Ibid., pp.58–68
15. Rennella & Walton (2004), pp.365–83
16. Bellmann (2015), pp.119–22
17. Wealleans (2006) pp.31–2, 66–7; Russell (2011), pp.227–56, 36–7
18. Bellmann (2004), pp.119–22
19. Davis (1914), pp.88–9
20. Wealleans (2006), p.60
21. Davis (1914), pp.89, 91
22. Wealleans (2006), p.61
23. Ibid., pp.66–7
24. Dawson & Peter (2010), pp.20–1
25. Wealleans (2006), pp.33–4
26. '"Imperator" und "Vaterland"', *Der Kunstwart 26* (1913), no. 19, pp.67–8; for a more extended discussion, see Russell (2011), pp.240–1
27. Paul (1914), pp.55–6
28. For a more detailed account of design reform on German ships, see Dawson & Peter (2010), pp.26–30
29. Rieger (2005), pp.168–75
30. Howarth & Howarth (2006), pp.47–52
31. On the origins of cruises, see Straub (2001), pp.107–9

INTER-WAR LINERS: THE POLITICS OF STYLE

1. 'Schiff des Friedens und der Freude "Wilhelm Gustloff"', *Arbeit und Staat* (9 June 1937)
2. See Wood (2003), pp.125–37
3. Rosenthal (1921), p.80
4. Ibid.
5. Mourey (1927), p.242
6. Ibid., p.246
7. Quoted in *Rassegna* (December 1990), vol. 44, p.34
8. Ibid., p.36
9. Bontempelli (1974), pp.327–8, quoted in ibid., p.28
10. Chavance (1931), p.155
11. Valette (1936), p.717
12. M.P. Malglaive quoted in ibid., pp.717–18
13. Dawson (2005), p.243
14. H.P. Shapland (1931), p.65
15. 'The "Queen Mary": Britain's Shipping Masterpiece', Akers (1936), p.14
16. See Lebovics (1992)
17. Beaton (1936), p.40
18. See Morris (1980), p.74
19. Anderson (1967), vol. 141, p.452
20. Tatton Brown (1935), vol. 78, p.138
21. Clonmore (1931), p.62

LINERS AT WAR

1. Harding (2007), p.106
2. Behrens (1999), p.53
3. Wilkinson (1920), p.264. There is no evidence to suggest that dazzle camouflage actually worked, but it is generally considered to have had a positive effect on morale.
4. Miller & Riding (2015), p.143
5. Harding (2007), p.147
6. Steele (2001), p.184

7. Interview with Linda Kitson for the Imperial War Museum, recorded by Lyn E. Smith, 19 January 1994, Imperial War Museum, catalogue no. 13727, reel 6

POST-WAR LINERS: 1945–1975

1. 'Skill: A Monthly Review of Building Techniques and Industrial Design', *Architectural Review* (February 1956), pp.133–40
2. Eliseo & Piccione (2001), pp.146–7
3. Ponti (1953), pp.17–24
4. Eliseo & Piccione (2001), pp.246–7
5. 'The 21-knot liner *Giulio Cesare*: First of two ships with double-acting Fiat machinery of 25,000 bhp using boiler oil', *The Motor Ship* (February 1951), vol. 31, p.355; 'The completion of the *Giulio Cesare*: An Italian liner of 25,000 tons gross, propelled by 26,000 bhp machinery', *The Motor Ship* (October 1951), vol. 32, p.259; 'Largest post-war motor liner: The *Giulio Cesare*, an Italian vessel of 27,700 tons gross, propelled by double-acting Fiat machinery of 26,000 bhp', *The Motor Ship* (January 1952), vol. 33, pp.424–9
6. American Export Lines brochure promoting the 'Four Aces', 1949, n.p.
7. Squarey (1955), p.89
8. Peter C. Kohler, 'Building Anew', Dawson & Peter (2010), p.108
9. Dawson (2005), p.161
10. 'The *Andrea Doria*', *The Shipbuilder and Shipping Record* (13 August 1953), vol. 82, pp.211–13. See also, Eliseo & Piccione (2001), pp.203–4
11. Eliseo & Piccione (2001), pp.248–52
12. Weinraub later took the name of Munio Gitai Weinraub.
13. For biographical details of Mansfeld, see Teut (1999)
14. '*The Secret Staircase*': The New Flagship *Rotterdam* (1959), p.3
15. 'Trans-Atlantic Liner "France": Luxury Passenger Liner for the French Line', *The Shipping World* (7 February 1962), p.171
16. Siriex & Conquer (1992), p.48
17. Garrett (1961), pp.155–8
18. Dawson (1990), p.65
19. Ibid.
20. Philip S. Dawson in discussion with Sir Hugh Casson, London, September 1981
21. *T/N Michelangelo* (1965), pp.30–107
22. Ibid.
23. Ibid.
24. Eliseo & Piccione (2001), p.268
25. Ibid., pp.267, 270
26. Potter & Frost (1969), p.49
27. Ibid., pp.124–5
28. Agnew (1969), p.418
29. Gardner (1983), p.128
30. *Queen Elizabeth 2* (1969)
31. Potter & Frost (1969), p.140

THE IDEALIZED SOCIETY OF THE OCEAN LINER

1. *Masterpieces* (n.d.)

2. Quoted in Seymour (2015) p.65
3. Gennep (1909)
4. Dale (1909), p.77
5. Henningsen (1961)
6. Aubert (1965)
7. One source notes that this restaurant was converted into a ballroom and reception room, suggesting that the artist created this scene before the ship's refitting was completed.
8. Dale (1909), p.31
9. Lindsay (1925), pp.4–5
10. MacDonald (1925)
11. Francis Lee Higginson Maritime Art and History donor files, Peabody Essex Museum (M18,692)
12. *The Ocean Ferry* (September 1925), vol. 5, no. 12, p.6
13. '*Normandie*' (1937), n.p.
14. Quoted in Sprague (2008)
15. 'To Open Ship Synagogue: Rabbis Dedicate Place of Worship on Polish Liner Today', *The New York Times* (23 February 1934); 'Polish Ship's Salon Made a Synagogue', *The New York Times* (25 February 1934), p.35
16. *The Daily Telegraph* (29 May 1936)
17. Rubinstein et al. (2011), p.256
18. Thanks to George Schwartz for identifying this visual symbolism.
19. 'Sea Going Synagogue', *The Spokesman* (27 March 1936), vol. 24, no. 3020
20. Tozier (1905), p.65
21. Sykes (2012)
22. 'Satisfying Transatlantic Equestrians', *Illustrated World* (September 1915)
23. *Ambassadors of Sport* (1925)
24. 'Notes for First Class Passengers on Board the Steamers of the White Star Line' (April 1913)
25. Kitchen (1927)
26. '*Normandie*' (1937), n.p.
27. *A Comparison: Gastronomy Afloat. Fifty Years Ago and Now* (1914)
28. *Ritz's Carlton Restaurant On Board the S.S. "Kaiserin Auguste Victoria"* ... (1906)
29. *The Economist* (10 November 1906); Dale (1909), p.59
30. 'Notes for First Class Passengers on Board the Steamers of the White Star Line' (April 1913)
31. Third-Class Menu, RMS *Scythia* (21 July 1922), Phillips Library, Peabody Essex Museum
32. Driscoll (2013), p.166
33. *Gourmet's Floating Paradise* (1937); *Sukiyaki: A Dainty Japanese Dish* (1938)
34. Eliot (2004), p.98
35. Rawson & Garrett (1892–4), p.664
36. Trubek (2001), pp.10–13
37. Finamore (2004), pp.30–47
38. MS *Gripsholm* Dinner Menu (14 December 1972), Peabody Essex Museum (M21,154)

SS *UNITED STATES*

1. Palmer (1952), p.14
2. Ujifusa (2012), pp.232–3
3. 'Two Women "Dress" New Luxury Liner', *Schenectady Gazette* (4 July 1952), p.4

4. Ujifusa (2012), p.246
5. Marckwald cited in Braynard (1981), p.63
6. 'Superliner Plans in Advanced Stage', *The New York Times* (17 July 1949); Palmer (1952)
7. As early as the 1920s, Navajo religious practitioners began making permanent representations of ephemeral sand paintings into textiles and other art forms for sale, Berlo (2012), pl. 26, p.95. The panels Ostuni created for the ship were directly drawn from sand-painting designs captured by anthropologists Franc J. Newcomb and Gladys A. Reichard, see Newcomb & Reichard (1937) and Reichard (1939). Though Ostuni took artistic liberties and changed the colour scheme and format slightly, the panel depicted here is based on 'Flint-armored Gods in Attack on Changing Woman', in Newcomb & Reichard (1975), pl. XVI
8. Clute (1952), p.11
9. Mira Jedwabnik Van Doren, unpublished excerpts from interview by Celebrity Cruises for "S.S. United States Restaurant" in the Van Doren collection, digital video, dir. Kenneth James Peterson, Celebrity Cruises, 2001.

FLOATING IN A DREAMLAND: FASHION AND SPECTACLE ON BOARD

1. Henriot (1926), pp.61–5, 124
2. 'The Paris' (1921)
3. Schweitzer (2012) p.253
4. 'Some Notable Passengers on Famous Ship', *The Ocean Ferry* (March 1926), vol. 5, no. 6, p.7
5. 'C.P.' (1935), pp.10–11
6. British Pathé Newsreels 'Ship Fashions', 1961, www.britishpathe.com/video/ship-fashions/query/ship+model and 'For Daughters in Search of the Sun', 1935, www.britishpathe.com/video/for-daughters-in-search-of-the-sun/query/ship+fashion (accessed 4 April 2016)
7. 'Les Mannequins à bord', *Femina* (15 May 1911), p.261; 'The Liner as a Substitute for the Racecourse: Models Aboard Ship', *Illustrated London News* (27 May 1911), n.p.
8. 'Ocean Going-Mannequins: How Enterprising French Houses Sell to Deep Sea Travelers', *Boston Daily Globe* (29 November 1914), p.SM15
9. Yates (1939), pp.193–4
10. 'The Paris' (1921)
11. Beaton (1936), pp.38–41, 87
12. 'Concerning Travelling Clothes and Some Others', *Vogue* (UK edition, January 1926), n.p.
13. Trowbridge Lewis (1921), pp.24–25; Fleming (1922), p.27; Yates (1939), p.201
14. In 1872, the company introduced a signature canvas with stripes, followed by a checked pattern, then the LV logo, www.us.louisvuitton.com/eng-us/la-maison/a-legendary-history (accessed 13 May 2016)
15. Compensation claim of Charlotte Cardeza, 1913, Record Group 21. In the Matter of the Petition of the Oceanic Steam Navigation Company, Limited, for Limitation of its Liability as owner of the steamship, TITANIC, https://research.archives.gov/id/6210868 (accessed 13 March 2016)
16. Tozier (1905), pp.35–8

17. 'Packing for Pleasure', *Vogue* (15 May 1934), pp.62–3, 89
18. Davis (2006), p.158; Etherington-Smith (1983), p.64
19. 'Cruise', *Harper's Bazaar* (February 1933), p.26
20. Friedman (2016)
21. Yates (1939), pp.195–6
22. 'Travel Advertising Addressed to Women Only', *The Ocean Ferry* (February 1926) vol. 5, no. 5, p.12
23. Mary Elizabeth Staples, Arrival at New York on the *Majestic* from Cherbourg, 19 April 1927. Ancestry.com. New York, Passenger Lists, 1820–1957 [database on-line]. Provo, UT, USA: Ancestry.com Operations, Inc. (accessed 29 March 2016)
24. Jenny receipt dated 22 July 1926, dress, 132655, object files, Peabody Essex Museum
25. Dale (1909), p.254
26. Ibid., pp.18–19
27. 'Shops on Ships', *Harper's Bazaar* (April 1934), pp.170–3
28. Schweitzer (2012), p.250
29. Tolini Finamore (2013), pp.84–6
30. Evans (2013), p.70
31. 'New Dances Inspire a Style in Skirts', *The New York Times* (2 November 1914), p.9
32. 'Paquin to Exhibit Here, Announcement Causes Resentment Among American Buyers in Paris', *The New York Times* (13 Feb 1914), p.4
33. Evans (2013), pp.125–7
34. Hawes (1938), p.38
35. 'New Styles Revive Sculptured Lines', *The New York Times* (20 Aug 1935), p.23
36. 'La Mode Française à New York', *L'Officiel de la Mode* (1935), no. 168, pp.24–5
37. Morelli, Della Cagna & Finamore (2015)
38. 'British Fashions Sail In', *The New York Herald Tribune* (5 November 1965) n.p.; John Bates Archive, Museum of Fine Arts, Boston
39. Henriot (1926), p.124

MODERNIST ARCHITECTURE AND THE LINER

1. Le Corbusier-Saugnier (1921)
2. Le Corbusier (2007), p.158
3. Janneau was Inspector of Public Monuments, General Manager of the Mobilier National and the Manufactures Nationales des Gobelins et de Beauvais, and then of the Manufacture Nationale de Sèvres. He also held the title of Professor at the Conservatoire National des Arts et Métiers.
4. Guillaume Janneau (1925), p.176 (author's translation)
5. Franz Kollmann (1929), p.158 (author's translation). A more favourable report can be found in Max Osborn's introduction to Fritz August Breuhaus de Groot et al. (1929), cited in Kaplan (1995), p.262
6. Le Corbusier (2007), p.152
7. Le Corbusier (1923), p.78 (author's translation)
8. Benton (2009), p.70; Le Corbusier (1987), p.158
9. Le Corbusier (1924), p.26
10. Le Corbusier (2007), p.149
11. See Benton (2009), p.74–5
12. Le Corbusier, 'Vivre! (Habiter)', *Plans* (4 April 1931), reproduced in altered form in *La Ville*

Radieuse (1935) quoted from the English edition, Le Corbusier (1967), p.117
13. Taut (1929), pp.4–5 (author's translation)
14. Ibid.
15. Le Corbusier to Monteiro da Carvalho (15 June 1936), (author's translation)
16. Le Corbusier to his wife Yvonne (24 September 1929) in Le Corbusier, Baudouï & Dercelles (2013), p.238
17. Le Corbusier to his mother (25 September 1929), ibid., pp.240–1
18. Ibid.
19. Le Corbusier to his mother (26 October 1935), ibid., p.518
20. Manuscript note on *Conte Biancamano* headed paper, Fondation Le Corbusier, F2(17)267. The curious can still inspect *Conte Biancamano* today, since a large section of the ship was saved from the scrapyard and installed in the Museo Nazionale della Scienza e della Tecnologia Leonardo da Vinci in Milan, albeit with its post-war decoration from a refit of 1949.
21. Le Corbusier to Austin (1 October 1936)
22. See Benton (2013)
23. Robert Mallet-Stevens (1935), pp.24–8
24. M. Nepveu, ibid., pp.11–23
25. Ibid., p.25
26. Benton (2011), pp.92–105

STREAMLINING

1. Bel Geddes (1932), p.35

THE LINER AS MACHINE

1. 'American's Eighteen-Foot Picture Nearly Splits Independent Artists', *New York Herald* (8 February 1924), p.1
2. The painting was left in storage in Paris and lost during the Second World War.
3. Tomkins (1962). The Murphys and their way of life famously inspired the Divers in F. Scott Fitzgerald's *Tender is the Night* (1934).
4. *New York Herald* (8 February 1924). Another critic described the funnels as 'violently coloured in minium' (a red pigment also called 'red lead'), 'Un incident aux Indépendants', *Petit Parisien: Journal quotidien du soir* (8 February 1924), p.3
5. Rubin & Lanchner (1974), p.24
6. Murphy's response to a question from Douglas MacAgy, October or November 1962, quoted in Rubin & Lanchner (1979), p.24. Murphy painted for less than a decade and was by no means prolific but the machinery of liners inspired two of his other known works. The artist himself later recalled that *Engine Room* sprung from a visit below decks on *Mauretania*, 'Autobiographical Notes by Gerald Murphy, from the Douglas MacAgy Papers', *Journal of American Art* (1999), vol. 39, no. 3–4, p.61; William Rubin has suggested that another lost work entitled *Pressure* was exhibited at the 1923 Salon des Indépendants and referred to liner machinery, Rubin & Lanchner (1979), p.16.
7. Marinetti (1909), quoted in Prampolini (1927), pp.9–10

8. Léger (2004), pp.81–5 (author's translation, the emphasis is Léger's). Machines and industrially produced objects were the central characters in *Ballet mécanique*, Léger and Dudley Murphy's avant-garde film made in 1924.

9. Mac Delmarle (1913) quoted in Lista (1973), p.178 (author's translation)

10. In *L'Evolution créatrice* (Creative Evolution, 1907) Henri Bergson developed an influential theory about the continuous evolution of life. Form, he explained, was never fixed but constantly changing, and what appeared to be successive states were in fact the uninterrupted change undergone as time flowed continuously.

11. The painting was lost in Cologne during the First World War but studies survive.

12. Belbachir (1992), p.839

13. Del Marle quoted in Belbachir (1996), pp.30–2 (author's translation)

14. 'Picabia, Art Rebel, Here to Present the New Movement', *The New York Times* (16 February 1913), section 5, p.9, in Picabia, *Écrits* (1975), pp.19–21

15. William A. Camfield in conversation with Gabrielle Buffet-Picabia, July 1968, in Camfield (1979), p.49

16. Picabia (1913), reproduced in Camfield et al. (2014), p.82

17. Paloma Alarcó, 'Albert Gleizes, *In Port*, 1917', www.museothyssen.org/en/thyssen/ficha_obra/392 (accessed 21 April 2016)

18. The experience of travelling also inspired Juliette Roche-Gleizes's poetry. 'Année' follows their journey from New York to Barcelona, from the Azores to Lisbon, Madrid and Barcelona before returning to New York via Havana. She evokes each place in succinct images and impressions juxtaposed in a manner comparable to her husband's painting, see Roche (1920).

19. Quoted in Brooke (2001), p.150 (author's translation)

20. Although Murphy's *Boatdeck* painted over a year later bears some comparison with Demuth's *Paquebot 'Paris'*, it seems unlikely that Murphy knew this work since they overlapped in Paris by only a few months in late 1921, before Demuth produced the painting on his return. There is no evidence they met or that Murphy saw a reproduction. Rather, *Boatdeck* owes its gigantic scale and graphic quality to posters and its subject to photographs whose role Murphy acknowledged. For an extended discussion of the reasons why Murphy is unlikely to have known Demuth's work, see Rubin & Lanchner (1974), p.22

21. Haskell (1987), p.132

22. Demuth to Stieglitz (10 October 1921), in Kellner (2000), p.28

23. Haskell (1987), p.131

24. Ozenfant & Jeanneret (1920), pp.373–4

25. Quoted from Sheeler's unpublished autobiography in Stebbins, Mora & Haas (2002), p.190

26. Little is known about this commission and the brochure has not been traced. Although it is frequently recorded as a commission for a German steamship company, *Majestic* belonged to the White Star Line. The construction of *Majestic* began in 1913 in German dockyards where it was intended to become the Hamburg-American Line's *Bismarck*. However, the vessel became British and was renamed *Majestic* when it was given over to the White Star Line in First World War reparations.

27. I am grateful to Dr Bruce Peter for identifying the machines.

28. Tsujimoto (1982), p.190

29. Evans (1958), p.122

30. Ibid.

THE AFTERLIFE OF SHIPS

1. Massey (2009), pp.207, 212

2. L. Miller (1984), p.36

3. 'Cruise Ship Jobs Have Boatloads of Benefits', *The Boston Globe* www.bostonglobe.com/lifestyle/travel/2016/09/12/cruiseworkers/E9NvHDlPlUfacou5ExSQFK/story.html?s_campaign=bdcglobewell_B (accessed 13 September 2016)

4. Personal communication between Daniel Finamore and architect Scott Wilson, 23 September 2015

5. Jackson (2008), p.81

6. 'Luna Park Opens: Livelier than Ever', *The New York Times* (24 May 1914)

SELECTED BIBLIOGRAPHY

PRIMARY SOURCES

A

Ambassadors of Sport, Cunard Line booklet (New York, NY, 1925)

American Export Lines brochure promoting the 'Four Aces' (1949)

'American's Eighteen-Foot Picture Nearly Splits Independent Artists', *New York Herald* (8 February 1924)

Colin Anderson, 'Ship Interiors: When the Break-through Came', *The Architectural Review* (June 1967)

'The *Andrea Doria*', *The Shipbuilder and Shipping Record* (13 August 1953), vol. 82

B

Jean Badovici & Eileen Gray, 'E. 1027, maison en bord de mer', *L'Architecture vivante*, (Autumn–Winter 1929)

Bassett-Lowke Ltd, 'Exhibition Ship Models', promotional text (London & Northampton, 1929), Bassett-Lowke Archive, Brighton Toy and Model Museum: www.brightontoymuseum.co.uk/info/File:Exhibition_Ship_Models,_Bassett-Lowke_%28BLB_1929-03%29.jpg

Bassett-Lowke Ltd, *R.M.S. Queen Elizabeth: The Largest Model of the World's Greatest Liner* (Manchester, 1949)

Cecil Beaton, 'Reviewing the Queen', *Vogue* (US edition, 1 July 1936)

Norman Bel Geddes, *Horizons* (Boston, MA, 1932)

Fritz August Breuhaus de Groot et al., *Fritz August Breuhaus de Groot; Dr. Herbert Eulenberg: Menschliches, Dr. Max Osborn: Kritik des Werkes* (Berlin, 1929)

'British Fashions Sail In', *New York Herald Tribune* (5 November 1965)

British Pathé newsreels: 'For Daughters in Search of the Sun' (1935), www.britishpathe.com/video/for-daughters-in-search-of-the-sun/query/ship+fashion; 'Queen Elizabeth Model 1949' (4 April 1949), www.britishpathe.com/video/queen-elizabeth-model/query/queen+elizabeth+cunard+model; 'Ship Fashions' (1961), www.britishpathe.com/video/ship-fashions/query/ship+model

C

'*California* is Herald of Electric Age in Sea Travel', *The Ocean Ferry* (February–March 1928), vol. 7, nos 5–6

John C. Callahan, '10 Shipbuilders Whittle at Job: Perfectionist Patience is Rule at Shop That Turns Out Master Models', *The New York Times* (3 April 1960)

Catalogue of Ship Models and Marine Engineering in the South Kensington Museum: With Classified Table of Contents and an Alphabetical Index of Exhibitors and Subjects (London, 1878)

'The Centennial', *Harper's Weekly* (8 July 1876)

Aurelio Cerdan, 'Ship Models to be Shown: Hobby of Building Tiny Copies of Big Boats Is Now Widespread', *The New York Times* (8 March 1936)

René Chavance, 'Le Paquebot "L'Atlantique" et les Beaux Métiers', *Art et Décoration* (July–December 1931), vol. 60

Lord Clonmore, 'Through Evolution to Reiteration', *Architectural Review* (September 1931), vol. 70

Eugene Clute, 'Murals in Vitreous Enamel', *Craft Horizons* (November–December 1952), vol. 12

A Comparison: Gastronomy Afloat. Fifty Years Ago and Now, Cunard Steamship Co. (1914)

'Compensation claim of Mrs Charlotte Cardeza' (1913), Record Group 21. In the Matter of the Petition of the Oceanic Steam Navigation Company, Limited, for Limitation of its Liability as owner of the steamship, TITANIC, www.research.archives.gov/id/6210868

'The Completion of the *Giulio Cesare*: An Italian liner of 25,000 tons gross, propelled by 26,000 bhp machinery', *The Motor Ship* (October 1951), vol. 32

'Concerning Travelling Clothes and Some Others', *Vogue* (UK edition, January 1926)

Le Corbusier (trans. James I. Dunnett), *The Decorative Art of Today* (Cambridge, MA, 1987)

Le Corbusier, *The Radiant City: Elements of a Doctrine of Urbanism to be used as the Basis of our Machine-Age Civilization* (New York, 1967)

Le Corbusier to Austin (letter, 1 October 1936), Fondation Le Corbusier R2(04)337

Le Corbusier to Monteiro da Carvalho (letter, 15 June 1936), Fondation Le Corbusier I3(3)15

Le Corbusier (trans. John Goodman), *Toward an Architecture* (Los Angeles, CA, 2007)

Le Corbusier, *La Ville Radieuse* (Boulogne-sur-Seine, 1935)

Le Corbusier, 'Vivre! (Habiter)', *Plans* (4 April 1931)

Le Corbusier, Rémi Baudouï & Arnaud Dercelles, *Correspondance. Lettres à la famille, Tome II, 1926–1946* (Paris, 2013)

Le Corbusier-Saugnier, 'Des yeux qui ne voient pas ... Les paquebots', *Esprit Nouveau* (1 May 1921), no. 8

Le Corbusier-Saugnier, *Vers une Architecture* (Paris, 1923)

C.P., 'And So I Went Tourist', *Vogue* (US Edition, 15 July 1935)

'Cruise', *Harper's Bazaar* (US Edition, February 1933)

'Cruise Ship Jobs Have Boatloads of Benefits', *The Boston Globe* (13 September 2016)

'The Cunard Building, New York', *Architecture and Building* (August 1921)

D

Arthur J. Davis, 'Planning, Decoration and Equipment' *The Architectural Review* (April 1914)

Charles Dickens, *American Notes* (New York, NY, 1883)

E

Walker Evans, 'Ship Shapes and Shadows', *Architectural Forum* (October 1958)

F

Ethel Fleming, 'Women's Fashions for the Crisp Brisk Days at Sea', *The Cunarder* (November 1922) vol. 3, no. 5

'Foreign News', *Time Magazine* (8 June 1936)

'$40,000 Ship Model is at Travel Show: Reproduction of the *Berengaria* is Complete to Smallest Details', *The New York Times* (10 April 1923)

Devon Francis, 'Ship Models Come as High as $50,000: Big Lines Spend Tidy Sums for Proud Miniatures', *Daily Boston Globe* (28 July 1935)

'The French Quadruple-Screw Turbo-Electric North Atlantic Liner "Normandie"', souvenir edition of *Shipbuilder and Marine Engine-Builder* (June 1935)

G

James Gardner, *Elephants in the Attic* (London, 1983)

W.A. Gibson-Martin, A.T. Wall & Ashby Tabb, *Ship-furnishing and Decoration: A Handbook for Shipowners, Naval Architects, Furnishing and Decorating Specialists and their Taffs* (Liverpool, 1932)

Gourmet's Floating Paradise, NYK Line 8-panel publicity brochure (1937)

A Guide to the Great Exhibition (London, 1851)

H

Elizabeth Hawes, *Fashion is Spinach* (New York, NY, 1938)

Francis Lee Higginson Maritime Art and History Donor Files, Peabody Essex Museum (M18,692)

'How Long is the "Queen Mary"?', *Pittsburgh Post-Gazette* (18 May 1936)

I

'"Imperator" und "Vaterland"', *Der Kunstwart 26* (1913), no. 19

'Un incident aux Indépendants', *Petit Parisien: Journal quotidien du soir* (8 February 1924)

'Introduction to English Architecture', *The Architects' Journal* (10 August 1950)

J

Guillaume Janneau, 'Introduction l'Exposition des arts décoratifs: considérations sur l'esprit moderne', *Art et Décoration* (May 1925)

K

Karl K. Kitchen, *Lido All the Way* (New York, NY, 1927)

Linda Kitson, Interview for the Imperial War Museum, recorded by Lyn E. Smith, 19 January 1994, Imperial War Museum (catalogue no. 13727, reel 6)

Franz Kollmann, 'Die Gestaltung moderner, Verkehrsmittel, IV: Schiffe', *Das neue Frankfurt* (1929), vol. 3, nos 7–8

L

'Largest post-war motor liner: the *Giulio Cesare*, an Italian vessel of 27,700 tons gross, propelled by double-acting Fiat machinery of 26,000 bhp', *The Motor Ship* (January 1952), vol. 33

Fernand Léger, 'A propos de l'élément mécanique' (1923) in *Fonctions de la peinture* (New edition, revised and expanded, Paris, 2004)

David Lindsay, 'Class Consciousness Fades from Transatlantic Travel', *The Ocean Ferry* (September 1925), vol. 4, no. 12

'The Liner as a Substitute for the Racecourse: Models Aboard Ship', *Illustrated London News* (27 May 1911)

'Luna Park Opens: Livelier than Ever', *The New York Times* (24 May 1914)

M

Machine-Age Exposition (New York, NY, 1927)

A.F. Mac Delmarle, 'La Peinture Futuriste', *Le Nord Illustré* (15 April 1913), no. 5

A.K. MacDonald, *My Cunard Trip*, Cunard Line (1925)

Robert Mallet-Stevens, 'Exposé' in 'Cabines en acier de paquebots', *Acier* (Special issue of the OTUA journal, 1935), 3 (8)

Lord Mancroft, 'Can Ocean Travel Survive?', *Journal of the Royal Society of Arts* (1971), vol. 119, no. 5178

'Les Mannequins à bord', *Femina* (15 May 1911)

'Marine Models at the Paris Exhibition', *Ships and Ship Models* (September 1937), vol. 6

Filippo Tommaso Marinetti, 'Le Futurisme', *Le Figaro* (20 February 1909)

'Maritime Station, Le Havre, France', *The Architect & Building News* (30 August 1935)

Masterpieces, Navigazione General Italiana brochure about *Augustus* (New York, NY, n.d.)

Mauretania factsheet (October 2013), Cunard Archive, Liverpool

The Mild South Route to Europe, Publicity Department of the Italian Line (New York, NY, 1933)

'La Mode Française à New York', *L'Officiel de la Mode* (1935), no. 168

Gabriel Mourey, 'SS. "Ile-de-France": A Floating Museum of French Decorative Art', *The Studio*, (October 1927), vol. 94, no. 415

N

The New Cunard Building, Commemorative Publication, Mewès & Davis Archive, Plymouth, UK, D42/PR10/13

'New Dances Inspire a Style in Skirts', *The New York Times* (2 November 1914)

'New Orient Line Building, Spring Street Sydney', *Art in Australia* (23 May 1940)

'New Styles Revive Sculptured Lines', *The New York Times* (20 Aug 1935)

'"Normandie", Chef-d'œuvre de la technique et de l'art français', *L'Illustration* (June 1935), special issue no. 4813 bis

'Normandie': The Ship of the Future Designed in the Present, French Line/Compagnie Générale Transatlantique (New York, NY, 1937)

'North German Lloyd Opens New Ticket Offices This Week', *Daily Boston Globe* (18 May 1931)

'Notes for First-Class Passengers on Board the Steamers of the White Star Line' (April 1913)

O

The Ocean Ferry (September 1925), vol. 5, no. 12

'Ocean Liner's Model', *Times-Picayune* (22 January 1911)

'Ocean Going-Mannequins: How Enterprising French Houses Sell to Deep Sea Travelers', *Boston Daily Globe* (29 November 1914)

Amédée Ozenfant & Charles-Édouard Jeanneret, 'Le Purisme', *L'Esprit Nouveau* (1920), no. 4

P

'Packing for Pleasure', *Vogue* (15 May 1934)

C.B. Palmer, 'The Building of S.S. *United States*: The Nation's Newest, Biggest and Fastest Liner is a Unique Maritime Contribution', *The New York Times* (30 March 1952)

Le Paquebot France (Paris, 1962)

'Paquin to Exhibit Here, Announcement Causes Resentment Among American Buyers in Paris', *The New York Times* (13 Feb 1914)

'The Paris', French Line brochure (c.1921)

Parliamentary Debates [Hansard], fourth series, vol. 127

'The Passenger Ship: Backward or Forward? A review of ship interiors, including some recent Cunarders, the Orient liner 'Oriana'; Designed by: Design Research Unit; and the P&O liner 'Canberra'; Designed by: Hugh Casson, with McInnes, Gardner & Partners', *Architectural Review* (September 1961)

Bruno Paul, 'Passagierdampfer und ihre Einrichtungen', *Jahrbuch des Deutschen Werkbundes* (Jena, 1914)

Georges Philippar, *La Décoration des navires*, conference given by Georges Philippar on 11 December 1926 at the Institut océanographique in Paris (Paris, 1927)

'Picabia, Art Rebel, Here to Present the New Movement', *The New York Times* (16 February 1913)

Francis Picabia, '"How New York Looks to Me" by Picabia', *New York American* (30 March 1913)

'Polish Ship's Salon Made a Synagogue', *The New York Times* (25 February 1934)

Gio Ponti, '*Alcuni interni dell'Andrea Doria*', *Domus* (April 1953), no. 281

Enrico Prampolini, 'The Aesthetic of the Machine and Mechanical Introspection in Art', translated by 'E.S.' (reprinted from *The Little Review*) in *Machine-Age Exposition* (New York, 1927)

Q

Queen Elizabeth 2, Cunard Line inaugural season brochure (1969)

R

William A. Rawson & Theodore Francis Garrett, *The Encyclopaedia of Practical Cookery* (London, 1892–4), vol. 7

Gladys A. Reichard, *Navajo Medicine Man: Sandpaintings and Legends of Miguelito from the John Frederick Huckel Collections* (New York, 1939)

Charles A. Richter, unpublished manuscript notebook, 1928 (in possession of one of Richter's five grandchildren, Sally Festing)

Ritz's Carlton Restaurant On Board the S.S. "Kaiserin Auguste Victoria" (Hamburg-American Line) Under the Management of the Carlton Hotel, London, Carlton Hotel & Hamburg-Amerikanische Packetfahrt-Actien-Gesellschaft (London, 1906)

John Robinson, *The Marine Room of the Peabody Museum of Salem* (Salem, MA, 1921)

Juliette Roche, *Demi Cercle* (Paris, 1920)

Léon Rosenthal, 'Le Paquebot "Paris"', *Art et Decóration* (January–December 1921)

S

'Satisfying Transatlantic Equestrians', *Illustrated World* (September 1915)

Karl Schaefer, 'Der Norddeutsche Lloyd und die moderne Raumkunst', *Dekorative Kunst*, 1908, vol. 16

'Schiff des Friedens und der Freude "Wilhelm Gustloff"', *Arbeit und Staat* (9 June 1937)

'Sea Going Synagogue', *The Spokesman* (27 March 1936), vol. 24, no. 3020

'The Secret Staircase': The New Flagship *Rotterdam*, Holland America Line guide booklet (Rotterdam, 1959)

H.P. Shapland, 'De luxe', a speech delivered to the Design and Industries Association, July 1930, quoted in *Architectural Review* (September 1931)

'Ship Model Exhibit Intrigues Visitors to Cunard Line Offices', *The Washington Post* (18 October 1936)

'Shops on Ships', *Harper's Bazaar* (US Edition, April 1934)

'Some Notable Passengers on Famous Ship', *The Ocean Ferry* (March 1926), vol. 5, no. 6

'Steamship Model Costs Run up to $25,000', *Daily Boston Globe* (24 November 1929)

'Steamship Model Worth a Fortune', *Baltimore American* (7 April 1911)

Sukiyaki: A Dainty Japanese Dish, NYK Line 6-panel publicity brochure (1938)

'Superliner Plans in Advanced Stage', *The New York Times* (17 July 1949)

T

William Tatton Brown, 'Architecture Afloat, The "Orion" sets a New Course', *Architectural Review* (October 1935), vol. 78

Bruno Taut, *Die neue Baukunst in Europa und Amerika* (Stuttgart, 1929), simultaneously published in English as *Modern Architecture* (London, 1929)

'The 21-knot liner *Giulio Cesare*: First of two ships with double-acting Fiat machinery of 25,000 bhp using boiler oil', *The Motor Ship* (February 1951), vol. 31

Third-Class Menu, RMS *Scythia* (21 July 1922), Phillips Library, Peabody Essex Museum

T/N Michelangelo, Italia Compagnia Navigazione, Ansaldo Cantiere Navale & La Marina Mercantile (Genoa, 1965)

'To Open Ship Synagogue: Rabbis Dedicate Place of Worship on Polish Liner Today', *The New York Times* (23 February 1934)

Josephine Tozier, *The Travelers' Handbook: A Manual for Transatlantic Tourists* (New York, NY, 1905)

'Trans-Atlantic Liner "France": Luxury Passenger Liner for the French Line', *The Shipping World* (7 February 1962)

'Travel Advertising Addressed to Women Only', *The Ocean Ferry* (February 1926) vol. 5, no. 5

Carolyn Trowbidge Lewis, 'When She Travels – Fine Women's Fashions for Ocean Liner Travel', *The Cunarder* (July 1921), vol. 1, no. 1

'Two New Docks at Home and Abroad', *The Architects' Journal* (3 August 1933)

'Two Women "Dress" New Luxury Liner', *Schenectady Gazette* (4 July 1952)

V

John de La Valette, 'The Fitment and Decoration of Ships from the "Great Eastern" to the "Queen Mary"', *Journal of the Royal Society of Arts* (22 May 1936), vol. 84, no. 4357

'Vor dem Auskunftsbureau des "Norddeutschen Lloyd" in Berlin', *Das Buch für Alle. Illustrierte Familien-Zeitung. Chronik der Gegenwart* (1893), vol. 28

W

Norman Wilkinson, 'Dazzle Painting of Ships', *Journal of the Royal Society of Arts* (12 March 1920), vol. 68, no. 3512

Y

Helen Eva Yates, *The World is Your Oyster: The Art of Traveling Smartly* (New York, NY, 1939)

SECONDARY SOURCES

A

Kenneth Agnew, 'Concept to Cunarder', *Architectural Review* (June 1969)

Alfred Auguste Janniot 1889–1969 (Paris, 2003)

Virginie Alliot-Duchêne (ed.), *Paquebot France* (Paris, 2011)

Anne Anderson, 'Fit for the Queens: Teawares for the Cunard Transatlantic Liners c. 1920–40', *Journal of the Decorative Arts Society* (1998), vol. 22

Mathilde Apelt Schmidt, *My Father, Hermann Apelt: The Legacy of a Great German Senator* (Bloomington, IN, 2011)

Ruth Artmonsky, *Shipboard Style: Colin Anderson of the Orient Line* (London, 2013)

Ruth Artmonsky & Susie Cox, *P&O Across the Oceans, Across the Years: A Pictorial Voyage* (Woodbridge, 2012)

Vilhelm Aubert, *The Hidden Society* (Totowa, NJ, 1965)

'Autobiographical Notes by Gerald Murphy, from the Douglas MacAgy Papers', *Journal of American Art* (1999), vol. 39, no. 3–4

B

C. Baecker, C. Jeanmaire & C. Väterlein, *Die Anderen Nürnberger: Technisches Spielzeug aus der "guten alten Zeit"* (Frankfurt am Main, 1988), vol. 7

Chris Howard Bailey, *Down the Burma Road: Work and Leisure for the Below-Deck Crew of the* Queen Mary, *(1947–1967)*, (Southampton, 1991)

Gregory Battcock, 'Ocean Liners: The Way They Were', *Art in America* (Summer 1980)

Roy R. Behrens, 'The Role of Artists in Ship Camouflage During World War I', *Leonardo* (1999), vol. 32, no. 1

Patricia Belbachir, 'A.F. Mac Del Marle: vision futuriste du port', *Revue du Nord* (July–December 1992), vol. 74, nos 297–8

Patricia Belbachir, *Félix Del Marle: Itinéraire d'une liberté* (Pont-sur-Sambre, 1996)

Dagmar Bellmann, *Von Höllengefährten zu schwimmenden Palästen: Die Passagierschifffahrt auf dem Atlantik* (Frankfurt am Main, 2015)

Tim Benton, *The Rhetoric of Modernism: Le Corbusier as a Lecturer* (Boston, MA, 2009)

Tim Benton, 'The Villa de Mandrot and the Place of the Imagination' in Michel Richard (ed.), *Massilia 2011: Annuaire d'Études Corbuséennes* (Marseilles, 2011, originally published in *Quaderns*, 1984)

Tim Benton, *LC Foto: Le Corbusier Secret Photographer* (Baden & London, 2013)

Janet Catherine Berlo, 'The Skies (from the Shootingway Chant)', *Shapeshifting: Transformations in Native American Art* (Salem, MA, 2012)

Massimo Bontempelli, *L'Avventura novecentista* (Florence, 1974)

Frank O. Braynard, *The Big Ship: The Story of the SS United States* (Newport News, VA, 1981)

Emmanuel Bréon & Philippe Rivoirard (eds), *1925, Quand l'Art déco séduit le monde* (Paris, 2013)

John Malcolm Brinnin, 'The Decoration of Ocean Liners: Rules and Exceptions', *Journal of Decorative and Propaganda Arts* (Spring 1990) vol. 15

John Malcolm Brinnin and Kenneth Gaulin, *Grand Luxe: The Transatlantic Style* (New York, NY, 1988)

Charles Brock, *Charles Sheeler: Across Media*, (Washington D.C. & Berkeley, CA, 2006)

Peter Brooke, 'Albert Gleizes à New York' in Christian Briend (ed.), *Albert Gleizes: Le Cubisme en majesté* (Paris, 2001)

Edward Burtynsky, *Burtynsky – Oil* (Göttingen, 2009)

C

Gabriele Cadringher & Anne Massey, *Ocean Liner Posters* (Woodbridge, 2011)

William A. Camfield, *Francis Picabia: His Art, Life and Times* (Princeton, NJ, 1979)

William A. Camfield et al., *Francis Picabia Catalogue Raisonné: Volume 1* (New Haven, CT & London, 2014)

Charles Demuth: Memorial Exhibition (New York, NY, 1937)

Charles Sheeler: Paintings, Drawings, Photographs, with an introduction by William Carlos Williams (New York, NY, 1939)

Martina Corgnati (ed.), *Arte a Bordo: La Collezione in viaggio di Costa Crociere/Art on Board: Costa Crociere Travelling Collection* (Milan, 2010)

Costa Crociere's Corporate Communication Department (ed.) with texts by Paolo Piccione, Gian Paolo Ceserani & Fiora Steinbach Palazzini, *Sessant'anni di crociere Costa/Sixty Years of Cruising with Costa* (Milan, 2008)

D

Alan Dale, *The Great Wet Way* (New York, NY, 1909)

Mary E. Davis, *Classic Chic: Music, Fashion and Modernism* (Berkeley & Los Angeles, CA, 2006)

Philip Dawson, *British Superliners of the Sixties: A Design Appreciation of the* Oriana, Canberra *and* QE2 (London, 1990)

Philip Dawson, *Canberra: In the Wake of a Legend* (London, 1997)

Philip Dawson, *The Liner: Retrospective and Renaissance* (London, 2005)

Philip Dawson & Bruce Peter, *Ship Style: Modernism and Modernity at Sea in the Twentieth Century* (London, 2010)

Guillemette Delaporte, *René Herbst: Pioneer of Modernism*, trans. by David Radzinowicz (Paris, 2004)

Gérard Destrais, *Chef-d'œuvre de l'architecture Art Déco des années 1930* (Cherbourg-Octeville, 2002)

Lawrence Driscoll, *The Last Great Race* (El Cerrito, CA, 2013)

Maldwin Drummond, *Salt-Water Palaces* (New York, NY, 1979)

E

Sarah Edington, *The Captain's Table: Life and Dining on the Great Ocean Liners* (London, 2005)

Marc Eliot, *Cary Grant: A Biography* (New York, NY, 2004)

Maurizio Eliseo & Paolo Piccione, *Transatlantici: The History of the Great Italian Liners on the Atlantic* (Genoa, 2001)

David Ellery, *RMS* Queen Mary*: 101 Questions and Answers about the Great Transatlantic Liner* (London, 2006)

Frederick E. Emmons, *American Passenger Ships: The Ocean Lines and Liners, 1873–1983* (Newark, NJ & London, 1985)

Meredith Etherington-Smith, *Patou* (New York, NY 1983)

Caroline Evans, *The Mechanical Smile: Modernism and the First Fashion Shows in France and America, 1900–1930* (New Haven, CT, 2013)

Glyn L. Evans, *The Maritime Art of Kenneth D. Shoesmith* (Kettering, 2010)

F

Peter de Figueiredo, 'Symbols of Empire: The Buildings of the Liverpool Waterfront', *Architectural History* (2003), vol. 46

Daniel Finamore, 'Pirate Water: Sailing to Belize in the Mahogany Trade' in David Killingray, Margarette Lincoln & Nigel Rigby (eds), *Maritime Empires: British Imperial Maritime Trade in the Nineteenth Century* (Woodbridge, 2004)

Michelle Tolini Finamore, *Hollywood Before Glamour: Fashion in American Silent Film* (London, 2013)

F. Scott Fitzgerald, *Tender is the Night* (New York, NY, 2003)

Alastair Forsyth, 'Floating Palaces: British Liners of the 1930s', *Thirties Society Journal* (1984), no. 4

Bruno Foucart, Charles Offrey, François Robichon & Claude Villers, *Normandie, l'épopée du 'Géant des mers'* (Paris, 1985)

Vanessa Friedman, 'Chanel Cruises into Havana, Showcasing Style and Questions', *The New York Times* (5 May 2016)

Roland Fuller, *The Bassett-Lowke Story* (London, 1984)

G

Stephen Garrett, 'Amid Ships', *Architectural Review* (September, 1961)

Bruno Gaudichon et al., *Carlo Sarrabezolles, 1888–1971: De l'esquisse au colossal* (Paris, 2008)

John Graves, 'Ship Models – Magnificent *Mauretania*', Royal Museums Greenwich, www.rmg.co.uk/discover/behind-the-scenes/blog/ship-models-magnificent-mauretania

Christopher Green, 'The Machine', in Christopher Wilk (ed.), *Modernism 1914–1939: Designing a New World* (London, 2006)

Basil Greenhill & Ann Giffard, *Travelling by Sea in the Nineteenth Century: Interior Design in Victorian Passenger Ships* (London, 1972)

H

Freda Harcourt, *Flagships of Imperialism: The P&O Company and the Politics of Empire From its Origins to 1867* (Manchester, 2006)

Stephen Harding, *Great Liners at War* (Stroud, 2007)

William Owen Harrod, 'Toward a Transatlantic Style: The Vereinigte Werkstätten für Kunst im Handwerk and German Modernism in the United States', *Studies in the Decorative Arts* (Fall–Winter 2004–2005) vol. 12, no. 1

E. Harryman, P. Lasley & M. Verdure, *The Art of Cruising: Fine Art and Antiques of Holland America Line* (Seattle, 2007)

Barbara Haskell, *Charles Demuth* (New York, NY, 1987)

Mark Haworth-Booth, *McKnight Kauffer: A Designer and his Public* (London, 2005)

Henning Henningsen, *Crossing the Equator: Sailors' Baptism and Other Initiation Rites* (Copenhagen, 1961)

Douglas M. Hinkey, with Cynthia B. MacMullin & Ronald L. Smith, *The Art of the RMS* Queen Mary (Long Beach, CA, 1994)

David Howarth & Stephen Howarth, *The Story of P&O* (London, 1986 and revised edition, 1994)

J

Anna Jackson, *Expo: International Expositions 1851–2010* (London, 2008)

Christopher Jordan, 'Tile Panels by William De Morgan for the Peninsular and Oriental Steam Navigational Company', *The Burlington Magazine* (June 2001), vol. 143, no. 1179

K

Wendy Kaplan (ed.), *Designing Modernity: The Arts of Reform and Persuasion, 1885–1945* (London, 1995)

Bruce Kellner (ed.), *The Letters of Charles Demuth, American Artists, 1883–1935* (Philadelphia, 2000)

D. Killingray, M. Lincoln & N. Rigby (eds), *Maritime Empires: British Imperial Maritime Trade in the Nineteenth Century* (Woodbridge, 2004)

Pierre Kjellberg, *Art Déco: Les Maîtres du mobilier, Le Décor des paquebots* (Paris, 1981)

Arnold Kludas, *Die Geschichte der deutschen Passagierschiffahrt: Band II: Expansion auf allen Meeren 1890 bis 1900* (Hamburg, 1987)

Peter C. Kohler, 'Building Anew' in Philip Dawson & Bruce Peter (eds), *Ship Style: Modernism and Modernity at Sea in the Twentieth Century* (London, 2010)

Leonard Koren & John Margolies, 'New Life for Luxury Liner: The *Queen Mary*', *Progressive Architecture* (July 1974), vol. 55, no. 7

L

Peter Laister, *Mariner's Memorabilia: A Guide to British Shipping Company China of the 19th & 20th Centuries*, vols 1 & 2, (Longfield, 2006)

Brian Lavery & Simon Stephens, *Ship Models: Their Purpose and Development from 1650 to the Present* (London, 1995)

Herman Lebovics, *True France: The Wars Over Cultural Identity, 1900–1945* (New York, NY, 1992)

Pierre Léonforte & Éric Pujalet-Plaà, *100 Legendary Trunks: Louis Vuitton* (New York, NY, 2010)

Sophie Lévy, *A Transatlantic Avant-garde: American Artists in Paris, 1918–1939*, (Berkeley, CA & Giverny, 2003)

Giovanni Lista, 'A.F. Delmarle, peintre futuriste', *L'Humidité* (July 1973), no. 16

Giovanni Lista, *Futurisme: Manifestes, proclamations, documents* (Lausanne, 1973)

Karen Lucic, *Charles Sheeler and the Cult of the Machine* (London, 1991)

M

Anne Massey, 'Nationalism and Design at the End of Empire: Interior Design and the Ocean Liner', in Penny Sparke et al. (eds), *Designing the Modern Interior: From the Victorians to Today*, (Oxford, 2009)

Yōko Masutani, Santorī Bijutsukan et al., *Fantastic Voyage: Luxury and Sophistication on the Ocean Liners* (Osaka, 1996)

Ered Matthew, 'The *Kronprinzessin Cecilie* Project: Restoring Fleischmann's Forgotten Masterpiece', www.kronprinzessin-cecilie.com/index.html

John Maxtone-Graham, *The Only Way to Cross* (New York, NY, 1972)

John Maxtone-Graham, *SS* United States*: Red, White & Blue Ribband, Forever* (New York, NY, 2014)

Harriet McKay, 'Conservative Flagship: Interior Design for RMS *Windsor Castle*, 1960', in C. Breward, F. Fisher & G. Wood (eds), *British Design: Tradition and Modernity after 1948*, (London & New York, NY, 2015)

Amy Miller & Christine Riding, 'Art, Artists and the Home Front', *Art and the War at Sea: 1914–45* (London, 2015)

Laurence Miller, 'Cunard: Nearly 150 Years of Cruise Excellence', *Cruise News* (6 May 1984)

William H. Miller, *The First Great Ocean Liners in Photographs, 1897–1927* (New York, 1984)

F. Morelli, L. Della Cagna & M. Finamore, *Gaetano Savini: The Man Who Was Brioni* (New York, 2015)

Charles F. Morris, *Origins, Orient and Oriana* (Sussex, 1980)

Henri Mouron, *A.M. Cassandre* (New York, 1985)

N

Franc J. Newcomb & Gladys A. Reichard, *Sandpaintings of the Navajo Shooting Chant* (New York, 1937, reprinted 1975)

O

Richard B. Oliver, *The Oceanliner, Speed, Style, Symbol* (New York, 1980)

F. Ollivier, A. Perroy & F. Sénant, *À Bord des paquebots: 50 ans d'arts décoratifs* (Paris, 2011)

Jürgen Osterhammel & Niels P. Petersson, *Globalization: A Short History* (Princeton, 2005)

P

Peter Padfield, *Beneath the House Flag of the P&O* (London, 1981)

Paul-Gérard Pasols, *Louis Vuitton: La Naissance du luxe moderne* (Paris, 2005)

B. Peter, P. Dawson & I. Johnston, QE2*: Britain's Greatest Liner* (Ramsey, 2008)

Paolo Piccione, *Crociere nell'arte: Arte a bordo delle navi Italiane / Cruising into Art: Art on board Italian Liners* (Genoa, 2002)

Paolo Piccione, *Nino Zoncada: Interni Navali 1931–1971* (Genoa, 2007)

Paolo Piccione, *Gio Ponti: Le Navi. Il progetto degli interni navali 1948–1953* (Viareggio, 2007)

Paolo Piccione, *Manifesti: Il Viaggio in mare, pubblicità e crociere in Italia 1885–1965 / Posters: The Sea Voyage: Advertising and Cruises in Italy from 1885 to 1965* (Milan, 2013)

Gérard Piouffre, *First Class: Legendary Ocean Liner Voyages Around the World* (London & New York, NY, 2009)

Philip Plisson, Queen Mary 2*: The Birth of a Legend* (New York, 2004)

Neil Potter & Jack Frost, Queen Elizabeth 2*: The Authorised Story* (London, 1969)

Q

Peter Quartermaine, *Building on the Sea: Form and Meaning in Modern Ship Architecture* (London, 1996)

Peter Quartermaine & Bruce Peter, *Cruise: Identity, Design and Culture* (London, 2006)

R

Rassegna (December 1990), vol. 44

Mark Rennella & Whitney Walton, 'Planned Serendipity: American Travelers and the Transatlantic Voyage in the Nineteenth and Twentieth Centuries', *Journal of Social History* (Winter 2004), vol. 38, no. 2

Bernhard Rieger, 'Floating Palaces: Ocean Liners as Icons of Modern Splendour', *History Today* (2005), vol. 55, no. 2

Bernhard Rieger, *Technology and the Culture of Modernity in Britain and Germany, 1890–1945* (Cambridge, 2005)

Constance Rourke, *Charles Sheeler, Artist in the American Tradition* (New York, NY, 1938)

William Rubin & Carolyn Lanchner, *The Paintings of Gerald Murphy* (New York, 1974)

W.D. Rubinstein, M.A. Jolles & H.L. Rubinstein (eds), *Palgrave Dictionary of Anglo-Jewish History* (Basingstoke, 2011)

Mark A. Russell, 'Picturing the *Imperator*: Passenger Shipping as Art and National Symbol in the German Empire', *Central European History* (2011), vol. 44, no. 2

S

George Schwartz, *'Collecting and Arranging a History of the Globe': A Reconsideration of the Salem East India Marine Society and Antebellum American Museology* (doctoral dissertation, Boston University, 2015)

Marlis Schweitzer, 'Networking the Waves: Ocean Liners, Impresarios, and Broadways' Atlantic Expansion', *Theatre Survey* (September 2012), vol. 53, no. 2

Susan C. Seymour, *Cora Du Bois: Anthropologist, Diplomat, Agent* (Lincoln, NE, 2015)

Daniel Sicard (ed.), *Décors de paquebots: Cadre de vie et arts décoratifs sur les paquebots d'hier et aujourd'hui* (Saint-Nazaire, 1998)

Françoise Siriex & Philippe Conquer, 'La Décoration du paquebot *France*', *303 Arts, Recherches et Créations* (Nantes, 1992), no. 24

'Skill: A Monthly Review of Building Techniques and Industrial Design', *Architectural Review* (February 1956)

Abbie N. Sprague, 'Modern Art Takes to the Waves', *Apollo* (1 May 2008)

C.M. Squarey, *The Patient Talks* (London, 1955)

Gail Stavitsky et al., *Precisionism in America, 1915–1941: Reordering Reality* (New York, NY, 1994)

T.E. Stebbins, G. Mora & K. Haas, *The Photography of Charles Sheeler: American Modernist* (Boston, MA, 2002)

James Steele, *Queen Mary* (London, 2001)

Eberhard Straub, *Albert Ballin: Der Reeder des Kaisers* (Berlin, 2001)

C.S. Sykes, *David Hockney: The Biography, 1937–1975* (New York, 2012)

T

Stefano Tettamanti, *Six Wonderful Days. Un Invito Al Viaggio Sulle Grandi Navi Italiane* (Tormena, 2002)

Anna Teut (ed.), *Al Mansfeld: An Architect in Israel* (Berlin, 1999)

William Makepeace Thackeray, 'De Juventute' (1860), in *The Roundabout Papers* (first US edition, New York, 1863)

Calvin Tomkins, 'Living Well is the Best Revenge', *The New Yorker* (28 July 1962)

Carol Troyen & Erica E. Hirshler, *Charles Sheeler: Paintings and Drawings* (Boston, MA, 1987)

Amy B. Trubek, 'Turtle Soup', *Gastronomica* (2001), vol. 1, no. 1

Karen Tsujimoto, *Images of America: Precisionist Painting and Modern Photography* (Seattle, 1982)

Elizabeth Hutton Turner, *Americans in Paris (1921–1931): Man Ray, Gerald Murphy, Stuart Davis, Alexander Calder* (Washington, D.C., 1996)

Mark Twain, *Life on the Mississippi* (London, 1883)

U

Steven Ujifusa, *A Man and His Ship: America's Greatest Naval Architect and His Quest to Build the SS* United States (New York, NY, 2012)

V

Jules Verne, *A Floating City* (London, 1876)

Louis-René Vian, *Arts décoratifs à bord des paquebots français, 1880–1960* (Paris, 1992)

Gregory Votolato, *Ship* (London, 2011)

W

Anne Wealleans, *Designing Liners: A History of Interior Design Afloat* (London, 2006)

Jeffrey Russell Willoughby, *Bremen & Europa: German Speed Queens of the Atlantic* (Surrey, 2010)

Richard Guy Wilson, Dianne H. Pilgrim & Dickran Tashjian, *The Machine Age America 1918–41* (New York, NY, 1986)

Ghislaine Wood, 'The Exotic' in C. Benton, T. Benton & G. Wood, *Art Deco 1910–1939* (London, 2003)

INDEX

PHOTOGRAPHY CREDITS

By plate number. All images © Victoria and Albert Museum, London. Except:

3 Peabody Essex Museum, Salem, Massachusetts. Photo by Allison White

4 Courtesy of the University of Liverpool Library, Cunard Archive, (Stuart Bale Photograph) D42/PR2/1/97/B14

5 Image Courtesy of Scandlines Danmark ApS.

6 Image © Gary Black

8 © Peabody Essex Museum, Salem, Massachusetts. Photo by Luke Abiol

10 © Ron Herron Archive. All Rights Reserved, DACS 2016

11 © Italia di Navigazione S.p.A. Photo by Kathy Tarantola

12 © 2016 Peabody Essex Museum, Salem, Massachusetts. Photo by Kathy Tarantola

13 Courtesy of The Mariners' Museum, Newport News, VA. Photo by Brock Switzer

14 © 2016 Peabody Essex Museum, Salem, Massachusetts. Photo by Kathy Tarantola

15 Courtesy Cunard

16 Münchner Stadtmuseum

17 Private Collection/Ken Welsh/Bridgeman Images

18 © Peabody Essex Museum, Salem, Massachusetts. Photo by Stephen Petegorsky

19 Courtesy of Peabody Essex Museum, Salem, Massachusetts

20 Courtesy of Peabody Essex Museum, Salem, Massachusetts. Photo by Bob Packert

22 © Compagnie Générale Transatlantique

25 Cliché Saint-Nazaire Tourisme et Patrimoine

26 © P&O Heritage Collection

28 Courtesy of Peabody Essex Museum, Salem, Massachusetts

29 © Historische Museum Bremerhaven

30 Robert Walker/The New York Times/Redux/eyevine

31 © 2016 Peabody Essex Museum, Salem, Massachusetts. Photo by Kathy Tarantola

32 © The Mariners' Museum, Newport News, VA. Photo by Brock Switzer

33 Peabody Essex Museum, Salem, Massachusetts. Photo by Allison White

34 © 2016 Peabody Essex Museum, Salem, Massachusetts. Photo by Walter Silver

35 Reproduced by permission of Historic England Archive

37 © P&O Heritage Collection

38 Reproduced by permission of Historic England Archive

39 © Peter Cowling

40 By courtesy of The University of Liverpool Library, Cunard Archive. D42/PR (uncatalogued)

41 © P&O Heritage Collection

42 Bruce Peter Collection

43 Collection French Lines

44 Bruce Peter Collection

45 Bruce Peter Collection

46 Bruce Peter Collection

47 © Collection French Lines

48 © Collection French Lines/Créapolis (2013)

49 © Collection French Lines

50 © Collection French Lines

51 © P&O Heritage Collection

52 © Wolfsoniana - Palazzo Ducale Fondazione per la Cultura, Genova

53 © National Maritime Museum, Greenwich, London

54 © National Maritime Museum, Greenwich, London

55 © 2016 Peabody Essex Museum, Salem, Massachusetts. Photo by Kathy Tarantola

56 © Imperial War Museums

57 Courtesy of John R. Hume

58 © Scottish Maritime Museum

59 © CSG CIC Glasgow Museums and Libraries Collections

60 © E. Phillips/Stringer/Hulton Archive/Getty Images

61 © Pierre Boucher – Cliché Musée d'Art Moderne/Roger-Viollet

62 © John Parrot/Stocktrek Images/Getty Images

63 Courtesy of Peabody Essex Museum, Salem, Massachusetts. Photo by Jarrod Staples

64 Paolo Piccione Collection

65 © Martin Stringer/Hulton Archive/Getty Images

66 Byron Company (New York, N.Y.)/Museum of the City of New York

67 Courtesy of Peabody Essex Museum, Salem, Massachusetts. Photo by Mark Sexton

68 © The Mariners' Museum, Newport News, VA. Photo by Brock Switzer

69 Public domain

72 © Peter Cowling

73 © dpa picture alliance/Alamy Stock Photo

74 © Laister Collection

76 © National Museums Northern Ireland/Harland & Wolff Collection, Ulster Folk & Transport Museum

77 Photograph by Paul Carter. Image © Victoria and Albert Museum, London

79 Private Collection/The Stapleton Collection/Bridgeman Images

80 From the collection of the Maritime Museum of the Atlantic, Halifax, Nova Scotia

81 University of Glasgow Archive Services, Stoddard-Templeton collection, GB248 STOD/DES/133/27

82 © National Maritime Museum, Greenwich, London

85 Münchner Stadtmuseum

86 Münchner Stadtmuseum

87 Peabody Essex Museum, Salem, Massachusetts. Photo by Allison White

88 © Cliché Saint-Nazaire Tourisme et Patrimoine

89 SLUB Dresden/Deutsche Fotothek

90 Yad Vashem Photo Archive

91 © Collection French Lines

92 © Cliché Saint-Nazaire Tourisme et Patrimoine

93 Image Courtesy of Cliché Saint-Nazaire Tourisme et Patrimoine/© ADAGP, Paris and DACS, London 2016

94 © Musées de la Ville de Boulogne-Billancourt

95 © 2016 Peabody Essex Museum, Salem, Massachusetts. Photo by Kathy Tarantola

96 © Cliché Saint-Nazaire Tourisme et Patrimoine

97 © Cliché Saint-Nazaire Tourisme et Patrimoine

98 © Cliché Saint-Nazaire Tourisme et Patrimoine

99 Paolo Piccione Collection

100 © Wolfsoniana - Palazzo Ducale Fondazione per la Cultura, Genova

101 © Collection French Lines

102 © RIBA Collections

103 © Collection French Lines/Créapolis

104 © 2016 Peabody Essex Museum, Salem, Massachusetts. Photo by Walter Silver

105 © Musée d'Art Moderne/Roger-Viollet

106 © Byron Company (New York, N.Y.)/Museum of the City of New York

107 Académie d'Architecture, Paris

108 © P&O Heritage Collection

109 Courtesy of Jonathan Quayle/image © Victoria and Albert Museum, London

112 © Williamson Art Gallery and Museum, Wirral, UK

113 © Peabody Essex Museum, Salem, Massachusetts. Photo by Tim Nighswander/Imaging4Art

114 © RIBA Collections

116 © National Maritime Museum, Greenwich, London

117 © Imperial War Museums

118 © Bettmann/Getty Images

119 © Imperial War Museums

120 © Giorgio Lolli

121 Bruce Peter Collection

122 © The Estate of Edward Bawden

123 © The Estate of Edward Bawden

124 © The Estate of Edward Bawden

125 Paolo Piccione Collection

126 © Paolo De Poli

127 Paolo Piccione Collection

128 Courtesy of Archivio Marcello Mascherini/Costa Cruises

129 Bruce Peter Collection

130 Bruce Peter Collection

131 SS United States Conservancy

132 Paolo Piccione Collection

133 Courtesy of Peabody Essex Museum, Salem, Massachusetts. Photo by Allison White

134 © Collection French Lines

135 © Collection French Lines

136 © Collection French Lines

137 © P&O Heritage Collection

138 © P&O Heritage Collection

139 Image courtesy of the Sainsbury Centre for Visual Arts, reproduced by kind permission of the owners P&O Heritage Collection © Estate of Mary Martin

140 © Ernest Race. Image courtesy of Collection, The Target Gallery, London

141 Archivio Storico della Pubblicità, Genova, Italy

142 Mary Evans Picture Library

143 Bruce Peter Collection

144 © Ernest Race/image © Victoria and Albert Museum, London

145 Paolo Piccione Collection

146 Paolo Piccione Collection

147 Paolo Piccione Collection

148 Paolo Piccione Collection

149 Courtesy of Peabody Essex Museum, Salem, Massachusetts. Photo by Allison White

150 © P&O Heritage Collection

151 The Mariners' Museum, Newport News, VA. Photo by Brock Switzer

152 © 2016 Peabody Essex Museum, Salem, Massachusetts. Photo by Walter Silver

153 © 2016 Peabody Essex Museum, Salem, Massachusetts. Photo by Kathy Tarantola

154 © Magnes Collection

156 Image courtesy of P&O Heritage Collection, Permission granted by the Ardizzone Estate © Edward Ardizzone

157 Bruce Peter Collection

158 © Peabody Essex Museum, Salem, Massachusetts. Photo by Luke Abiol

159 © National Maritime Museum, Greenwich, London

160 © R. Holman & Co./Museum of the City of New York

161 © 2016 Peabody Essex Museum, Salem, Massachusetts. Photo by Kathy Tarantola

162 © Byron Company (New York, N.Y.)/Museum of the City of New York

163 Courtesy of Peabody Essex Museum, Salem, Massachusetts. Photo by Allison White

164 Courtesy of Peabody Essex Museum, Salem, Massachusetts. Photo by Stephen Petegorsky

165 Private Collection/The Stapleton Collection/Bridgeman Images

166 By courtesy of The University of Liverpool Library, Cunard Archive. D42/PR2/10/7/6/10

167 © Peabody Essex Museum, Salem, Massachusetts. Photo by Luke Abiol

168 © Laister Collection

169 © Laister Collection

170 © Peabody Essex Museum, Salem, Massachusetts. Photo by Luke Abiol

171 © Cliché Saint-Nazaire Tourisme et Patrimoine

172 © RIBA Collections

173 Courtesy of Peabody Essex Museum, Salem, Massachusetts. Photo by Allison White

174 © The Mariners' Museum, Newport News, VA. Photo by Brock Switzer

175 Courtesy of Peabody Essex Museum, Salem, Massachusetts

176 Mira Jedwabnik Van Doren Collection. Image © Peabody Essex Museum, Salem, Massachusetts. Photo by Tim Nighswander/Imaging4Art

177 © 2016 Peabody Essex Museum, Salem, Massachusetts. Photo by Kathy Tarantola

178 © Edward Steichen/Conde Nast Collection/Getty Images

179 Courtesy of Peabody Essex Museum, Salem, Massachusetts

180 © Eduardo Garcia Benito/Conde Nast Collection/Getty Images

181 © Woods/Express/Getty Images

182 Courtesy of The Elizabeth Taylor Trust and Christie's, Inc.

183 © Cité de l'architecture et du patrimoine

184 © Laziz Hamani

185 © Bettmann/Getty Images

186 LOUIS VUITTON MALLETIER

187 Marian Gérard, Cartier Collection © Cartier

189 © 2016 Peabody Essex Museum, Salem, Massachusetts. Photo by Kathy Tarantola

191 © 2013 Peabody Essex Museum. Photo by Walter Silver

192 © 2016 Museum of Fine Arts, Boston

193 © 2016 Museum of Fine Arts, Boston

194 © Collection Schall

195 © Collection Schall

196 © Les Arts décoratifs, Paris/Jean Tholance

197 Private Collection

198 © Museum of London

199 © FLC/ADAGP, Paris and DACS, London 2016

200 © FLC/ADAGP, Paris and DACS, London 2016

204 © Eileen Gray/Image © Victoria and Albert Museum, London.

205 © FLC

206 Courtesy of Peabody Essex Museum, Salem, Massachusetts. Photo by Allison White

207 Courtesy of Peabody Essex Museum, Salem, Massachusetts. Photo by Allison White

208 Courtesy of Peabody Essex Museum, Salem, Massachusetts. Photo by Jarrod Staples

209 © Musées de la Ville de Boulogne-Billancourt – Photo Philippe Fuzeau

210 Courtesy of Musées de la Ville de Boulogne-Billancourt/Photo Philippe Fuzeau © FLC/ ADAGP, Paris and DACS, London 2016

211 © Peabody Essex Museum, Salem, Massachusetts. Photo by Luke Abiol

212 © Jeffrey Sward

213 © Museum of the City of New York

214 Columbus Museum of Art, Ohio

215 Courtesy of Boston Public Library/DACS

216 © National Maritime Museum, Greenwich, London

217 Photo © RMN-Grand Palais/René-Gabriel Ojéda

218 © Tate, London 2016

219 Private Collection/Bridgeman Images © ADAGP, Paris and DACS, London 2016

220 © Museo Thyssen-Bornemisza, Madrid/ADAGP, Paris and DACS, London 2016

221 © 2016. Image © The Metropolitan Museum of Art/Art Resource/Scala, Florence

222 © President and Fellows of Harvard College

224 Photo © Centre Pompidou, MNAM-CCI, Dist. RMN-Grand Palais/Philippe Migeat

225 British Airways Heritage Collection

226 © Allan Baxter/Getty Images

227 Collection of the Nantucket Historical Association, Gift of Alfred Lowden, 1970.9.1

228 © Cunard

229 © Cunard

230 © Geoff Williamson SuperPrime/Alamy Stock Photo

231 © United Archives GmbH/Alamy Stock Photo

232 © AF archive/Alamy Stock Photo

233 © 2016 Peabody Essex Museum, Salem, Massachusetts. Photo by Kathy Tarantola

ACKNOWLEDGEMENTS

Several years in development, the *Ocean Liners* project has involved a huge number of people and we are grateful to everyone who has helped to see this exhibition and book come to fruition. Above all we would like to thank the curatorial and exhibition teams. At the Peabody Essex Museum, George Schwartz, Curatorial Scholar, and Sarah Chasse, Associate Curator, have worked alongside Brittany Minton and Rachel Miller in the Registration department. At the V&A, Anna Ferrari, Project Curator, and Meredith More, Research Assistant, have worked closely with Vanessa Baldwin, Alexandra Kaspar and Roo Gunzi in the Exhibitions department. Both teams have worked assiduously to produce this exhibition and book.

We are immensely grateful to all the institutional and private lenders to the exhibition for their support and generosity, many of them are mentioned in the book and listed below. Special mention should be made of Stephen Lash and Susie Cox who from the early stages have generously given of their time and expertise. Thanks to Judy Aitken, Sharon Ament, Kevin Andris, Iris Apfel, Réjane Bargiel, Beatrice Behlen, Laura Bennett, Ian Blatchford, Jane Bradbury, Emmanuel Bréon, Barbara Bundy, Mark and Cleo Butterfield, Stéphane Caron, Marie-Sophie Carron de la Carrière, Richard Chamberlain, Nancy Chauvet, Damien Cordier, Peter Cowling, Dorian Dallongeville, Susannah Darby, John H. Davey, Duncan Dornan, Agathe Doufils, Clémence Ducroix, Tony Dumitru, Thérèse Dumont, Courtney Ercolino, Richard Fain, Gretchen Fenston, Kevin Fewster, Lyles Forbes, Renée Frank, Julie Franklin, Olivier Gabet, Kirsten Gade, Nonie Gadsden, Dominique Gagneux, Afsaneh Girardot, Eric Giuily, Isabelle Godineau, Vadim Goncharenko, Kelly Gonzalez, Marc Goutierre, John Graves, Paul Gross, Vincent Hadot, Anna-Klara Hahn, Miranda Hambro, Meghan Grossman Hansen, Michael Harrison, Anette Hellmuth, Sarah Henry, Fabrice Hergott, Charles Hind, Jan Jacobsen, Mira Jedwabnik Van Doren, Ernest Jolly, Kevin Jones, Susan Henshaw Jones, Sarah Kavanagh, Capt. Will Kayne, Konstantin Kleinichen, Peter Knego, Marilena Kourniati, Harri Kulovaara, Peter and Pam Laister, Anne Lamarque, Ethan W. Lasser, Diane Lees, Paul Liss, Nannette V. Maciejunes, Richard MacMichael, Ferdinando Maffii, Christa Mahar, Emily Malcolm, David Mann, Roger Marsters, Emmanuel Mary, Bleue-Marine Massard, Jennifer Davis McDaid, Abigail McIntyre, Jeremy Michell, John Miottel, Helle Mølgaard, Marina Morgavi, Gaëlle Naegellen, Maria Newbery, Fiona Orsini, Clare Paterson, David Peyceré, Paolo Piccione, Claire Poirion, Evelyne Possémé, Søren Poulsgaard Jensen, Sue Prichard, Roberto Prili di Rado, Mario Pulice, Jonathan Quayle, Paul Quintrand, Alexandre Ragois, Jimmy Raye, Geoff Rayner, Rebecca Rhodes, Marie-Pierre Ribere, Lynn-Marie Richard, Michel Richard, Kathy Richmond, Christine Riding, Claudia Rivola, Lauren Robinson, Maria Rollo, David Rooney, Joanna S. Rose, Linda Ross, Moshe Safdie, Mary Schneider Enriquez, Lisa Shepherd, Colin Simpson, Richard Slocombe, Stephanie Smith, Guillermo Solana, Francesco Spagnolo, James A. Squires, David Stark, Simon Stephens, Kirsten Strachan, Fritz Straub, Angus Struthers, Martha Tedeschi, Matthew Teitelbaum, Jonathan Thomas, William J. Tramposch, Lindsay Turley, Simon Vaillant, Carrie Van Horn, Melanie Vandenbrouck, Antonia Voit, Jeanne Willoz-Egnor, Marie Wurry and Tiphaine Yvon.

We are deeply indebted to the authors, listed on p.288, who have contributed to this book. Many of them generously shared their expertise and helped with the selection of works for the show. Although it is difficult to single out one person, Bruce Peter deserves special thanks and we are grateful to him for his knowledge, passion and enthusiasm.

A host of scholars, curators and collectors have contributed to the project over the years. For their invaluable help, we would like to thank Simon Andrews, Alexis Ashot, Wendy Atkin-Smith, Paul Atterbury, Gilles Barnaud, Alastair Battson, Fiora Bellini, Tulga Beyerle, Anneli Blom, Christine Boydell, Rose Carver, Dinah Casson, David Clampin, Sarah Copplestone Wood, Daniel Davies, Jean-François Delamarre and Béatrice Delamarre-Levard, Anne Demeurisse, Gregg Dietrich, Roja Dove, Diane Dowgielewicz,

Joe Farcus, Sally and Michael Festing, Joy Fleischmann, Matteo Fochessati, Michael Gallagher, Susan Gibbs, Frédérique Gontier, Anne Gros, Tony Guanci, Karine Hagen, Anne Hoben, Charles Howland, Irene Jacobs, Paul Jarvis, Richard Kelton, Pierre Lagrange, Claire Longworth, Harry Lyons, Charles E. Mac Kay, Caroline Maniaque, Doris May, Karen B. Metheny, François Michaud, Brian W. Mock, Keith Morgan, Klara Nemeckova, Elizabeth Padjen, François Paillé, Agnès Paris, Stephen Payne, Patricia Pince van der Aa, Côme Remy, Geneviève Sarrabezolles-Appert, Lucia Savi, Lars U. Scholl, Joshua M. Smith, Aya Soika, Peter Spang, Dominique Suisse, Barbara Tomassi, Laura Tunbridge, Carina Villinger, Gregory Votolato, Lynne Warren, Rosemary Watt, Ali Wells, Nick White, Lesley Whitworth, Siân Wilks, Scott Wilson, Carola and Roger Zogolovitch, and Chiara Zuanni.

For the book, we would especially like to thank Jane Ace, Philip Contos and Sophie Kullmann, formerly of V&A Publishing, and Sophie Sheldrake, Emma Woodiwiss and Tom Windross for their work on various aspects of the publication; Fred Caws and Liz Edmunds for assembling images for the book; Linda Schofield for proof-reading the text; and Irena Hill and Trista Selous for translating essays. At the Peabody Essex Museum we would like to thank Kathy Fredrickson, Claire Blechman and Rebecca Bednarz in Exhibition Research and Publishing. We are extremely grateful to Richard Davis and Robert Auton of the V&A Photographic Studio, and to Bob Packert, Walter Silver, Kathy Tarantola and Allison White at the Peabody Essex Museum for the new photography. Our thanks to Peter Dawson of Grade Design for the elegant book design.

We are very grateful to the volunteers and interns who have assisted with research over the course of the project. Our thanks to Joanie Ingraham and Jim Vaccarino, as well as Nicole Nietzel, Olivia Kiers, Isaiah Krieger and Theresa Mitchell at the Peabody Essex Museum; and to Joel Moore and Isabella Russel at the V&A.

Numerous colleagues from across departments have supported the exhibition. At the Peabody Essex Museum, we would like to thank our executive director and CEO Dan L. Monroe and our deputy director Lynda Roscoe Hartigan; Priscilla Danforth and Annie Lundsten in Exhibition Planning; Dave Seibert, Karen Moreau-Ceballos, Richard Pepin and Jackie Traynor in Exhibition Design; Juliette Fritsch, Gavin Andrews, Lisa Incatasciato, and Jeanne Goswami in Education and Interpretation; Ed Rodley and Chip Van Dyke in Integrated Media; John Childs, Kathryn Carey, Mimi Leveque, Angela Lowther, Donald McPhee, Darcey Moore, J. David O'Ryan, Francesca Williams and Eric Wolin in Collections Services and Registration; Julie Diewald, Jay Finney, Susan Flynn,

Whitney Van Dyke, Kristen Levesque and Melissa Woods in Marketing; Amanda Clark MacMullan, Anne Butterfield, Janet Mallett Natti and Rebecca Ehrhardt in Development.

At the V&A, we would like to thank Sherrie Eatman who has played an important role coordinating the considerable conservation requirements. We would particularly like to thank all members of the Exhibitions department. Such a project would not have been possible without the expertise of many curators across the Collections at the V&A and we are immensely grateful to them for their advice, suggestions and support. We wish to thank Johanna Agerman Ross, Martin Barnes, Victoria Bradley, Victoria Button, Oriole Cullen, Cassie Davies-Strodder, Max Donnelly, Richard Edgcumbe, Edwina Ehrman, Alun Graves, Elizabeth-Anne Haldane, Kirsty Hassard, Ruth Hibbard, Olivia Horsfall Turner, Nick Humphrey, Anna Jackson, Eoin Kelly, Daniel Milford-Cottam, Joanna Norman, Linda Sandino, Gill Saunders, Bill Sherman, Suzanne Smith, Sonnet Stanfill, Deborah Sutherland, Margaret Timmers, Eric Turner, Rebecca Wallis and Claire Wilcox. We are very grateful to Roger Mann and Craig Riley from Casson Mann, Netia Jones from Lightmap and David Ellis and Kate Rogers from Why Not Associates for their exciting exhibition design and graphics, to Zerlina Hughes from Studio ZNA for the lighting and to Sor Lan Tan and Keith Flemming from Flemming Associates for their invaluable help.

We would also like to thank Kathy Flynn, Tamara Gaydos, Catherine Robertson, Ruth Stewart and Jennifer Hornsby at the Phillips Library (PEM), and all the staff at the National Art Library for their help with research and advice.

Special thanks to Philip Long, Director, V&A Museum of Design Dundee, who has been hugely supportive of this project from the outset and to the Sainsbury Centre, University of East Anglia, for generously allowing Ghislaine to continue to work on the project.

Moira Gemmill was a champion of the *Ocean Liners* exhibition at the V&A and it would not have happened without her support and advocacy. She is greatly missed.

Finally, we would like to thank our families for their patience.

GHISLAINE WOOD
FELLOW OF THE RESEARCH DEPARTMENT, VICTORIA AND ALBERT MUSEUM AND DEPUTY DIRECTOR OF THE SAINSBURY CENTRE FOR VISUAL ARTS, UNIVERSITY OF EAST ANGLIA

DANIEL FINAMORE
THE RUSSELL W. KNIGHT CURATOR OF MARITIME ART AND HISTORY, PEABODY ESSEX MUSEUM, SALEM, MASSACHUSETTS

TIM BENTON is Emeritus Professor of Art History at the Open University. A noted scholar of the works of Le Corbusier he has also acted as associate curator for several major exhibitions including *Art and Power* (1995), *Art Deco 1910–1939* (2003) and *Modern Taste: Art Deco in Paris 1910–1934* (2015). His recent books include *The Rhetoric of Modernism: Le Corbusier as Lecturer* (2007), *The Villas of Le Corbusier and Pierre Jeanneret, 1920–1930* (2007), *LC Foto: Le Corbusier Secret Photographer* (2013), and *E-1027 La restauration de la villa en bord de mer de Eileen Gray et Jean Badovici* (2016).

SARAH N. CHASSE is Associate Curator for Exhibitions and Research at the Peabody Essex Museum. She has contributed to numerous exhibitions for the museum including *Samuel McIntire: Carving an American Style* and *American Epics: Thomas Hart Benton and Hollywood*. Her research is focused on American and European decorative arts and design as well as early twentieth-century American art.

DORIAN DALLONGEVILLE is Senior Curator at French Lines in Le Havre which preserves and promotes the heritage of the French merchant shipping companies. He has curated many exhibitions dealing with maritime heritage, including *Légendes des Mers* (Evian, 2013), *Palaces on the Seas*, (Maritime Museum, Hong Kong, 2014) and *Lalique et l'Art du Voyage* (Musée Lalique, Wingen-sur-Moder, 2016).

ANNA FERRARI is Project Curator for *Ocean Liners* and a member of the Research Department at the V&A. She wrote her PhD thesis on the French modernist sculptor Henri Laurens (1885–1954) and has previously worked at Kettle's Yard, Cambridge and Barbican Art Gallery, London, where she co-edited *Barbican: Life, History, Architecture* (2014).

DANIEL FINAMORE is Co-Curator for *Ocean Liners* and The Russell W. Knight Curator of Maritime Art and History at the Peabody Essex Museum where he has organized more than 15 exhibitions. He holds a master of arts and doctorate in the field of archaeology and is the author and/or editor of five books, including *Maritime History as World History* (2004) and *Fiery Pool: The Maya and the Mythic Sea* (2010).

MICHELLE TOLINI FINAMORE is Penny Vinik Curator of Fashion Arts at the Museum of Fine Arts, Boston where she has curated *#techstyle*, *Hollywood Glamour* and *Think Pink*. She is the author of several books, including *Hollywood Before Glamour: Fashion in American Silent Film* (2013), *Gaetano Savini: The Man Who Was Brioni* (2015), as well as articles for *Fashion Theory*, *European Dance and Performance Studies*, *Architecture Boston* and *Gastronomica*.

CATHERINE FLOOD is a Prints Curator in the Word and Image Department at the V&A where she specialises in posters and design and politics. She co-curated the V&A exhibition *Disobedient Objects* (2014) and co-edited the accompanying publication. She has curated exhibitions and displays on political posters and various aspects of nineteenth-century print culture. She is the author of *British Posters: Advertising, Art & Activism* (V&A, 2012) and co-author of *Style and Satire: Fashion in Print 1776–1925* (V&A, 2012).

JOHN R. HUME was formerly Professor of Economic and Industrial History at Strathclyde University. He is the author of several books including *Clyde Shipbuilding from Old Photographs* (1975), co-authored with Michael S. Moss. In the mid-1980s he was involved in establishing the Scottish Maritime Museum at Irvine and has recently been appointed as Vice-Chairman. He served for a time on the National Historic Ships Committee. Since then, he has maintained a close interest in the history of shipbuilding.

MEREDITH MORE is Research Assistant for *Ocean Liners* and Assistant Curator for the Scottish Design Galleries at V&A Museum of Design Dundee (opening 2018). She has a first-class honours degree from the University of Glasgow, and an MA from the Courtauld Institute of Art, London. Her research is focused on Scottish design and regional museum collections.

BRUCE PETER is Reader in Design History at The Glasgow School of Art. He has a long-standing interest in naval architecture and the interior and industrial design of modern merchant ships. He has researched and published extensively on these subjects, as well as modern commercial architecture, transport design and architecture and design for leisure.

PAOLO PICCIONE is an architect specialising in ship interiors and exhibition design. He is an ocean liners scholar and has curated exhibitions and authored books in this field, including: *Transatlantici: The History of the Great Italian Liners on the Atlantic* (2001); *Cruising Into Art: Art on Board Italian Liners* (2002) and *Floating Art Déco. Interior Design and Decoration in the Golden Age of Sea Travels 1925–1940* (2013).

BERNHARD RIEGER is Professor of Modern and Contemporary History at University College London. He is the author of *Technology and the Culture of Modernity in Britain and Germany, 1890–1945* (2005) and *The People's Car: A Global History of the Volkswagen Beetle* (2013). He has contributed to *The New York Times*, *Foreign Affairs*, and *Bloomberg News* as well as to BBC television and radio.

GEORGE SCHWARTZ is Curatorial Scholar at the Peabody Essex Museum, where he has contributed to several of the museum's most successful exhibitions including *Fiery Pool: The Maya and the Mythic Sea*. He holds a master of arts in historical archaeology and a doctorate in American Studies, and is the author of *Collecting the Globe: The Salem East India Marine Society Museum* (forthcoming).

GHISLAINE WOOD is Co-Curator for *Ocean Liners* and Deputy Director of the Sainsbury Centre for Visual Arts, University of East Anglia. A Fellow of the V&A Research Department and formerly a Senior Curator, she has curated many exhibitions for the Museum, including *Art Deco 1910–1939* (2003), *Surreal Things: Surrealism and Design* (2007) and *British Design 1948–2012: Innovation in the Modern Age* (2012). She has published extensively on twentieth-century art and design.